ANCIENT GREECE
State and Society

Nicholas F. Jones
University of Pittsburgh

PRENTICE HALL, Upper Saddle River, New Jersey 07458

Library of Congress Cataloging-in-Publication Data

Jones, Nicholas F.
  Ancient Greece : state and society / Nicholas F. Jones.
    p.   cm.
  Includes bibliographical references.
  ISBN 0–13–339748–3 (pbk.)
    1. Athens (Greece)—Civilization.   2. Greece—Civilization—To 146
  B.C.   3. Democracy—Greece—Athens—History.   I. Title.
  DF275.J66   1996
  938′.5—dc20   96-33678
                                                              CIP

To My Mother

Editorial director: Charlyce Jones Owen
Acquisitions editor: Sally Constable
Editorial assistant: Justin Belinski
Editorial/production supervision
  and interior design: Darrin Kiessling,
  P.M. Gordon Associates
Copy editor: Sue Gleason
Cover design: Kiwi Design
Buyer: Lynn Pearlman
Marketing manager: Chaunfayta Hightower

This book was set in 10/12 Baskerville by D.M. Cradle
Associates, and was printed and bound by Courier
Companies, Inc. The cover was printed by
New England Book Components, Inc.

© 1997 by Prentice-Hall, Inc.
Simon & Schuster/A Viacom Company
Upper Saddle River, New Jersey 07458

Printed in the United States of America
10   9   8   7   6   5   4   3   2   1

ISBN   0-13-339748-3

Prentice-Hall International (UK) Limited, *London*
Prentice-Hall of Australia Pty. Limited, *Sydney*
Prentice-Hall Canada Inc., *Toronto*
Prentice-Hall Hispanoamericana, S.A., *Mexico*
Prentice-Hall of India Private Limited, *New Delhi*
Prentice-Hall of Japan, Inc., *Tokyo*
Simon & Schuster Asia Pte. Ltd., *Singapore*
Editora Prentice-Hall do Brasil, Ltda., *Rio de Janeiro*

Contents

Preface   vii
Chronology   ix
Introduction   1
   "State" and "Society"   2
   Ancient Greece and Classical Athens   3
   Sources of Our Knowledge   5
   Goals of Study   7
   Suggested Readings   7

PART   I   FROM PALACE STATE TO CITY-STATE

1 Prehistory: Minoans and Mycenaeans   8
   The Minoans   10
      The Archaeological Record   11   Minoan Society: The People   14   Minoan
      Society: The Social Structure   16   Minoan Religion   17   Thera: "Pompeii
      of the Ancient Aegean"   18   The Eruption of Thera and the Decline of Minoan
      Civilization   20
   Mycenaean Civilization   22
      The Archaeological Record   23   The Linear B Tablets and Mycenaean Society   24
      The Mycenaean Economy   27   The Later Mycenaeans (The Late Helladic Period)   28
      The Trojan War   30   The Destruction of Mycenaean Civilization   32
      Suggested Readings   33

2 The Renaissance of Greek Civilization   35
   The Dorian "Invasion"   35
   The Great Migrations   37
   The Emergence of the City-State   37
   Colonization   41
   The Rediscovery of Literacy   45
   The Rise of Historiography   47
   Iron Age Society   49
   Suggested Readings   53

PART   II   CLASSICAL ATHENS: STATE AND SOCIETY

3 Attica and Athens: The Built Environment   55
   The Built Environment: The Big Picture   55
      Attica   55   The Acropolis   56   The Agora   56
      The Port Town of Peiraeus   58

The Built Environment: State and Society   60
  Public Architecture and the Pervasiveness of Religion   61   The Agora: Diversity
  of Function   63   Public Architecture Outside the Urban Center: The Gymnasia   68
Architecture and the Outdoor Culture of Athens   69
Domestic Architecture and Athenian Society   70
  Suggested Readings   72

4 The Development of the Athenian Democracy   73
From Aristocracy to Democracy   74
  The Sources   74   Competing Models of Political Conflict   75
The Aristocracy   76
Cylon's Failed Coup d'État (632 B.C.)   77
The Legislation of Draco (621 B.C.)   78
The Reforms of Solon (594 B.C.)   79
  The System of Income Classes and the Constitution   81   Measures to Strengthen
  the Economy   82   The Administration of Justice   83
The Tyranny of Pisistratus and His Sons   84
  Background: Regions, Ideology, and Personal Ambition   84   The Rise of Pisistratus
  and the Three Periods of the Tyranny   86   The Third Tyranny at Athens
  (546–510 B.C.)   87
The Creation of the Democracy   90
  Suggested Readings   90

5 Citizens, Resident Aliens, and Slaves   91
Classical Athenian Society: "Classes" or "Orders"?   91
Citizens   93
  The Athenian Citizenship Law   93   Diversity of Wealth   94
  Holders of the Liturgy   95   The Aristocracy   95   The New Rich   98
  "Middle" and "Low" Classes   99
Metics (or Resident Aliens)   102
Slaves   104
Sparta   108
  Suggested Readings   111

6 The Democracy of Classical Athens   113
The Clisthenic Organization of Attica   113
  The Pre-Clisthenic Organization   113   The Clisthenic Organization   114
  The Purposes of Clisthenes' Organization   115
The Organs of Government   118
  The Assembly   118   The Council of Five Hundred   119
  The Magistrates   120   The Courts and Ostracism   121
Qualities of the Athenian Democracy   124
  Voluntary Participation   125   Opposition to One-Man Rule   125
  Egalitarianism   126   High Level of Participation   126
  Promulgation of the Acts of Government   127   The Urban Bias   127
The Urban Minority and the Demes   128
  Suggested Readings   128

7 The Family, Women, Children, and the Old 129

The Family 129

*Family or Household? 129 Nuclear or Extended Family? 129
Size of the Athenian Family 130 State Intervention in Family 130
Three Features of Athenian Family Life 132 Kinship Beyond the
Extended Family 133*

Women 133

*Betrothal and Dowry 133 The Athenian "Wedding" Ceremony 135
Age at First Marriage and Marital Ideals 136 A Married Woman's Work
and Daily Routine 137 The Seclusion of Women 137 Women at Work
Outside the Home 138 The Economic Rights of Athenian Women 139
Widowhood, Divorce, and Remarriage 139*

Children 140

*Why Have Children? 140 Childbirth, Birth Control, Exposure, and
Infant Mortality 141 Rites of Passage 144 The Conceptualization
of Childhood 145 The Education of Children 146 Integration of the Child
into the Athenian Community 147 Rites of Passage (continued) 148*

Old Age 150

*Public Roles of the Old 151 Popular Attitudes About the Old 151
Legal Protection of the Old in Athens 152 Suggested Readings 154*

8 Farmer, Crafter, and Soldier 155

Phases of the Athenian Citizen's Life Course 155

Farming and the Citizen Farmer 157

*The Athenian Farm 158 Crops and Stock 159 The Rural Village 161
Agricultural Labor 162 The Mentality of Ancient Greek Farmers 164
Town Versus Country 167*

Industry 169

Mining 169 Industrial Workplaces 171 Order and Status 174

The Military Organization 176

*Infantry 177 Naval Service 180 The Cavalry 181
The Athenian Military Organization: Ideology and Motivation 183
Suggested Readings 184*

9 Athenian State and Society: The Economy 185

The Coinage of Classical Athens 185

The Uses of Coinage 186 The Value of Athenian Coinage 186

Wages, Compensation, and the Cost of Living 187

The Economy of Subsistence Farming 191

"Subsistence Crisis Insurance" 192 "Patrons" and "Clients" 194

The Rich 196

*Sources and Uses of Wealth 196 The Precarious Condition
of the Wealthy 199*

Imports and Exports 200

The Athenian State Treasury: Income and Expenditure 202

The Athenian Empire 203

Suggested Readings 205

PART III   **EPILOGUE**

Epilogue: State and Society in the Hellenistic Era   206
    The Athenian State: The Democracy   206
    The Hellenistic Greek World: Society   208
        Citizenship and the Citizen Body   208   The Individual   210
        Hellenistic Associations   211
    The Hellenistic Greek Polis: Education, Economy, and Culture   212
        Suggested Readings   214

Preface

The guiding assumption of this textbook is that as much may be gained from an intense and multifaceted study of a single state and society as from a broader and necessarily more superficial sweep over space and time. Rather than attempt coverage of all Greek antiquity, from the Stone Age to the fall of the Roman Empire, from Cadiz to Bactria, my focus is narrowed to a single city—Athens—during the so-called classical era of the fifth and fourth centuries B.C. The book's comprehensiveness resides in its examination of its subject, classical Athens, in terms of prehistoric and archaic antecedents; physical infrastructure; the development and nature of its government; the gross societal regime; the family and the individual's life course; work as represented by farming, crafts, and the military; the economy; and major trends influencing its future development during the Hellenistic and Roman eras.

The foundation of the text is my own research, two years of study in modern Greece, and, most importantly, nearly twenty years of teaching the topics introduced for discussion. Against this backdrop, my primary goal has been to introduce the reader to the serious academic study of the subject as reflected in the scholarly writings of present-day historians of ancient Greece. Referencing of some type is therefore required. Many topics, problems, and proposed solutions are so well known and widely discussed as to require no specific reference to their ultimate source. But where my discussion is dependent on a particular investigator's theory or research, especially if that work is recent, I have acknowledged the fact with such formulations as "a recent study" or "an English scholar." Full reference to author and writing may be found within the "Suggested Readings" appended to each chapter. It should go without saying that a textbook of this type is necessarily the end product of generations of scholarly research.

Acknowledgment of another kind is also in order. Two advanced graduate students in the Department of Classics at the University of Pittsburgh, Karen Hoover and John Newell, conscientiously critiqued, and improved, a penultimate draft; that I was not able to follow all their suggested changes does not mean that I am any the less grateful. My wife, Marilyn Jones, herself a trained classicist, subjected the text to careful scrutiny, detecting many errors and other inadequacies. Throughout its writing, she also joined in spirited discussion of many of the issues raised by our subject. My gratitude to her, too, is immense. I alone am responsible for all that remains.

All translations of ancient Greek texts are my own. A date given in the form 508/7 B.C. designates an ancient Greek year comprising roughly the second half of 508 B.C. and the first half of 507 B.C. The spelling of most Greek proper names is given in a more familiar latinized (and sometimes anglicized) form, but rarer words are usually simply transliterated.

N. F. J.

Chronology

DATE B.C.	EVENT	STATE AND SOCIETY
From Palace State to City-State		
ca. 6500	Neolithic revolution	Agriculture and domestication of animals introduced
ca. 3000	Bronze Age begins	
ca. 1900	Greeks enter Greece	
ca. 1700–1400	Zenith of Minoan age	Palace states on Crete
ca. 1600–1200	Zenith of Mycenaean age	Palace states in Greece, including Athens
ca. 1220	Trojan War	
ca. 1250–1200	Mycenaean palaces destroyed	End of palace state
ca. 1100	Dorian invasion (or uprising)	Cultural innovations, including introduction of iron
ca. 1100	Iron Age begins	
ca. 1100–800	Dark Age of Greece	Low level of civilization
ca. 800–525	Archaic Age of Greece	Renaissance of civilization
ca. 800	Emergence of city-state	Settled communities; social stratification
ca. 750	Alphabet acquired from Phoenicians	Homer, Hesiod, and first examples of writing
ca. 750–550	Colonization	City-states established over Mediterranean
ca. 632–508/7	Development of government at Athens	From aristocracy to democracy
ca. 600	Rise of historiography	Historical events recorded in written form
Classical Athens: State and Society		
ca. 525–322	Classical Age	Zenith of Greek civilization
ca. 550–500	Persian Empire expands	
508/7	Democracy established at Athens	
490	Battle of Marathon	Greatest Athenian infantry victory
490–479	Greece repels Persian invasions	Athens assumes leadership of Greek alliance
479	Battle of Salamis	Greatest Athenian naval victory
478	Delian League founded	Athens converts league to empire

DATE B.C.	EVENT	STATE AND SOCIETY
	Classical Athens: State and Society	
451/0	Citizenship law	Creation of citizen caste
447–432	Parthenon constructed	Imperial funds spent on Athens
431–404	Peloponnesian War	Athens loses war, and empire, to Sparta
404–338	Hegemonies of Sparta, Thebes, and Macedon	Athens second-class power
377–338	Second Athenian league	Athens regains maritime supremacy
338–323	Conquests of Alexander the Great	Old Persian Empire overrun by Macedonians
322	Macedonian takeover of Athens	Athenian democracy overturned
	Epilogue: State and Society in the Hellenistic Era	
323–272	Alexander's successors seek domination	Hellenistic kingdoms (Egypt, Syria, Macedon) established
ca. 200	Romans begin to intervene in Greece	
146–30	Greece and Macedon fall to Rome	
146–30	Romans conquer Hellenistic kingdoms	Greece reduced to Roman provinces
88	Athens sacked by Sulla	Much of Athens demolished

Introduction

The history of ancient Greece has been told many times, beginning in antiquity even as the events themselves were unfolding and continuing today in an unabating stream of publications. With few exceptions, however, the story was, until recently, usually told in much the same way. Ancient Greek history was customarily viewed in political, diplomatic, and military terms. But this narrowness of viewpoint was not entirely as arbitrary or unjustified as it might at first appear. Some of the Greek historians, such as Thucydides and Xenophon, were themselves actors in the arenas of public life. Thus when they turned to the description and interpretation of events, they naturally kept close to the subjects they understood from their own personal experience. Besides, their readership was generally confined to an upper class of educated men whose interests in history probably likewise reflected the preoccupations of their class—again, politics, diplomacy, and military matters. Not surprisingly, when modern scholars, beginning in the Renaissance, next undertook the task of reinterpreting for their own ages the story of ancient Greece, they tended to follow the ancient Greek authors' agenda of topics, questions, and viewpoints seen as appropriate to the business of ancient history. Wars in particular held a central place in the reconstruction of ancient Greece. The Persian wars, the Peloponnesian War, and the conquests of Alexander the Great—the first two celebrated by the splendid and still-extant writings of Herodotus and Thucydides—emerged as the centerpieces of the story, the epochal events to which all else was relegated to the status of prologue, interlude, or aftermath.

There is, of course, another, substantive reason why this perception of history was not entirely lacking in justification. Those familiar with the military episodes just mentioned will realize that, had certain decisions been made differently, had the historical actors acted otherwise, the future course of the Aegean and (in part) Near Eastern, and eventually European, civilizations would have been drastically altered. These were the true turning points, literally decisive moments, on which the course of subsequent developments depended. But from a broader societal perspective this traditional perception of history was woefully incomplete. Politics, interstate relations, and battles inevitably elevated free adult men—whether a great leader or an entire adult male citizen body—to the status of principal, indeed sole, historical actors. But the concerns of the investigator of ancient Greek society do not end here. What of the ongoing, more or less continuous substratum of ancient Greek life that underlay the discontinuities and upheavals of revolutions and wars? What about domestic life? What of work? What about those elements of the Greek population who, by reason of age, gender, or constitutional status, could play no direct role in the events that had captured the attention of traditional historians: children, women, and slaves? With the rise of *social* history, some of these deficiencies have begun to be corrected. The last three decades have witnessed a dramatic widening of the scope of subjects and questions that may properly be termed "historical."

"STATE" AND "SOCIETY"

Given this enlarged scope of ancient Greek history, which is by now familiar among most students of ancient Mediterranean civilization, how should we go about our study? Since the subject is large, one is initially tempted to divide it in two, along the line separating the traditional approach from that of more recent investigators of society in its wider dimensions. One study would deal with elections, treaties, and wars; the other, with the household and family, women, slaves, and private life in general. But such an approach will not do in this textbook. The two imaginary studies just mentioned correspond roughly to what would, in modern parlance, be termed "state" and "society," yet in ancient Greece, state and society were not, as in our own experience, so sharply separated. In fact, ancient Greek state and society were integrated to such an extent as hardly to be separable.

Modern Western experience typically equates "the state" with a more or less permanent complex of governmental organs and bureaucracies. Even with periodic elections, the same elected officers or representatives are often returned to office again and again, and most candidates belong in any event to a well-defined class of politicians. Bureaucracies, staffed by experts and professionals, change very little over time. Government is commonly identified with a specific physical seat of administration, whether Washington, D.C., or city hall. This complex, along with a network of agencies, police forces, and so forth, is charged with the governance and regulation of society. The latter, by contrast, is generally characterized in terms of the pursuit of personal or even private ideals, whether by the individual, in the context of some household or familial unit, or within the still larger setting of different types of voluntary associations. By and large, the business of society is distinct from and often out of the reach of the state, and many insist that, in principle and in point of law, it should remain so. Witness current discourse regarding religious beliefs and practice, household and family composition, sexual orientation and expression, and lifestyle variations generally.

The same distinction in conceptualization and practice does *not* apply to the developed civilization of ancient Greece. To be sure, *state* and *society* can in their classical context be given precise definition. Distinct political or social institutions correspond to them, and in general they prove to be useful, indeed necessary, analytical tools. But in the actual life of the Greek city-state, the two are inextricably intermeshed. For one thing governments in the period covered by our study were not staffed by well-defined cadres of professional career politicians or expert bureaucrats. As we will see in our examination of the Athenian democracy (Chapter 6), with very few exceptions the boards of officers or organs of government were filled with ordinary private citizens, with a rapid turnover of personnel and a resulting high rate of citizen participation. Athenian "society" in effect staffed the "state." No citizen could legitimately complain about "city hall" or "big government," because he himself was part of that government and had in one way or another helped make it what it was.

Nor was "private" life insulated from the impact of public policy, laws, or other intervention. The Athenian family was actively promoted and shaped by constitutional and legal regulations; and a citizen's career was punctuated by public rites of passage on a schedule synchronized with those of private civil society. Far from acknowledging a separation of church and state, an individual's only gods were the state's gods, and virtually all religious ceremonies of importance were conducted under the aegis of the central government or one of its units. In the place of voluntary associations, the internally organized segments of the state itself, such as the constitutionalized village, served as the hubs of local social and cultural groups. The public square and seat of government doubled as the venue of a wide range of athletic, dramatic, artistic, intellectual, and commercial activities. The great Athenian tragedies and comedies were first produced in the context of a state religious festival staged in a public theater. It is thus obvious that ancient Greek "state" and "society" were inseparable. Hence the orientation—and the subtitle—of this textbook.

ANCIENT GREECE AND CLASSICAL ATHENS

To describe and attempt to understand the state and society of any polity, historical or living, requires a substantial body of evidence. At once a major problem arises. Greek antiquity witnessed the emergence of over a thousand city-states, but the documentation of those city-states, when measured against the demands made by our subject, is exceptionally fragmentary. For our purposes, fragments are all but useless. Archaeology provides an instructive parallel. An isolated physical artifact—a piece of pottery, architectural member, tool, or coin—tells us little unless it can be related to a *context*, to a specific place and time, to an assemblage of physical remains, societal structures, and cultural norms in relation to which it acquires significance. The same is true of historical facts. Without a context, isolated events, personalities, and institutions are essentially meaningless. But "without a context" is a phrase that fairly accurately describes the situation for all but a few of our thousand or so city-states. My comprehensive study of the public administrative systems of the Greek city-states illustrates the point. For only about two hundred city-states does evidence of any kind survive, and for only a handful of these is it possible to reconstruct the form and development of the system. And of this handful, only one case, that of Athens, is sufficiently documented to permit in-depth description and analysis.

For precisely the same reason, Athens provides the only possible subject of any in-depth examination of ancient Greek state and society. Sparta might be thought an exception, but that city's early history is not documented by contemporary texts, records, or artifacts, and those written sources that appear later are notoriously compromised by exaggeration, speculation, or outright invention. Athens, then, it must be. But there are positive advantages to dealing with just this one city. Athens alone of major ancient Greek polities enjoyed substantial continuity from the first great era of Greek civilization, the Bronze Age (the era of the Trojan War), down to and through the zenith of that civilization, the classical period, and beyond, to the end of antiquity. The Athenians of the halcyon days of the fifth century B.C. are the lineal descendants of the Athenians of the time of the Trojan War. This fact opens up the possibility of constructing a more or less continuous and uniform account of ancient Greek state and society, even if it is based on but one of the thousand known polities.

Doing so will, however, require two significant departures from what might be expected in such an enterprise. First, although the memory of Bronze Age Athens is preserved in both the archaeological record and later Greek legend, other centers, as will become clear in Chapter 1, are far better preserved and documented. Thus it will be to them, to Mycenae in particular, that we will turn at the beginning of the story. Second, what we know of pre-historic Greece depends to an extraordinary degree on the findings of archaeology, on the physical remains of that era. Without the record of these remains, one would have to delay the beginning of the narrative to a much later time, when the contemporary accounts of the Greek historians first become available. But this will not do. Not the nature of the source materials—archaeological or written—but rather the subject itself, the ancient Greek people and the Athenians in particular, must determine the parameters of our study. The findings of archaeology are, and always should have been, essential ingredients in the reconstruction of ancient Greek state and society.

So much for the scope of our study and where to begin it. Where will it end? Because a major strand of the subject, the state, embodies the government and related institutions, the most natural end point, given a focus on Athens, is the suppression of the democracy in 322 B.C. Democracy, Athens' original and most distinctive contribution to Aegean government, underlay the institutions, social forms, and public life that constitute the subject matter of most of this textbook. With the democracy gone, much else necessarily changes as well. Besides, the ensuing phases of Greek antiquity represent distinctive epochs deserving treatment in their own right. With the death, in 323 B.C., of the Macedonian king Alexander the Great, who had conquered a vast eastern territory roughly corresponding to the old Persian Empire, begins the so-called Hellenistic Age. Its major political development, the rise of the monarchies (attended by decline of the city-state), and the dissemination over the East of Hellenism precipitated major dislocations of Greek civilization. With the year 146 B.C. and the beginning of the incorporation of Greece as imperial provinces, the history of ancient Greece becomes part of the larger history of the Roman Empire. Athens, to be sure, survived the upheavals. But with the loss of democracy, its intermittent subjugation to imperial powers, and the opening up of its once insular community to foreign influences, it is clear that the year 322 B.C. marked the dawn of a new age. Accordingly, our text will end in a final Epilogue which looks ahead to the trends that lay in store for state and society at this watershed of ancient Greek history.

SOURCES OF OUR KNOWLEDGE

Our study will be concerned with historical matter of all kinds—models, theories, cause-and-effect relationships, current problematic areas, and so on. It is less concerned with the source materials forming the basis of these models and theories. The student nonetheless needs at least a general idea of the nature and extent of the sources, for ultimately much of what is controversial about ancient Greek history—and there is much—comes down to what they do or do not indicate.

It is in part the sources that account for the distinctiveness of the study of ancient Greece compared with other areas of historical study. Both the quantity and the quality of those sources are in question. An American or modern European historian may be able to draw on newspapers, magazines, diaries, baptismal records, death certificates, censuses, commercial receipts, voting records, and government documents, in addition to existing historical writings, some of them contemporary with their subjects. For the historian of ancient Greece, such documentation is for the most part nonexistent. True, the Greek Bronze Age is sporadically documented by the Linear B tablets, and several of the Greek city-states—above all, Athens—have left relatively rich records of inscriptions engraved on stone. But the breadth of coverage, continuity of that coverage over time, and level of detail fall far short of the expectations of historians of many other societies. Written histories survive in the writings of Herodotus, Thucydides, Aristotle, Xenophon, and others, yet, as already noted, their subject matter is almost exclusively geared to the experiences and interests of the upper-class male citizen elites. Thus both the volume and the character of the ancient Greek source materials are subject to severe limitations.

Quantity of information has an important impact on the methods available for analyzing that information. Historians of modern societies have long subjected their bountiful funds of data to statistical analysis. Such quantitative procedures permit the asking and often the answering of questions that can be successfully approached by no other route. The historian of ancient Greece, by contrast, often finds himself or herself confronted by an isolated fragmentary inscription or a single unsupported statement by a Greek historian. Not only is quantification out of the question, but unsettling problems arise concerning the accuracy and general dependability of that single, isolated source. Thus some topics are never broached, some questions never asked, because little or no evidence has survived on which to base an inquiry, much less bring it to a satisfactory conclusion. For the most part, the historian of ancient Greece must follow the available evidence, wherever it leads. At various points in this textbook, references to the Mycenaean Linear B tablets, or to the archaic poet Hesiod, or to the constitutional writings of the polymath philosopher Aristotle will impart an idea of this distinctive and often exasperating characteristic of historical study in this field.

Then there is the qualitative aspect. It cannot be overemphasized that virtually all ancient Greek historical writings were composed by authors conforming to a single profile: Greek, free, citizen, and male. Some, such as Thucydides and Xenophon, were upper-class aristocrats as well. It is less an accusation of bias than merely acknowledgment of the limitations of our humanity to observe that their choice of topics, organization of material, point of view, and of course opinions reflect the authors' nationality, constitutional status, gender, and socioeconomic standing. The consequences for ancient Greek history, in particular for that of classical Athens, are profound. No works relevant to our subject are known to have been written by a foreigner, woman, or slave. Equally seriously, the representations of foreigners, women, or slaves that do survive are without exception the production of the Greek male authorial elite. We are thus put at a great disadvantage if, say, we attempt to reconstruct the life, not to mention the attitudes, viewpoints, or feelings, of an ancient Athenian woman. Not a single such woman is known to have participated in the creation of any of the sources from which her own history might be reconstructed—such as forensic speeches, tragedies, comedies, Platonic dialogues, painted pottery, and funerary inscriptions. The same applies to children, slaves, and non-Greek foreigners, as well as to most males below the upper echelons of Greek society. The point here is not to denigrate ancient Greek society but merely to call attention to another distinctive feature of the doing of history in this place and time—one that must be kept in mind throughout the relevant sections of this textbook. Much of our story, to borrow from the language of the courtroom, depends on hearsay evidence, with all the limitations implied by that phrase.

GOALS OF STUDY

With these preliminaries in mind, let us now embark on our investigation. By way of a chronological framework in which to set our various discussions, a chart indicating the dates of principal events and developments mentioned in the text may be found at pages ix–x. But our concerns throughout will be less with chronology and events, and far more with the environmental forces, societal goals, and cultural ideals that helped shape the course of ancient Greek history, above all as evidenced in the achievements and experiences of Greece's premier city, Athens. At the end, after we have tried to understand the development, nature, and function of ancient Greek state and society, it is hoped that the reader will have gained an appreciation of the contribution made by the study of ancient Greece to an understanding of human civilization.

Suggested Readings

To complement the approach of the present book, several excellent traditional histories are available. J. B. Bury and R. Meiggs's *A History of Greece to the Death of Alexander the Great* (London, 1975), is now in its fourth edition. Another is N. G. L. Hammond, *A History of Greece to 322 B.C.*, 3rd ed. (Oxford, 1986). More comprehensive in scope, detailed, and fully documented is the standard general history of Greece and Rome in English, *The Cambridge Ancient History*, with Volumes 1 and 2 now in their third edition and the remaining volumes in their second.

Chapter 1. Prehistory: Minoans
and Mycenaeans

The story of ancient Greek history does not begin with the earliest surviving written accounts of Greek historians. Those accounts make a relatively late appearance, leaving unrecorded, among other subjects, the most advanced stage of Greek civilization prior to the classical period. By the term *prehistory* we mean those early eras of history, prior to the survival of the earliest *contemporary* documents. The italicized word makes the important point that, for a written text to be of value, it must itself belong to the time it describes; it is not enough to have access (as we do) to much later attempts to reconstruct the unrecorded period. Although, as we will see, contemporary documents have in fact survived from this era, there are no formal written histories; thus it is reasonable to continue to use the term *prehistory*.

In the absence of histories, the ancient historian is almost entirely dependent on the findings of *archaeology*, the recovery, study, and interpretation of the physical remains of the past. Archaeologists' goal is the reconstruction, in all its dimensions, of the human society that produced those remains. Archaeologists are concerned not so much with isolated, individual physical artifacts (as one might gather from viewing displays in a museum) as with those same artifacts in their original ancient context. By *context* is meant the time and place of an object's original (or later) use, whereby the archaeologist can determine its relationship to other objects and therefrom its place and function in the total societal framework. Excavation is not random "gold digging" in search of precious finds for collection or display; it is rather the systematic reconstruction on the basis of all recoverable physical remains, however humble, of an entire society and its culture.

Excavation, so understood, is largely confined to what archaeologists call *stratified* sites; that is, sites of successive human habitation, with each phase of such habitation corresponding to a distinct and detectable layer, or *stratum*. (Single-period sites are, by contrast, quite rare.) Ideally, the excavator will, beginning with the modern layer at the surface, systematically remove it and each succeeding layer one at a time, carefully noting the exact location and disposition of every artifact within it. Near the bottom, beneath the modern, medieval, late antique, and Roman levels, the archaeologist at last reaches Hellenistic, classical, Archaic, and, finally, prehistoric Greek strata. Below them, virgin soil.

Now, an extremely crucial feature of prehistoric strata is that, with very rare exceptions, they yield no objects or other material bearing evidence of an *absolute* date (expressed, in our tradition, by years B.C.). Greek archaeologists working in later periods regularly recover inscriptions bearing names of officials who served during a single, known year; coins bearing the portrait of a king of known regnal dates (indeed, the exact year within his reign is sometimes given); or other artifacts associated with historical events of previously established chronology. No such objects are customarily encountered by prehistoric archaeologists. What the excavator does know is that a given stratum and its contents are later than the stratum (and its contents) below it and earlier than that above it. In other words, the prehistoric era as reconstructed by archaeologists is based on a system of *relative* chronology, whereby a given period of human occupation (including human remains, houses and other structures, pottery, religious objects, and graves) is definable in terms of the periods preceding or following it, with the *absolute* date or dates unknown or debated. (Indeed, at the time this book is being written, the chronology of the Greek Bronze Age is being debated by two opposing camps of prehistorians, whose calculations of absolute dates differ by more than a century.) For this reason, historians must follow the archaeologist's system and its special nomenclature for the relative chronology of the prehistoric era (see Table 1–1). This system is based on the dimensions of time (Stone Age, Bronze Age, Iron Age, and their subdivisions) and place (mainland of Greece and Peloponnesus, Cyclades islands, and Crete).

The assignment of absolute dates to these temporal and regional phases is a tricky business. What is needed is to establish a linkage between the Greek

Table 1–1. Prehistoric Chronology of Ancient Greece

	MAINLAND AND PELOPONNESUS	*CYCLADES*	*CRETE*
Stone Age	Palaeolithic		
	Mesolithic	Same	Same
	Neolithic		
Bronze Age	Early Helladic	Early Cycladic	Early Minoan
	EH I A,B,C	EC I A,B,C	EM I A,B,C
	EH II A,B,C	EC II A,B,C	EM II A,B,C
	EH III A,B,C	EC III A,B,C	EM III A,B,C
	Middle Helladic	Middle Cycladic	Middle Minoan
	MH I A,B,C	MC I A,B,C	MM I A,B,C
	etc.	etc.	etc.
	Late Helladic	Late Cycladic	Late Minoan
	(Mycenaean)		
	LH I A,B,C	LC I A,B,C	LM I A,B,C
	etc.	etc.	etc.
	Sub-Mycenaean		Sub-Minoan
Iron Age	Protogeometric		
	Geometric		

relative chronology and external (that is, non-Greek) evidence, for which there is a secure absolute date. Once a number of such correlations have been secured, it is then possible to work out the absolute chronology for all of Greek prehistory. Fortunately, such linkages exist, most notably in connection with the chronologically fixed reigns of Egyptian pharaohs. For example, the latest datable Egyptian object in Crete prior to the destruction marking the boundary between the end of LM II and the beginning of LM III is a seal of Queen Tiy, consort of Amenophis III, regnal dates 1417–1379 B.C. Thus LM III can have begun no earlier than Amenophis' reign, or approximately 1400 B.C.

With these fundamentals in mind, let us very briefly touch on some landmark events and developments of Greek prehistory. The Stone Age, of indeterminable starting date, reaches its climax with the Neolithic, or "New Stone," Age, a phase ushered in about 6500 B.C. by two great cultural innovations: agriculture and the domestication of animals. Stone Age indigenous populations underwent the transition to the Bronze Age around 3000 B.C. About a millennium later, probably at the break between Early Helladic II and III, absolute date around 1900 B.C., the first Greeks (defined as the carriers of the culture that included the Greek language, distinctive physical artifacts, institutions, and religion) arrived in Greece. About another half-millennium later, this mainland Greek civilization reached its zenith in the Late Helladic, a period extending from about 1600 to 1200 B.C. Prehistorians call the Late Helladic by the specialized term "Mycenaean," with reference to the mainland palace center at Mycenae. In terms of physical culture, wealth, societal complexity, and engagement overseas, this was the high point of Greek civilization before the classical period.

Meanwhile, developments in Greek lands outside the mainland and Peloponnesus proceeded on a somewhat different schedule. For our purposes, the crucial venue is Crete, the long island that defines the Aegean on the south. Crete, too, at a somewhat earlier date, attained a high pitch of societal and cultural development, yet its people, whom prehistorians call "Minoans," were almost certainly *not* Greek. Nonetheless, the Minoan presence in Greek lands would prove significant for the early development of Hellenic civilization. Thus, paradoxically, it is appropriate that our story of ancient Greece begin with the record of these non-Greek island settlements.

THE MINOANS

To ancient Greeks, and to Western civilization until the beginning of the twentieth century, the people we now call the Minoans were known mainly for their roles in a number of entertaining and seemingly unhistorical myths. The best-known of these told of a king of the Phoenician city of Tyre (at the eastern edge of the Mediterranean). The king's daughter Europa, the story went, had been abducted by the god Zeus, who appeared to her in the form of a white bull. The bull, with Europa on its back, had swum to Crete, where Europa gave birth by it to a son, Minos. Minos went on to become lord of the kingdom of Cnossus. When, later, Minos' claim to the throne was challenged, the god Poseidon, in answer to Minos' prayer, sent a bull from the sea as a sign validating his right to rule. But Minos, overawed by the beauty of the animal, failed to honor the god (as he had agreed to do) by sacrificing it in Poseidon's name. So, to punish Minos, Poseidon made Minos' wife Pasiphae (the "All-Shining One," daughter of the Sun) conceive a passion for the bull. Pasiphae, aided by the exiled Athenian carpenter Daedalus, who constructed for her a hollow wooden cow into which she climbed to mate with the bull, bore by the bull a half-human, half-animal monster, the Minotaur. Minos kept the Minotaur in a maze called the Labyrinth. Later episodes of the myth bring Athens into play. When his brother was murdered while abroad in Athens, Minos punished the Athenians by compelling them to send to Cnossus each year seven boys and seven girls to be thrown into the Labyrinth. But Athens was finally freed from this oppression when Theseus, the son of the Athenian king, volunteered to be one of the sacrificial youths. At Cnossus he was assisted by Minos' daughter Ariadne, who provided him with a ball of thread and a sword. Tying the end of the thread to the entrance, Theseus entered the maze, met and killed the Minotaur with the sword, and followed the thread back to its entrance. With Theseus' safe escape from Crete, Athens was thenceforth freed from oppression by King Minos.

The fantastic quality of this story is apparent, particularly when one considers the presence in it of several traditional elements called by folklorists "motifs" (as, for example, when the hero falls in love with his oppressor's daughter, who helps him carry out his task). Is it any wonder that not until 1900 was there any serious attempt to search for the material remains of Minos' kingdom? In that year, Arthur Evans, the son of a wealthy British industrialist, commenced excavation at a site known in later antiquity as Cnossus. Evans soon exposed a vast palace complex, thereby substantiating the historicity of a prehistoric Cretan civilization. Evans coined the term *Minoan* to distinguish this civilization from the contemporary Bronze Age civilization of Greece and more northern Aegean islands. Thus, although the tale of Minos had admittedly been subjected to considerable embellishment, it was an embellishment with a core of historical truth. And in the following sections, the reader will see how Evans (and later scholars) were able to detect historical analogues even for some of the story's specific details.

The Archaeological Record

The site excavated by Evans is situated near the midpoint of the northern shore of Crete, about three miles inland from the coast (see Map 1–1). The site had been occupied since at least Neolithic times. Near or at the end of Middle Minoan I B (about 1900 B.C.), the site was leveled and the basic lay-

Map 1–1.   The Minoan-Mycenaean World

out of the complex established: a central court surrounded by a network of corridors, rooms, and storage compartments. During Middle Minoan II, this first complex was destroyed, probably by natural causes (in all likelihood an earthquake), but was subsequently entirely rebuilt, marking the beginning of the second palace period, which extended from Middle Minoan III to Late Minoan III A (that is, from about 1700 to 1400 B.C.). It is to this three-century period, the zenith of Minoan civilization, that we will direct our attention.

Evans identified the Cnossan complex as a palace, by which term is meant that it served, among its other functions, as the residence of the head of state and family; and, despite one archaeologist's recent argument in favor of its having been a temple, this point appears beyond doubt. Among Evans's earliest discoveries was a large room with a throne positioned against one wall, and although the room in its present form appears to belong to the later, Mycenaean phase of the palace, it is difficult to believe that the complex had previously been without such a function. Elsewhere within the palace, furthermore, were other rooms identified as domestic in function and thus natural candidates for the residence of the royal family. If there is a question, it concerns the identity of the throne's occupant. The myth speaks of King Minos; some historians even suppose that *minos* was a generic term for "Minoan king." However that may be, the ruler would have been a male. But it is a fact, as we will see, that women enjoyed an unusual prominence in Minoan society, in secular as well as in religious capacities. Could the occupant of the throne have been a woman? The theory of an Aegean pre-Greek matriarchal order—a literal "rule of women"—no longer enjoys the popularity it once did, particularly since a bona fide example of such a society, historical or living, has yet to be discovered. Yet even if the head of state was a man (as seems more likely, in view of the myth), it would be rash to conclude further that Minoan society *in other aspects* necessarily resembled the thoroughgoing patriarchal order of the Greeks.

Evans's later palace covered several acres, and the number of its compartments distributed over at least three stories may have exceeded one thousand. (Evidently, as Evans realized, it was the palace itself that had inspired the tale of the Labyrinth). Not surprisingly, the functions of so vast an installation were not exclusively domestic. The palace was a center of economic activity. In the west wing were storage rooms equipped with enormous jars, tall as a man, which had originally contained grain, oil, and wine. Additional rectangular, covered compartments, sunk into the floors, were probably used for the safekeeping of more valuable items. Storage on such a scale cannot be explained solely in terms of the needs of the palace itself, however large it was. Rather, archaeologists have come to think of the palace as a redistribution center to which produce or other goods were brought from the port or the dependent countryside, stored, and subsequently, under the direction of the central authority, reallocated to various destinations in the kingdom.

Still other spaces—such as those adduced in support of the complex as a temple—were dedicated to the performance of various religious acts and rituals. The successful performance of some of these acts and rituals was evidently believed to serve the well-being of the entire community. Consider, for example, the physical evidence from another Cretan palace interpreted to indicate the performance of human sacrifice. According to an archaeologist's reconstruction, in anticipation of an earthquake a victim had been sacrificed, evidently in the hope that the divine recipient, if satisfied, would avert the disaster that, as it turned out, did visit the site. Presumably Minoans believed that forces of such great potential for good or ill were accessible from the palace and so could be brought under the immediate control of the priests and priestesses, and ultimately of the king himself. But Minoan religion could also be practiced well outside the palatial centers, notably in caves and on mountaintops, where divine beings were thought to reside.

Public entertainment, finally, is yet another possible function. One of the several wall paintings from the interior of the palace depicts a curious activity descriptively labeled "bull leaping." A scantily clad adult faces a charging bull and, literally taking the bull by the horns, executes a full somersault over its back, to land safely behind the animal. Evans reasonably supposed that bull leaping was staged in the central court of the palace. Other wall paintings depict people, including elaborately coiffed women, viewing some activity from bleachers; and this may well be the activity and the place. If we have learned anything from the experience of ancient Greece and Rome, it is that heads of state are quick to reap the benefits of sponsoring public entertainments. To this end, the interior of the palace provided the optimum venue.

Excavation has thus revealed a centralized and apparently self-contained political, economic, religious, and cultural hub within the palace. But the site explored by Evans at Cnossus, although the largest, most complex, and most famous on Crete, was not the only population center. Subsequent explorations have revealed impressive complexes at Phaistos, Mallia, Zakro, and elsewhere; and outside these major centers a substantial segment of Minoan society resided in towns, villages, and the occasional private villa. These facts give rise to a pressing question. Were these settlements independent of one another? Or were they components of a larger organizational entity, perhaps embracing the entire island, and possibly administered from Cnossus?

It might be possible to answer this and many other questions about the Minoans were scholars able to solve a most perplexing puzzle of the archaeological record: the Linear A script. Examples of the script, a writing system in part resembling Egyptian hieroglyphs and used to record texts on a wide variety of objects, have been discovered at about two dozen Minoan sites on Crete, including Cnossus. Although some of these texts, to judge from the articles on which they are inscribed and from their archaeological context, probably had little or nothing to do with administrative matters, certain others, like the Linear B tablets of the Mycenaean Greeks that they closely resemble, are certainly accounts of some kind. Something could be learned, then, if the language recorded by this script were known. The fact that it is *not* is, incidentally, the most persuasive indication that the language and its users were not Greek. But, for the historian, it is primarily the content of the texts that is at issue. The decipherment of Linear A remains to this day one of the major challenges in the study of Mediterranean prehistory.

Minoan Society: The People

The conclusion forced on us by the resistance of Linear A to decipherment, that the users of that script, the Minoans, were not Greeks, is of potentially major significance for our understanding of the later history of classical Greece. The presence in this corner of the Mediterranean world of a non-Greek people, and one that had achieved a high order of development, opens up the possibility of a substantial foreign contribution to classical Greek civilization. All the more importance, therefore, is attached to the question of the ethnic identity of the Minoan people.

According to the Greek story that opened this chapter, the Greeks made King Minos the son of a Greek god, Zeus, and of Europa, daughter of the king of Tyre, in Phoenicia. The implication is that not only the king but also his people were at least partially of Eastern origin. To an appreciable extent, this inference is supported by the relevant archaeological material. Study of the pottery of the Early Minoan period has suggested affinities with Western Anatolia, Syria, and Palestine; and somewhat later (Early Minoan II), the appearance of stone vases, seal stones, and amulets seems to point to contact with Egypt. Still later, in the palace period, architectural features of the palaces themselves (such as the inverted, tapered columns and the use and execution of wall paintings) reaffirm the Egyptian influence on a larger scale.

But for the historian the crucial question remains. How is one to account for such affinities? Trade is, of course, always a possibility. Foreign goods (and ideas), once introduced into the home culture, may be assimilated and worked into its cultural repertoire. This mechanism is so familiar as not to require illustration. A second mode of transmission involves the movement of people, not of whole populations, but of a select group of culture carriers—for example, travelers, pilgrims, businesspeople, or emissaries—by whose report a new cultural artifact might be introduced. Again, this is a familiar concept requiring no illustration and one that, like trade, is amply supported by the known circumstances of eastern Mediterranean life.

The point is that the archaeologist can go a long way toward explaining cultural affinities without having recourse to a third, more drastic, model of explanation: the physical relocation of entire populations. With this model in mind, some prehistorians have written of a Cretan "melting pot" or of a Cretan "New World" to which foreign groups of various origins fled from their native homelands. Two factors admittedly favor this model. The non-Greek features of the Minoan script and language, particularly the language, would not easily have been established through either the mechanism of trade or occasional travelers. And the southerly and eastern location of Crete, at once relatively isolated from the Greek homeland yet within easy reach of Asia Minor, the Levant, and the northern coast of Africa, would have made Crete a convenient destination for immigrants from the eastern Mediterranean region. At the same time, however, mass immigration, though it can and does occur in antiquity, is a less economical hypothesis than the other two and for that reason should not be invoked unless there are compelling grounds for so doing.

Furthermore, all three models may in some instances be superfluous, if, as certain archaeologists believe, some of the apparent foreign cultural "imports" were in reality the products of local innovations by the indigenous (though still non-Greek) Cretan populations. Interest in these competing modes of explanation is currently at a high pitch, and ancient Greek historians eagerly await the results of this ongoing research.

Minoan Society: The Social Structure

Owing to the absence of contemporary documentation, the Minoan social structure is discernible only in its broadest outlines. Mention has been made of the palace in its roles as residence of the king and royal family, as hub of a redistribution network, as scene of cultic activities and popular entertainment, and generally as bureaucratic nerve center of a complex society. Some of the palaces, like that at Cnossus, were adjacent to towns, though others were not. Excavation and surveys have revealed their sometimes-substantial size. The population of Mallia, for example, may have approached ten thousand; that of Cnossus, eighteen thousand. Archaeologists have also recovered the layout of streets, the plans of public and private buildings, sophisticated water delivery and sewage systems, and, beyond the town limits, networks of roads. Domestic architecture, only rarely preserved above the foundation level, is vividly portrayed by a series of ivory and faience plaques from Cnossus. They depict multistory dwellings complete with sleeping quarters on the roof, windows above the ground floor, colorful exterior paint, and even timber framing with (on one archaeologist's interpretation) built-in earthquake-resistance features. It is with the towns, too, that we are presumably to associate the workplaces of the numerous craftspeople indicated by the surviving products of their work—pottery, metalwork, stone vases, and various other artifacts. Outside the towns, the Cretan countryside was dotted by villages, tiny hamlets, and (in contrast with the classical Greek practice) even isolated farmsteads. Aided by the plow and other bronze implements, Minoan farmers produced cereals, grapes (for wine and perhaps raisins), olives, and figs, among other crops. Livestock included goats, sheep, pigs, poultry, and cattle. Visitors to rural regions of modern Greece would be surprised only by the final item on this list, but the bull (and its horns) are so prominent a fixture in Minoan cult iconography and myth that the animal's presence and importance can hardly be doubted. Some of this produce supplied the rural settlements themselves; the rest found its way to the storage magazines of the palaces.

Royal family, prosperous residents of villas and townhouses, craftspeople, religious personnel, scribes charged with the keeping of the Linear A records, and a large farming population—these are the readily identifiable components of Minoan society. Pending, however, the decipherment of Linear A, details on such subjects as the organization of labor, the practice of slavery, magisterial titles and functions, and so on (that is, the sorts of information provided by the parallel Linear B tablets of the Mycenaean Greeks, shortly to be discussed) will continue to elude us. What further clues we have about the Minoan people are provided by artifacts, above all by the wall paintings that decorated some of the interior surfaces of the palaces. They reveal a wealth of clues about physical type and features, cultural stereotypes (subjects, whether male or female, are usually young and seemingly idealizations of physical beauty), clothing and grooming, and social roles.

Most striking, especially when compared with the condition of their classical Greek counterparts (see Chapter 7), are the Minoan women. They are depicted (in sculpture as well as in wall paintings) in young adulthood, with heavy makeup and elaborate hairdos, dressed in richly tailored flounced dresses that partially or wholly expose the wearer's prominent breasts. It is safe to say that, if the setting were not Minoan Crete but classical Greece, these women could not have been members of respectable (that is, free and citizen) society. But before concluding that we are dealing with a less-than-reputable segment of society, it would be well to consider the contexts in which these Minoan women appear. Some are in public view, participating in or attending events of an assured or probable cultic nature, such as the massed throng of women who, from within a sanctuary wall, raise their arms seemingly in supplication. A connection with religion is underscored by the presence of sacred attributes (as seen, for example, in the figurines of the "snake" goddess or priestess brandishing serpents in her hands) or by wearing the hair in the so-called sacred knot. Keep in mind that it was precisely on occasions of a religious nature—weddings, funerals, processions—that respectable women of classical Greece were regularly seen outside their homes. Thus the public visibility of Minoan women might, were the full truth known, make sense in its broader Mediterranean context. Details of deportment are another matter, and here we may have to look to local (but thus far not well understood) Minoan practice. The exposure of the breasts, in particular, may carry cultic or other cultural significance unknown to later Greeks, not to mention to our own society.

Minoan Religion

Religion indeed seems to have pervaded the Minoan world. Places of worship abounded—in caves, on mountaintops, in sanctuaries and shrines of varying location and arrangement. But whereas the fact of worship is manifest, the reconstruction of the rituals themselves is problematic. Some have found in bull leaping not a gory exhibition but a kind of dance, acting out a human struggle with the divinity embodied in the animal. Some have found in the palace wall paintings a program of rites and ordeals of initiation. Divine epiphanies in humanlike or animal form seem to be depicted by various artifacts. And the apparent ecstatic gyrations of the Minoan priestesses might portray their possession by a divinity—a notion that will reappear dramatically in classical Greek religion. Still more controversially, some have interpreted certain archaeological remains, as noted above, to signify the practice of human sacrifice to a god in anticipation of a divinely sent earthquake. The gods, it seems, were everywhere. All the more necessity for the historian to under-stand the hierarchy of the Minoan religious establishment and, in particular, that religious hierarchy's position in the larger pyramid of power headed by the king. The continuing study of excavated material, the opening of new sites, and (hopefully) the decipherment of Linear A may one day provide us with this understanding.

Thera: "Pompeii of the Ancient Aegean"

According to the tale of King Minos recounted at the beginning of this chapter, during that king's reign, Cnossus received tribute from Athens in the form of human victims to be fed to the Minotaur. The alleged tributary status of Athens is but one datum among many testifying to Minoan influence beyond the shores of Crete. Homer's and other literary texts link Crete with the Greek mainland, with some of the islands, and with Asia Minor. The name Minoa is found as a place name throughout the Aegean and as far afield as the Syrian coast, Arabia, and, in the west, the island of Corfu and the coast of Sicily. Archaeological investigation has revealed physical evidence of Minoan culture at several sites in the Aegean basin, especially on the islands of Melos, Kea, Kythera, Rhodes, and Thera. Minoan overseas presence or at least influ-ence would thus seem undeniable, but the specific nature of such presence or influence is not easily determined. Some, partly on the basis of ancient liter-ary evidence, have postulated the existence of a Minoan *thalassocracy* (literally, "rule of the sea")—a maritime empire established and presumably patrolled by a mighty Minoan navy. Alternatively, Minoan colonies, outposts, or trading stations serving as conduits for the transmission of Minoan culture have been imagined. As is so often the case, it is not merely a question of the existence or nonexistence of significant data. The problem is one of choosing from among a spectrum of equally plausible competing hypotheses.

In this instance, significant progress has been made in recent decades, largely due to the truly miraculous preservation of a Minoan town contempo-rary with the Late Minoan period on Crete. The site is located near the mod-ern village of Akrotiri on the island of Thera in the southern Cyclades, some seventy-five miles due north of Crete. At a time now hotly disputed by archae-ologists (see p. 20), the island, a long-dormant volcano, exploded in the great-est eruption in the documented human history of the planet. Preliminary shocks had apparently given advance warning of the coming disaster, for no human or animal remains or portable valuables have been found on the site. According to a recent reconstruction, the inhabitants, following the initial evacuation, returned to do repair work, only once again to flee with the full-scale awakening of the volcano, this time without possibility of return. The town was eventually buried beneath a thick layer of pumice and ash, to remain undiscovered (except for a few chance finds) until the commencement of sys-tematic excavation in 1967 by the Greek Archaeological Service. After nearly three decades, only a small fraction of the site has been exposed, yet even so it is evident that Akrotiri may some day live up to its billing as the "Pompeii of the ancient Aegean."

But that day has not yet arrived. So far, although indications are that the site, once fully uncovered, will prove to be an intact and complete Late Bronze Age town, only domestic architecture has been revealed. No public structure or space has been identified; no industrial establishments; no agricultural sites. Nonetheless, the private dwellings tell an interesting, if fragmentary, story.

The buildings were large, some rising originally to a height of four stories. Division of so large a space into multiple-family units, rendering them accessible to a lower-income group, is of course a possibility, but it is clear that at least some of the buildings were occupied by relatively affluent Therans. This is demonstrated most clearly by the presence in several of the houses of superbly executed wall paintings (a feature, we have already seen, of Minoan Cretan architecture). Besides the high level of disposable wealth implied by such costly decorations, the subject matter of the paintings suggests a certain freedom from the tiresome pursuit of daily necessities. Some paintings reveal an interest in the natural world—not the interest, however, of a poor dirt farmer concerned with next year's crops, but an elevated interest that expressed itself in exotic or stylized forms. (The exotic forms include blue monkeys swinging through the trees; the stylized ones represent biologically unknown or impossible formations.) Others depict human subjects, often in the pursuit of cultivated or leisurely activities. Thus we find people performing elaborate religious rituals or boys boxing or displaying strings of fish. Reminding us of their counterparts at Cnossus, the women of Akrotiri are elaborately and expensively bedecked in cosmetics, jewelry, and gowns (again, as on Crete, with breasts exposed). Uniquely, and unlike anything thus far discovered on Crete, the walls of one room carry two panels depicting, respectively, a sea battle and the voyage of a flotilla from one seacoast town to another. These last two subjects add a public, even a political, dimension and also provide a hint as to the interests or occupation of the home's owner, if the original excavator was right in suggesting that person was none other than the admiral of the flotilla. All told, it is clear that the Therans occupying these dwellings belonged to a relatively high socioeconomic stratum.

Nor is this the only deduction of societal significance that may be coaxed from the paintings. Because they were found, not in an isolated villa or two, but throughout the excavated portion of the town, it is possible to speak of a democratic or egalitarian tendency, even if it was confined to an upper class of prosperous free Therans. At the same time, one of the excavators has noted that the paintings do not adhere rigidly to a set of standard conventions but rather exhibit a striking individuality that presumably expresses the tastes of the artist's patron. Now, Minoan and (as we will see) Mycenaean society appear to have been highly regimented and subject to bureaucratic monitoring and control. But these wall paintings would seem to show that, at least within the confines of one's own home, it was still possible to give expression to a personal and individualistic impulse.

If the historian were to look for the sources of Theran individualism, it might be found in the high degree of societal differentiation, especially as revealed by the specialization of trades. A historian might deduce such specialization not from the existence of industrial workplaces or from contemporary documents, for neither is as yet known. But the wide range of artifacts discovered on the site—pottery, stone objects, woven materials, metal goods, furniture, and so on—suggests, *if those artifacts are of Theran manufacture,* a large and diverse community of crafters. Accordingly, each worker in that community might be expected to develop tastes corresponding to the specific nature of his or her craft. Hence a high degree of individualism.

But there is one major unanswered question regarding the physical record and the Theran economy in general. What was the source of the prosperity so evident in these visible private dwellings? That so small an island could have produced sufficient goods—raw materials, agricultural produce, finished goods, or otherwise—to support its evidently robust standard of living seems unlikely. An alternative mode of explanation, alluded to earlier, is that Thera (and other Aegean sites) had been colonized from Cnossus and that, if we apply the model of maritime thalassocracy to this particular case, Akrotiri owed its prosperity to the larger prosperity of the empire as a whole. Adequate support for this hypothesis, however, is not forthcoming from the archaeological record. But another possibility remains: that the Cyclades (including Thera), which at that time produced little that was in demand in foreign markets, acquired their wealth by transporting by ship the products of those societies that did, namely, Crete and Mycenaean Greece. As islanders, the Therans would have had long experience in shipbuilding and navigation; and if confirmation of this point is needed, one need only look at the two naval wall paintings from Akrotiri. Besides, if the settlement at Akrotiri were a mere offshoot of King Minos' palace at Cnossus, one should find greater uniformity of material culture between Thera and Crete than one does. Indeed, recent archaeological opinion finds stronger affinities with Thera's suggested partners in the carrying trade, to wit, the other islands of the Cyclades group. The conclusion that seems to be emerging is that the "Pompeii of the ancient Aegean" offers little support for traditional models of a Minoan maritime empire, or thalassocracy.

The Eruption of Thera and the Decline of Minoan Civilization

The eruption of the volcanic island of Thera had an impact reaching far beyond the settlement at Akrotiri. But for so catastrophic an event, the extent and historical consequences of its impact have proved surprisingly controversial. What is at stake for the historian is nothing less than the causes of the decline (and eventual disappearance) of Minoan civilization and—a development inextricably bound up with that decline—the concurrent rise of the Mycenaean Greeks. Two somewhat different problems are involved: the date and the effects of the eruption.

Absolute Chronology. The first problem is the date of the eruption. One might at first think that there could be little doubt about when so stupendous an event occurred, either absolutely or in relation to other events. But the absolute date remains up in the air pending an answer to a fundamental question of method. By what factors or tests is the date to be calculated? The pottery sequence provides the primary basis for the traditional method. Once pottery types (according to fabric, profile, decoration, and so on) have been arranged in an agreed-upon chronological sequence, it is possible to date an event by observing the latest known pottery type associated with the event in question. The event must be contemporary with or later than that pottery, and it must be earlier than the next type in the sequence, if that type is not found on the site. Prior to the beginning of the excavation at Akrotiri in 1967 there could be disagreement in this matter, but the material accumulated since then hardly leaves room for doubt. The latest imported Minoan pottery (and its local Theran imitations) coincides with the types in use in Late Minoan I A Crete; but the pottery of the following Late Minoan I B period (the so-called marine style) is found nowhere on the site. Thus, according to the traditional system of dating, the eruption must have occurred near or at the end of Late Minoan I A; that is, around 1500 B.C.

In recent years, however, this method and its specific result have been challenged, some would say successfully so. Three nontraditional dating techniques have been applied to the Theran material: radiocarbon (carbon 14) dating, dendrochronology (the establishment of dates by the counting of tree rings), and oxygen isotope measurements of ice samples from the Greenland icecap contemporary with the event. Although technical objections might be, and have been, lodged against some or all of these methods, it is an astonishing fact that they, entirely independently of one another, yield almost exactly the same result: the late 17th century B.C. One dendrochronological calculation, in fact, dates the eruption to the precise year 1628 B.C.—a full century and a quarter earlier than the pottery date. It might be possible to ignore a conflicting result of a single technically objectionable test, but the threefold agreement makes a powerful argument in favor of revising the date of the eruption upwards. Because, furthermore, the relative pottery record at Akrotiri is unassailable, something has to give, that "something" being the entire edifice of the traditional absolute chronology of the earlier Greek Bronze Age. In other words, all the events of the period, if the higher chronology is accepted, would have to be dated about 125 years earlier.

Effects of the eruption.   Whatever the absolute date, we still need to know the relation of the eruption to other events, especially those on Minoan Crete. The relevant facts available to us are the destructions of Cnossus by earthquake in Late Minoan I A and of about a dozen other Cretan sites in Late Minoan I B, in each case (where determinable) by fire. The latter events collectively represent the greatest single disaster on Crete in antiquity, one from which the island would never fully recover. What role, if any, was played by the eruption of Thera? Destruction by fire may have more than one possible cause, one of which is human agency. But (to consider an obvious scenario), if occupation of the rich island was the objective of invaders, they would not have so utterly destroyed the economic infrastructure; and, in any case, the sites would remain unoccupied for at least a full generation after the destructions. If human agency was the cause of the fires, the motive must have been punitive or piratical. But the eruption, provided the chronology fits, affords an alternative explanation. The difficulty here is the half-century gap between the eruption (traditional date, about 1500; revised date, late seventeenth century) and the Cretan disasters (traditional date, about 1450; revised date, early or mid-sixteenth century). A number of investigators have attempted to close the gap by supposing that the destruction and abandonment of Akrotiri were the result of a preliminary phase of the eruption and that the final explosion did not come for another fifty years, by which time Crete had entered the Late Minoan I B period.

This is in itself plausible, but a whole new set of questions arises concerning the precise mechanisms of the destructions on Crete. Did an earthquake accompany the eruption and, if it did, did it inflict damage on Crete, perhaps (as some suggest) overturning lamps and causing the fires? Did a tidal wave inundate the shore and destroy any Minoan ships sitting in northern harbors at the time, thereby crippling Cretan naval might? Did a fallout of pumice and ash choke out crops and render the land unusable for long periods? Technical difficulties arise for each of these proposed mechanisms. But it is the more general question that engages the attention of the ancient Greek historian. Are we justified in attempting to link to each other just those two events that we happen to know something about? And what if those two events—the eruption of Thera and the destructions on Crete—were the full truth known, turned out to have little or nothing to do with each other?

At any event, the eventual outcome appears beyond doubt. In the ruins of the palace at Cnossus were found unmistakable signs of the presence of another people—the Mycenaean Greeks.

MYCENAEAN CIVILIZATION

At the beginning of this chapter we learned of the first entry into Greece of the true Greeks, absolute date about 1900 B.C. These first Greeks, or the people who emerged from the intermingling of the new arrivals with the indigenous peoples, were the ancestors of those Greeks archaeologists call "the Mycenaeans." The word *Mycenaean,* the reader will recall, is used technically to refer to the latest phase of the Helladic—of the Bronze Age in Greece proper. Beyond technical terminology, however, *Mycenaean* denotes a well-defined historical epoch with a distinctive social-political organization, economy, cultural style, and, last but not least, legacy for later Greeks.

The Mycenaean civilization was, like the Minoan on Crete, centered on the palace. As can be seen on Map 1–1, the palaces thus far discovered were situated across the full breadth of the Greek mainland and into the central and far western Peloponnese. Some of the palaces will be familiar to readers of the heroic tales of Greek mythology: Mycenae of King Agamemnon and Queen Clytemnestra, Tiryns of King Eurystheus (for whom Hercules performed his Twelve Labors), Thebes of Oedipus the King, Sparta of King Menelaus (brother of Agamemnon) and his wife Helen, and Pylos of the elderly King Nestor. This correspondence between Mycenaean center and Greek heroic legend is no accident. For ancient Greeks of later times, the Bronze Age was the resplendent era of the larger-than-life achievements of semihistorical men and women. Our fundamental task, then, will be to try to reconstruct the reality that could have given rise to this enduring conception of an exalted heroic past.

The Archaeological Record

Today's visitor to the sites of Bronze Age Greece is struck by the sheer immensity of the physical remains of the palace centers. At Mycenae, Tiryns, Gla (and, across the Aegean, at Troy), the sites are defined by massive, towering walls constructed of giant blocks and up to forty feet thick at their base. Later Greeks, whose own constructions were on a far less massive scale, called the masonry style "cyclopean" because they believed that only superhuman beings like the Cyclopes could have erected walls of such gigantic proportions. Obviously, the existence of the belief implies not only that the technology had been lost but also, and importantly for our concerns, that the source of that technology, if not home grown, had been forgotten. The Egyptians, architects of the pyramids, are attractive candidates. This possibility will, as we will see, fit neatly into the overall pattern of extensive Mycenaean contacts with the nonclassical world throughout the Late Helladic period.

Be that as it may, it is appropriate to investigate the function of the walls. Manifestly, they were defensive: they sat atop a low hill; the circuits are punctuated by gates designed to maximize the effectiveness and safety of defenders and the risk to attackers; and, at a time still centuries before the advent of siege machinery, fortifications so colossal could stand up to any known human force. Archaeological study of the citadel at Mycenae leaves little doubt about what the Mycenaeans went to such lengths to defend. At its heart was the palace, organized around a large, rectangular room called the *megaron*, with a low, circular hearth in the center and a throne to one side. Around the megaron were arranged corridors, bedrooms, and other components of the palace's domestic complex. Below the palace were other compartments, identified by archaeologists as storage spaces, a granary, and rooms for the use of officials. Provision for the burial of the royal family (and perhaps others) was made, first, outside the citadel and, later, within it. In the final phase, the burials were shifted outside again to more massively constructed enclosures. The great bulk of the population dwelt in clusters of houses surrounding the citadel, with easy access to their fields while remaining within reach of the protective shield of the citadel in times of danger.

The Linear B Tablets and Mycenaean Society

It is therefore evident that we are dealing with a palace-centered complex fundamentally similar to the Minoan site at Cnossus. But, unlike Crete, in this instance there are contemporary documentary sources that shed valuable further light on the internal workings of the complex. The Minoan Linear A script, again, remains undeciphered despite the efforts of several generations of scholars. We are more fortunate with the Mycenaeans. Tablets inscribed with a script similar to, and at least in part derived from, Linear A were found in the destruction layers of Mycenae, Thebes, Pylos, and on Crete, with the Mycenaean occupation of the palace, at Cnossus. This script is called Linear B. Archaeologists assume that the tablets, originally in the form of unfired clay, were not intended to be preserved, but that, in the conflagrations that destroyed the palaces, they were fired like pottery and thereby assured of survival. From the discovery at the turn of the century of the first Linear B tablets at Cnossus, Arthur Evans and his successors struggled with the problem of decipherment. But it was not until 1952, in one of the great breakthroughs of classical studies, that Michael Ventris, a British cryptographer, deduced that the language inscribed in the script was an early form of Greek. At once the ethnic identity of the Mycenaeans was established, and a flood of light was shed on the administrative workings of the palace systems.

With the translation of the tablets, it became clear that they were the accounts, or books, of the Mycenaean palace. They record, for example, inventories, assessments, deliveries, records of distributions of materials for production and of the goods produced, and particulars regarding parcels of land and flocks of animals. Additionally, the tablets preserve much incidental information regarding the political and priestly hierarchy, details of religion and cult, personal names, and so on. In one isolated instance, which comes closest to capturing an account of a contemporary event, they preserve instructions given at Pylos in anticipation of an attack from the sea. But the texts are overwhelmingly administrative, with no trace of the historical (or literary) material characteristic of the parallel texts from contemporary Near Eastern civilizations. Nonetheless, above and beyond the procedural details that they preserve, the tablets establish what is probably the fundamental fact about Mycenaean civilization: Mycenaean palace society was governed by a highly stratified and compartmentalized bureaucracy, administered from the top down and meticulously monitored through a detailed accounting system.

At the peak of the pyramid of power was the *wanax*, or king. Mention of the king in the tablets, however, is exceedingly infrequent. Occasional uses are made of the adjective meaning "royal" to designate (for example) a potter or textiles, suggesting a degree of personal control by the king within the palace. The basis of his authority is not recorded, but the fact that the word *wanax* (like the English "lord") was sometimes applied to divinities is consistent with the supposition that he was regarded as a kind of god and ruled by divine right. No such associations, however, apply in the case of the *basileus*. Although, strangely, *basileus*, in both Homer and standard Greek, would become the normal prose word for "king," at Cnossus he appears to be a local chief and at Pylos, merely a low-level functionary—a warning of the possible anachronisms if one argues back from later to earlier times. In fact, the principal wielder of secular power is likely to have been the *lawagetas* (or "leader of the people"). Such a term might designate a commander-in-chief of the military forces, but he might equally well be a political or administrative officer complementing a primarily religious or ceremonial *wanax*. Of unknown functions were the *telestai*, who, perhaps incidentally to their magisterial authority, are recorded to have owned large parcels of land; just possibly, if the meaning of the word in later Greek is any indication, they were cultic officials of some kind. Another probable religious person was the *klawiphoros*, or "key-bearer." The fact that this officer was sometimes recognizably a woman anticipates the striking prominence of women in religion in historical Greece (see Chapter 7).

These examples are sufficient to establish the high degree of differentiation in the upper echelons of the social-political order. But beyond these officers, the tablets also provide some hints concerning larger social classes of Mycenaean society. One, the *hequetai*, or "followers," should be, if the term is taken more or less literally, a sort of entourage, presumably of the king. The ascription to the "followers" of slaves, clothes, and wheels suggested to the tablets' editor, respectively, the personal ownership of slaves, a distinctive style of dress, and access to the use of chariots. Personal property, the public advertisement of high status, and an important military function—all combined in a single class of people—would seem to justify our use of a term such as *nobility* to characterize them. But what about the lower classes?

Tablets from Pylos refer to the *damos*, a word that, to judge from its meaning in later Greek in such terms as *demokratia* ("the rule of the people"), could denote the entire population, more likely the entire free population. But in classical Greek, *damos* may also mean a village or, technically, a territorial administrative unit. Therefore, following this lead, some have proposed that the Mycenaean word more narrowly specifies, for example, the sixteen districts of the kingdom of Pylos. If so, we would then be without a word for "the people." But whichever way the term is understood, the tablets imply that it was the "plot holders"—that is, the owners of landed property—who spoke for the people (or Pylian district). Mycenaean society was therefore certainly not democratic in any sense that we attach to that concept (although, interestingly, the idea of restricting rights to those meeting a certain standard of property ownership would enjoy an enduring popularity in later Greece).

The Mycenaean population embraced a large force of specialized tradespeople. The tablets are especially rich in terms for occupations or crafts. Examples include shepherd, goatherd, and ox driver; woodcutter, carpenter, mason, bronzesmith, and potter; carder, spinner, and weaver; bath attendants and serving women. This evidence is ample enough to support some general observations. First, some tasks were allocated by gender. As scholars have noted, only women manufactured cloth but only men were fullers (although, inconsistently, both men and women were garmentmakers); whereas the grinding and measuring of grain were women's work, bread was made only by men; and so on. Although the bases (physical, economic, or otherwise) for these allocations, which to us sometimes appear so arbitrary, are not recoverable, we are perhaps at liberty to find the beginnings of the gender roles that would be developed to such an extreme degree in classical Greece. In a traditional society, precedents, especially if those precedents belong to an exemplary heroic age, may count for much, however ill justified they may originally have been. Second, and more generally, the simple fact that the division of labor was so highly developed again illustrates the fundamental trait of Mycenaean society: its high degree of differentiation. This was a society of specialists. Negatively, on the other hand, it is often remarked that the tablets, despite the multitude of occupational titles, preserve no word for a person who raises crops—for a farmer. Yet, for all its sophistication, the Mycenaean Greek economy remained fundamentally agrarian. These facts suggested to the editors of the tablets that everyone, in addition to the specialized occupational role, was also a farmer, and so no notice needed to be made of the fact.

Whether tradespeople or farmers or both, the social status of these Mycenaeans remains unknown. Were they free or slave? Slaves certainly existed. The male and female forms of the classical Greek word for "slave" occur numerous times in the tablets. But what do we know about these slaves? Involuntary servitude need not necessarily imply either impoverishment or inhumane treatment. At least one Mycenaean slave is listed alongside free men as a contributor to his master's revenue; and the numerous "slaves of the god (or goddess)" enjoy, like free men, the privilege of leasing and living on the lands of Pylos. What does distinguish slaves from the free is the fact that they in some or all cases were obtained either by raids or by purchase at slave markets (located, for example, along the western coast of Asia Minor). Some slaves are explicitly labeled "captives" in the tablets. It was the facts of capture or of purchase and ownership, then, that made a slave and distinguished him or her from a free person. Significantly, too, the preponderance of slaves were women and children. This suggests that some slaves were captured following battles in which adult males were killed or after which they were executed (the latter coinciding with the practice of later Greece). But beyond these simple facts the tablets tell us little. Before we can learn something of the condition and quality of life of the servile populations, we must wait until we reach the far richer source materials of classical Greece.

The Mycenaean Economy

From the tablets and from archaeological evidence it has been possible for archaeologists to recover information about the principal elements of the local economy. This includes information about the lands and population centers dependent on the palaces; holdings of property by the king, *lawagetas, telestai,* and other individuals; the identity of crops and livestock holdings; the movement, as indicated by the tablets, of goods and personnel into and out of the palaces; and, again, something of the nature of Mycenaean industry as revealed by mention of physical artifacts, inventories, and tradespeople. This is a truly vast store of data, and by no means has its analysis been carried to completion. Yet, even without a definitive reconstruction of the economy, it is necessary to confront and try to answer one of the perennial questions of Greek prehistory. What was the source of that wealth that seems so suddenly to have vaulted the Mycenaeans into prominence in the Late Helladic period?

The royal cemeteries. The clearest evidence of that wealth is provided by the royal cemeteries at Mycenae. The earliest of these, Grave Circle B (so designated because it was the second of the circles to be discovered, though earlier in date), is situated a short distance to the west and outside of the fortification wall. Of the twenty-eight burials, fourteen are of the "shaft" type and so thought to contain the bodies of royalty (in fact, the skeletons are reported to be generally of big, tall males). Among the grave goods (including pottery and weapons) were articles of gold (mostly thin foil) and a death mask of electrum (a natural alloy of gold and silver). Overlapping chronologically with the later of these burials and extending down to the end of the fifteenth century is Grave Circle A, which was eventually (though not originally) brought within the fortification wall. Discovered and excavated by Schliemann in the nineteenth century, its six deep shafts contain nineteen burials. The grave goods continue the tendencies of Grave Circle

B, but on a vastly richer scale: large quantities of weapons, pottery, and, most conspicuously, a multitude of gold objects, including (again) a death mask of one of the deceased—presumably the king of Mycenae, though not, for chronological reasons, Agamemnon, as Schliemann thought. Wealth of this magnitude is without precedent in Greece. What, again, is the explanation for its relatively sudden appearance?

Foreign contacts.   Any attempt at an answer must begin by acknowledging the foreign influence evident in the burials, beginning with the latest phase of the use of the shaft graves of Grave Circle B and embracing much of the contents of the burials of Grave Circle A. So varied are these influences that the aggregate of styles represented in the grave goods has justly been characterized as international. Minoan Crete, the Near East, Egypt—all are represented. Granting, however, the fact of foreign influence, we still need to understand the mechanism by which that influence was transmitted. Are we to think of commercial relations, resulting in the importation of foreign artifacts? And if these precious objects were obtained through peaceful exchange, what role, if any, was played by the Minoans, who may at this time, as some think, have dominated the Aegean seas? Did the Minoans facilitate or obstruct the Mycenaeans' contacts with their trading partners? Or, to take a different tack, perhaps some of the goods are of local manufacture, executed in imitation of well-known foreign styles by Mycenaean artisans. Alternatively, perhaps the grave goods are the fruits of Mycenaean piracy, or of raids on fortified towns such as that immortalized in the story of the Trojan War? Or did the Mycenaean kings receive these riches from foreign potentates in exchange for the service of Mycenaean mercenaries? The jury is still out, and of course we may never find out the truth. But the fact of foreign influence, whatever the medium of transmission, remains and must be factored into the mix of elements out of which Mycenaean civilization in its highest period of development would emerge. At the same time, care must be taken not to overstate the implications of those influences. These are mere grave goods. Their impact, if any, on the larger developments, cultural or otherwise, of Greek Bronze Age civilization, not to mention later classical Greek civilization, can only be established by rigorous demonstration.

The Later Mycenaeans (the Late Helladic Period)

With periods A and B of Late Helladic III (traditional chronology, about 1400–1200 B.C.), Greece arrives at the greatest phase of Mycenaean civilization. At Mycenae (to continue with this single, but illuminating, case), this was the time of the massive reconstruction of the citadel. The existing royal palace was erected on the summit; the great cyclopean walls were built, later to be extended to include within them Grave Circle A; and, among other constructions, the so-called Lion Gate, evidently symbolizing the warlike tendencies of the current regime, was installed. Beyond the walls, and breaking away from the earlier circles of shaft graves, a new design (possibly imported from Minoan Crete), was introduced for royal burials: the *tholos*, or "beehive" tomb. The two most well-preserved examples were enthusiastically dubbed by Schliemann the Tomb of Clytemnestra and the Treasury of Atreus, with reference to the wife and father of the Homeric king Agamemnon. Elsewhere, at Tiryns and Gla, the erection of massive fortification systems and, near Gla, the construction of a system of dikes and canals to drain the Copaic Basin date to the same era. If the greatness of a polity may be measured by the dimensions of its building projects, this was truly the great era of Mycenaean civilization.

In conjunction with the physical growth of the palace complex, the Late Helladic was marked by the penetration of Mycenaean civilization into neighboring and sometimes far-flung regions. Mycenaean settlements were established around the Aegean littoral. Products of Mycenaean manufacture surfaced over a wide expanse of the eastern, central, and perhaps western Mediterranean. Mycenaeans also evidently entered into relations with foreign powers. The Ahhijawans, with whom the Hittite kings of central Asia Minor maintained relations at this time, are widely suspected to have been "Achaeans"—that is, Mycenaean Greeks from Mycenae or other centers. Again, as with our characterization of the grave goods of the Middle Helladic grave circles at Mycenae, the term *international* is entirely justified. But now the term is no longer narrowly applied to the range of styles in an accumulation of luxurious keepsakes. With the Late Helladic it has a much broader reference to a wide spectrum of cultural, economic, and even military affairs.

The last-mentioned item, military affairs, is of vital importance for an understanding of the later Mycenaeans. Dispositionally, there can hardly be any doubt that the Mycenaeans were a particularly aggressive, even a violent people. The subjects of some of the paintings decorating the interior walls of the palaces (particularly at Pylos) and of some of the grave goods found in royal burials at Mycenae and elsewhere are unambiguous in this regard. Hunting of large game and warfare are among the most popular themes. And even if some of this material is of foreign origin or inspiration (as is probably true of the wall paintings, obviously indebted to Minoan prototypes), the choice of subjects nonetheless testifies to the tastes and inclinations of the Mycenaean consumers. Weapons, too, are frequently encountered in the royal burials; the shafts from Grave Circle A alone yielded about 150 bronze swords or daggers. Nor can there be any doubt about the military nature of the fortification systems, although the precise identification of the real or contemplated enemy from whom they were meant to offer protection will continue to be debated. Finally, the Homeric *Iliad* and *Odyssey*, the surviving masterpieces of an originally much vaster poetic celebration of the Trojan War, speak eloquently of the militaristic propensities of the Mycenaean people.

Aggressive ambitions on the part of the Mycenaeans would inevitably have invited competition—and perhaps conflict—with the Minoans. Some scholars have imagined various forms of cooperation (particularly in matters of trade) between the two powers, but, if there was ever any such understanding, it eventually deteriorated into Mycenaean aggression and ultimately conquest. The question for the historian is, again, when and under what circumstances. The one major datum we have is that Linear B tablets were claimed by Evans to have been discovered in association with the ruins of the palace at Cnossus. It would be difficult to deny the inference that the users of the script—namely, the Mycenaeans—had occupied the palace and that, further, by commandeering the centralized administrative machinery, they established control over all of Crete.

Again, assumptions concerning chronology and the unfolding of events are involved. For one, as we saw, a gap of about half a century separates the abandonment of the volcanic island of Thera and the eventual destruction by fire of the palace at Cnossus. Perhaps, a plausible reconstruction would go, the natural disaster severely weakened Minoan power, with the result that, after an interval, the militaristic Mycenaeans were able to marshal their forces and take over the palace nerve center of their peaceable island competitor. But this popular reconstruction has by no means been universally accepted. A furious debate has raged over the chronology of the Cnossan Linear B tablets, some archaeologists maintaining that they belong to a much later time, around 1200 B.C., about the time when, as we will shortly see, the mainland Mycenaean centers were visited with violent destruction. Consensus has yet to emerge. All we can be fairly confident about is that, at some point, whether soon after the eruption or not until much later, Mycenaeans occupied the palace at Cnossus and that this was probably the pivotal event in the ultimate extinction of Minoan civilization.

The Trojan War

The most famous event of Greek prehistory is the Trojan War. According to the legendary tradition beginning with Homer's *Iliad* and *Odyssey*, the war was precipitated by the abduction of Helen, wife of Sparta's King Menelaus, by Paris, a son of the king of Troy. The cuckolded Menelaus then appealed to his more powerful brother, Agamemnon, king of Mycenae, and under the latter's direction a great armada of "Achaeans" was assembled from all over the Greek world. It was Helen whose face launched a thousand ships. Crossing the Aegean (after a delay at Aulis, where Agamemnon sacrificed his daughter Iphigeneia to appease the offended goddess Artemis), the Greeks laid siege to the fortified citadel of Troy. In the tenth year of the war, through the brilliant ruse of the Wooden Horse, the Greeks violently sacked Troy.

Does this story preserve the memory of an actual historical event? Excavations undertaken by Schliemann in 1876 convinced him, and many others since, that indeed it does. Schliemann's site, near the modern Turkish town of Hissarlik in the northwestern corner of Asia Minor, enjoyed a long history of occupation extending back into the Stone Age, but a consensus has emerged that, of the many levels of settlement, Homer's Troy corresponds to that numbered VII A. The occupation ended in an apparently violent destruction by fire, and among the debris were found human skeletons and weapons reputedly of Achaean—that is, Mycenaean Greek—origin. Moreover, the archaeological date (according to the traditional chronology) for the destruction of VII A, around the middle of the thirteenth century, corresponds roughly to the beginning and ending dates for the war, 1194–1184 B.C., calculated by ancient scholars on the basis of independent nonarchaeological evidence. Skeptics remain, but more recent debate has concerned not the historicity of a war that most now accept as a fact, but its causes and its place within the context of the final chapters of Mycenaean civilization.

That a war of such dimensions and duration could have been fought over Helen should not, despite skepticism extending back to the ancient Greeks themselves, be readily dismissed as a poetic embellishment. For the Greeks, most marriages, certainly marriages involving kings, were the products not of affection or attraction, but of various political, social, and economic considerations. Thus the abduction of a king's wife was on general grounds bound to have major consequences unrelated to her or her husband's personal feelings on the matter. Besides, Helen's particular case was unusual (by the standards of Greek antiquity) in that she was the daughter of the previous king of Sparta and it was by virtue of the fact that Menelaus was her husband that he had succeeded his father-in-law as king. Technically put, the Spartan royal house operated on the principle of matrilineal succession. For this reason, there was more at stake for Menelaus than merely the recovery of his wife.

Yet Helen need not of course have been the only concern motivating the Greeks. Economic factors may well have been at work. Troy's strategic location on a land route between Europe and Asia and on the straits (the Hellespont) giving access from the Aegean to the rich resources of the Black Sea region is obviously relevant. Perhaps Troy had exploited its position, possibly through extracting tolls from commercial traffic, and the Mycenaeans wished to appropriate its wealth. Perhaps the Mycenaeans had commercial ambitions of their own and hoped, by eliminating the obstructing presence of Troy, to establish their own access to the region. Some recent speculation has focused on the local fishing grounds, over which the Mycenaeans may have wished to assert control. Or, to cite a rather different approach, perhaps the Mycenaeans had somehow become embroiled in the power politics of Asia Minor and were thereby drawn into war with Troy. The debate continues. But at least we can say that, on any of these (or related) approaches to the problem, whether economic or political, the Trojan War would fit comfortably with the aggressiveness and overseas expansion that we have found to be particularly characteristic of the Mycenaeans in the Late Helladic period.

The Destruction of Mycenaean Civilization

The Trojan War, though it comes near the end of the Mycenaean era, is not the last identifiable event of that era. During the century from about 1250 to 1150 B.C. the palace complexes suffered widespread violent destruction from which the civilization was never to rebound. Particularly affected were Mycenae, Tiryns, Pylos, Gla, and Thebes, in addition to a number of the smaller settlements. A major exception was Athens, which by this time was heavily fortified; indeed it was to Athens, the tradition records, that Mycenaeans fleeing from Pylos escaped en route to their new homes in Asia Minor. But elsewhere the destruction was general and, though not attributable to any natural cause, more or less simultaneous. The highly stratified and compartmentalized bureaucracy was destroyed, never to be seen again. Eventually, too, although some sites were temporarily reoccupied by Mycenaeans, there occurred a widespread depopulation from which Greece would not recover for centuries. To the historian in search of the agents of so catastrophic a series of events, it is especially puzzling that over the immense area of the destructions no clue has been discovered that might establish their identity. This is the final mystery of the Greek Bronze Age.

Some scholars believe that the destructions were the work of foreign invaders. Evidence of an emergency exists at Pylos, where a series of Linear B tablets records measures taken by the king in anticipation of a raid from the sea. Since, like the tablets from the other palaces, the Pylian texts belong to the time just prior to the destruction by fire that baked them, it is reasonable to infer that the raid did indeed take place and that the raiders were the agents of destruction for whom we are searching. Some have identified these with the so-called Sea Peoples (actually a collective term designating, it has been suggested, Lycians from Asia Minor, and Sardinians and Sicilians from the West, among others), known from Egyptian records to have been active in the eastern Mediterranean at this time. Did these Sea Peoples venture into the Aegean region and attack Greece?

Another possibility, that the agents were a Greek population called the Dorians, was widely favored among classicists until fairly recently. However, despite the explicit support this theory receives from later Greek written sources, the notion of a Dorian "invasion" at this time has been questioned by some scholars on both archaeological and linguistic grounds (see further, Chapter 2). For one thing, as with the Sea Peoples hypothesis, no trace of a Dorian presence has been found anywhere in the destroyed ruins of the palaces. Is it not strange that invaders, having incurred such risks, should then fail to occupy the conquered territory and exploit the resources of their Mycenaean victims?

For alternative hypotheses, the historian turns to the Greek literary tradition. According to the Homeric and classical poetic texts, Agamemnon, upon his return from Troy to Mycenae, was slain by Clytemnestra, taking vengeance for the sacrifice of their daughter Iphigeneia; and Odysseus, upon his arrival at his kingdom on Ithaca, had to slay over a hundred suitors for the hand of his wife, Penelope, before resuming the throne. Perhaps these are embellished reminiscences of internal conflicts within the palaces which exploded into all-out civil wars? The immediate cause of the strife might have been a power struggle among noble dynasts for ascendancy (thus foreshadowing the revolutionary era of historical Greece); or, as some have speculated, the wars possibly pitted a united ruling elite against an uprising of prosperous but nonnoble merchants, peasants, or even slaves. Somewhat differently, and departing from the literary tradition, the palace centers may have made war *against each other.* But any model of domestic rebellion or conflict founders once again on the same paradox. If land, wealth, or power was the object of the strife, why did the Mycenaean winners not rebuild and occupy the conquered or successfully defended citadels and territories?

A way out of these difficulties is possible if, following the lead of more recent, nontraditional approaches to the subject, we can identify an element in the situation that might have rendered Mycenaean lands at least temporarily uninhabitable. Two recent theories are applicable. Deforestation (and its consequences) is one. Large-scale loss of timber would inevitably have attended the clearing of land for agriculture and the cutting of old-growth forests for construction of palaces and navies. Deforestation would lead in turn to erosion, thus making the land unarable. (Somewhat more hypothetical are suggestions of epidemics, major droughts, a change of climate, earthquakes, or, again, the chronologically disputed effects of the eruption of Thera.) The second approach is more closely tied to the distinguishing feature of Mycenaean society: its complexity. The theory of *systems collapse* states that the various components of a complex society may be so interdependent that the removal or failure of one might cause irremediable damage to the system as a whole. In the ancient Mediterranean context, for example, a succession of crop failures could have brought down the whole house of cards that was Mycenaean society. Either development—collapse of the system or environmental disaster—could, in combination with foreign invasion or civil war, have crippled the civilization beyond recovery.

Suggested Readings

A recent detailed and scholarly account of prehistoric Greece will be found in the third edition of the *Cambridge Ancient History*, vols. 1–2 (Cambridge, 1970–1975). More accessible and accompanied by many excellent photographs is the "coffee table" overview by a recognized authority, P. Warren, *The Aegean Civilizations:* Phaidon (Oxford, 1975).

For the monumental publication on the site at Cnossus by its excavator, see A. Evans, *The Palace of Minos,* 4 vols. (London, 1921–1935; reprinted 1964). Despite the questionable identification of the palace as a temple and the use of the Linear B tablets as sources for Minoan civilization, R. Castleden's *Minoan Life in Bronze Age Crete* (London and New York, 1990) presents a useful overview of its announced subject. A more conventional, but now dated, account is S. Hood, *The Minoans: The Story of Bronze Age Crete* (New York, 1971). Excavations at Akrotiri from 1967 to 1979 are insightfully described and interpreted by C. G. Doumas, *Thera: Pompeii of the Ancient Aegean* (London, 1983), to which the text refers for the views of the site's excavator.

For an excellent account of the Mycenaean civilization, based mainly on the evidence of the Linear B tablets, there is J. Chadwick, *The Mycenaean World* (Cambridge, 1976). The tablets themselves are accessible in Chadwick's *Documents in Mycenaean Greek,* 2nd ed. (Cambridge, 1973), Chapter 5 of which, "The Evidence of the Tablets," pp. 106–150, has been drawn upon in the account above. More broadly based accounts include G. E. Mylonas, *Mycenae and the Mycenaean Age* (Princeton, 1966); J. T. Hooker, *Mycenaean Greece* (London, 1976); and R. H. Simpson, *Mycenaean Greece* (Park Ridge, N.J., 1981). A scholarly but readable account of the Mycenaean excavations is W. A. McDonald and C. G. Thomas, *Progress into the Past. The Rediscovery of Mycenaean Civilization,* 2nd ed. (Bloomington and Indianapolis, 1990).

A classic, penetrating, and beautifully crafted account of Greek prehistory, E. Vermeule, *Greece in the Bronze Age* (Chicago, 1972; originally published in 1964), remains valuable despite its age.

Chapter 2. The Renaissance
of Greek Civilization

The destruction of Mycenaean civilization had not been a single cataclysmic event. Destruction had come in waves, first at Pylos and elsewhere around 1250 B.C.; later, around 1200 B.C., with much greater devastation at Mycenae, Tiryns, Gla, and Thebes, among others. A few places—notably Argos and, significantly for this book, Athens—escaped for the time being. At these sites and at Mycenae and Tiryns, which were soon rebuilt, Mycenaean culture lived on for another century, although in a far less elevated form. Gone were the complex, sophisticated bureaucracies; gone, the Linear B writing system; gone, the cultivated expressions of wealth and leisure earlier evidenced in wall paintings, sculpture, stone vessels, and other decorative articles. All perished forever with the disappearance of the palaces. Nonetheless, there is considerable evidence of continuity—for a time, anyway. Mycenaean society, as documented by surviving signs of its physical culture, was not dead. For one thing, the pottery record continues intact, despite the replacement of the uniform styles of the palace period by distinct regional styles. Beyond Greece, Late Helladic III C pottery was exported to the Near East and, to the west, as far away as Tarentum in Italy. Something of the old order remained alive.

THE DORIAN "INVASION"

Eventually, however, change overwhelmed the Mycenaean Greek world. Outmigration from the Mycenaean centers occurred on a vast scale. Evidence of the historical Greek dialects (as well as of material culture) shows that Mycenaean people dispersed to Cyprus; and evidence of Mycenaean presence is also found in Achaea, the Ionian islands, and the Cyclades. Meanwhile, beginning in the later twelfth century, new peoples were making their first appearance in Greece. Some have looked to the northwest of Greece for the source of these peoples, but on the basis of strictly archaeological indications, their origins remain obscure.

Greeks of the classical period, however, were less uncertain about what had happened. Thucydides, an Athenian historian of the fifth century B.C., wrote of the arrival in the Peloponnese of the Dorians eighty years after the Trojan War. This date—in the later twelfth century B.C.—would coincide with signs of new peoples in the physical record. Furthermore, with Thucydides' (and other writers') evidence may be linked to the distribution of that Greek dialect called "Doric" in the historical period. This is consistent with the supposed movement of speakers of that dialect from the northwest, through the Peloponnese, and from the Peloponnese across the southern Aegean islands (including Crete) to Asia Minor. With these givens, next, historians have traditionally associated the legendary event preserved in the ancient tradition as "the Return of the Heraclidae" (the sons of Heracles). Translated into nontraditional language, the return of the Heraclidae became "the Dorian invasion"—a mass incursion of Greeks that, a century in the wake of the destruction of Mycenaean civilization, repopulated much of mainland, Peloponnesian, and southern Greece. This has always been an attractive, even a beguiling, reconstruction. These invaders would have brought with them the host of cultural innovations now appearing in the archaeological record for the first time—the use of iron in place of bronze, cremation of the dead in place of burial, and a variety of intrusive artifacts—as well as the Doric dialect of Greek. And, most beguilingly, the hypothesis constructs a neat and easily imagined scenario that conforms to the model—so familiar in later, historical Greece—of the massive movement of an entire population. Thus Thucydides' evidence, the legendary tradition, the physical record, and the known distribution of the Doric dialect can all be combined in a single familiar and eminently plausible historical reconstruction.

But plausibility and truth need not coincide. Over the years, a host of problems have arisen with the invasion hypothesis. If the Dorians, entering Greece en masse, had introduced all the abovementioned innovations, we would expect to find traces of *all* of them at the *same* site at the *same* time. But this does not happen. Nor is it clear that all the alleged innovations are to be attributed to the Dorians. Archaeological evidence suggests that iron, for example, was introduced from the east, by way of Cyprus; if so, the innovation could no longer be associated with an invasion from the north. Perhaps most unsettling is the evidence of the dialects. If the Dorian Greeks were in fact invaders originating in a location outside of Greece proper, their form of Greek should differ substantially from that of the Mycenaean Greeks. But, in truth, the evidence of the later dialects proves that they shared many linguistic features. When one considers, finally, that the ancient sources speak not of a Dorian "invasion" but of the *return* of the descendants of Heracles, it is easy to see the attractions of a modern alternative hypothesis: that the Dorians had always been in Greece and that (more hypothetically) they were originally an under or lower class that had either risen up and overthrown the Mycenaean ruling class. Alternatively, the Dorians may, at an interval following the destructions by other, unidentified agents, have filled the void created by the collapse or emigration of the Mycenaeans.

The new hypothesis is equally able to account for the facts at our disposal, while avoiding the pitfalls of the invasion model. At the same time, its acceptance does involve a cost. What of the movement of the Dorians into the Peloponnese, mentioned by Thucydides? And what is to be done with the return of the Heraclidae? Ultimately, the choice between the traditional or the revisionist hypothesis will come down in large part to how much faith one is willing to place in the ancient literary traditions.

THE GREAT MIGRATIONS

The rise (or entry) of the Dorians was soon followed by a massive eastward expansion across the Aegean to the seaboard of Asia Minor. This expansion may be pictured in the form of three broad bands of emigration, extending from Greece in a due easterly direction (see Map 1). To the north, Greeks from in and around the region of Thessaly, who spoke the Aeolic Greek dialect, expanded to occupy the island of Lesbos and the northern segment of the coastal region of Asia Minor. Peoples from the Peloponnese and Isthmus region—under the leadership of Mycenaeans from Pylos who, fleeing from the destructions at the end of the twelfth century, had taken refuge at Athens—settled the islands of the central Aegean (including the Cyclades) and the central seaboard of Asia Minor, now called Ionia. These Greeks, like the Athenians, spoke the Ionic dialect. The Dorians, comprising the third band, spread, as mentioned, from the Peloponnese across the southern Aegean, occupying the islands of Melos, Crete, and Rhodes and its group, before coming to rest in the southwestern region of Asia Minor.

These movements, although only imperfectly understood, were evidently unorganized undertakings which bore little relation to the formal colonial ventures of later times (see p. 41). Their cause is uncertain, because the most likely explanation, population pressure, is inconsistent with the observed *de*population of Greece at the end of the Mycenaean era. And a second hypothesis, that the Aeolians and Ionians were pushed out by the Dorians, who themselves were carried by their own momentum across the southern Aegean, is obviously dependent on acceptance of the (as we have seen) currently debated notion of a Dorian "invasion." It may be that we will have to think less in terms of the avoidance of undesirable conditions at home and more in terms of the attractions of those regions to which the migrations led the Greeks. In any event, the result was the permanent establishment of Greek populations in island and Asian coastal regions that had previously been only spottily occupied by Mycenaeans of the Bronze Age.

THE EMERGENCE OF THE CITY-STATE

The period following the Mycenaean collapse, down to the middle of the eighth century B.C., is traditionally known as the Dark Age. At its beginning, the physical infrastructure of Greek civilization lay in ruins. Throughout the following four centuries, except for those short-lived reoccupations of

Mycenaean sites mentioned above, the evidence of settlement in Greece points to a drastic deterioration of conditions. A survey of known sites provides a graphic illustration: for the century 1300–1200, 320 sites are known; for 1200–1100, 130 sites; for 1100–1000, 40 sites. At the same time, what sites are recognized for the later periods are significantly smaller. Many existing sites had been abandoned and, whether by mortality, a falling birthrate, or emigration, the settled population underwent a dramatic reduction. Nor, to state the obvious, had new palaces or other settlements of comparable dimensions appeared to fill the void left by the decline of the Mycenaeans.

By the outset of the classical period, however, the situation had undergone an equally dramatic reversal. The Greek world, now greatly enlarged, was by this time dotted with hundreds, perhaps more than a thousand, cities or, more precisely, *city-states*. (These were cities that, by virtue of their political independence and general economic self-sufficiency, were legally and for all practical purposes autonomous states in their own right.) Nor was growth simply a matter of numbers. Although the great majority of the new cities were small, with citizen bodies of no more than a few hundred, a few others, such as Athens, Argos, Sparta, Syracuse, and Miletus, boasted populations in the tens of thousands, massive public infrastructures, vibrant economies, large holdings of valuable land or accumulations of wealth, and impressive military arsenals. How had this happened? What factors precipitated so stupendous a reorientation and process of growth?

No simple answer, no easy formula, of course, is to be found. Too many variables are involved, differing in character or combination from case to case. Some cities were situated on or near old Mycenaean sites; others were planted on virgin ground. Some grew up on the coast; others were confined to all or part of an island; still others lay far inland without access to the sea. Sometimes the territory of a city was well defined (and defended) by mountains or other natural formations; others occupied but a fully exposed segment of a vast, unbroken plain. Some cities were endowed with rich arable land or valuable natural resources, such as timber or minerals, whereas others were entirely without such advantages. One city might be ringed by actual or potential enemies; in another place, conditions favored peaceful cooperation with neighboring populations. Such variation obviously rules out the possibility of a single line of development from beginnings to fully functioning city-state. Nonetheless, it does make sense to try to reconstruct those basic conditions underlying the variations among the individual cases that, in most instances, were probably sufficient to snap the Greeks out of the unproductive lethargy of the Dark Age.

An absolutely necessary condition was growth of population. Archaeological opinion agrees that such growth occurred at about the time the earliest cities were beginning to develop. The study mentioned earlier in connection with Dark Age settlements estimates that, between about 780 and 720 B.C., the population of Athens multiplied *sevenfold*. What precipitated such growth? The same study conjectures as the economic basis for the rise of the city-state the transition from pastoralism (the raising of grazing animals—in Greece's case, sheep and goats) to the resumption of arable farming. Such a change would, if successful, account for rapid population growth. The rise of farming would help account for much else as well. Greek farmers historically did not, on the pattern familiar to observers of the rural United States, establish their homes on their land in isolation from their neighbors. Instead, they congregated in nucleated, or clustered, villages. Villages might next (and sometimes did) coalesce into larger communities. Sparta, in fact, not only started out as an aggregate of four such settlements but even retained that basic structure throughout the remainder of antiquity. Many other states, such as Athens, "synoecized," or coalesced, out of a mass of towns and hamlets, continued to recognize those original components as unitary elements of government in their developed constitutional organizations. And where, finally, were these clusters of villages likely to be situated? In many instances they were at the base of, or near, a defensible height, a fortified citadel, to which the villagers might flee with their movable property in times of danger. Indeed, the Greek word for "city-state," *polis*, originally denoted such a place of refuge, as illustrated by the case of Athens where, as late as the classical period, the word *polis* could still be used to refer to the city's fortified citadel, the Acropolis.

Thus the first communal public project of the young city-state was typically its fortifications. Once these were in place, archaeological dates favor the first public building's being a temple or shrine of some kind. General probabilities also point this way. Classical cities often recognized a particular divinity as a patron, as Athens for instance recognized Athena. It was to Athena that Athenians ascribed (among other acts) the creation of the first olive tree on the slopes of the Acropolis, and it was she whom they identified as *promachos*, their leader in warfare. So, too, Sparta and the Dioscuri, Argos and Hera. Similarly, citizens of colonies sometimes worshiped their departed human founder as a hero or demigod. Both types of cults could be housed in sanctuaries in the urban center. Temples on the Athenian Acropolis included the "Old" Athena temple and an earlier and later Parthenon—the shrine of the Virgin Athena. The citizens of Amphipolis, a colony founded from Athens, worshiped, first, the heroized Athenian founder and, later, after a Spartan takeover, the successful Spartan general in whose honor, on his death, a shrine was erected "as to a hero." The sanctuary would serve as the site of offerings to the divinity in the hope of obtaining benefits for the community; it would be the natural venue for any communal expressions of thanksgiving; it would play a central role in public gatherings—sacrifices, festivals, processions—in the patron's name.

Subsequent developments, however, are more difficult, for want of physical evidence, to reduce to a pattern. At some early point, efficiency would presumably have dictated the emergence or growth of trades and crafts at some centralized location, typically at or near the now-developing urban center. Agricultural implements, pottery and other utensils, or military weaponry—the hardware without which this community could not function—could obviously not be produced efficiently or in adequate quality by a farmer working in his barn. Smiths and potters and other full-time specialists, echoing their Mycenaean forerunners, would have emerged, and, again for the sake of efficiency, their workplaces would have been centrally located on or near the citadel.

So far, the physical infrastructure and permanent population of the nascent city is beginning to take shape. But fortifications, public buildings, even an urban populace do not singly or in combination make a polis. There is also the element of mentality. In classical times, the city was to be marked by internal cohesion, particularly solidarity among the citizen population, and, in general, the recognition of the polis (in distinction from Greek nationalism or, at the other extreme, from the individual person) as the proper focus of loyalty and the standard of correct conduct. It is attitudes like these that distinguish a physical concentration of building materials and human bodies from a community. Thus any account of the origins of the city-state must identify at least the beginnings of these attitudes. What, in the absence of contemporary written sources, can be conjectured?

One contributing factor was the essentially *defensive* nature of the city. The polis started out as a place of refuge, and elements of this defensive mentality are arguably still to be detected centuries later. Nothing makes for solidarity, even among people with scant or nonexistent shared interests, like the perception and fear of a common enemy. Religion, too, added a vital ingredient of communal solidarity. Because ancient Greeks were polytheistic, a multitude of divinities (the result of the multiple village or other diverse origins of the citizens) could be accommodated within a single religious establishment. Besides, the major Olympian deities (Zeus, Hera, Poseidon, Artemis, and the others) were acknowledged by all Greeks. But it was the patron divinity that perhaps contributed most to the unification of the community, since it was to a single divinity—Athena, say—that all Athenians looked for the furtherance of their common interests. An individual Athenian might privately maintain observance of an ancient village hero, but if he or she wished by appeal to the gods to promote the interests of the polis of Athens, it was necessary to participate in the *communal* observance of the cults of the state. Still a third, closely related factor is the Greeks' propensity to invent and to transmit to succeeding generations a body of lore—myth and legend—that served in various ways to identify and ennoble their specifically civic origins. Modern religions may spotlight and dignify the individual worshiper or, again at the opposite extreme, an entire nation or community of faith. Ancient Greek myth and legend, by contrast, tended to target the city-state as the focus of interest. Many, perhaps all, cities developed so-called foundation legends whereby the city's origins were traced to some miraculous, divinely caused event. The legend of Thebes was justly famous. It told how the founder, Cadmus, slew a dragon, collected its teeth, and sowed them, and how from the ground sprang up the "sown men." These men would ultimately be the ancestors of all Thebans, or at least of the Theban nobility. Thus legend created for Thebans of the historical era a common heritage, a shared past.

To conclude, it is in such factors that we may find the wellsprings of the civic—and nonindividualist and non-nationalist—solidarity and sympathies of the developed city-state. They, together with the material circumstances we have isolated, represent only the common denominator of factors shared by these very diverse communities, but they are sufficient to make comprehensible the relatively sudden appearance of this new political form. With this conclusion in mind, then, let us turn to the other major political development of the era, the exportation of the new city-state in the form of colonies beyond the limits of the Greek world.

COLONIZATION

The generally agreed-upon facts about Greek colonization may be stated briefly. Chronologically, the vast majority of colonies of known date fall within the two centuries from about 750 to 550 B.C. Thus the movement belongs to the formative period of the city-state, suggesting that the primary precipitating factor leading to the emergence of the polis, the surge in population growth, had continued unabated. With regard to the spatial extent of colonization, it would be no exaggeration to say that virtually the entire littoral of the Mediterranean Sea, plus the Black Sea region, was affected. Historians of the Roman Empire are fond of terming the Mediterranean a "Roman lake." By the onset of the classical period, the spotty distribution of the outposts of Hellenism were enough to suggest the emergence of a "Greek lake."

The earliest colonies were sent westward to southern Italy (to the extent that later Greeks termed the region "Big Greece") and Sicily. Here the most active colonizers included the Euboean cities Chalcis and Eretria, Corinth, Sparta, Rhodes, and Crete. Among the colonies were Cumae (from Chalcis), Syracuse (from Corinth), Tarentum (from Sparta), Gela (from Crete and Rhodes), and, an example of a secondary colony, Acragas (from Gela). Corinth was also active in northwestern Greece, founding Corcyra (modern Corfu) late in the eighth century and other colonies (including Corcyra's secondary colony, Epidamnus) a century later. To the far west, the coasts of Spain and France received settlers, notably at Massalia (modern Marseilles) from Phocaea. Another Phocaean settlement, at Alalia on Corsica, however, was expelled by a combined force of Carthaginians and Etruscans. Overseas expansion in this quarter had embroiled the Greeks in political conflict on an international scale.

To the east, colonies were dispatched thick and fast. Closer to home, colonies were established on the northern Aegean coast, especially along the three prongs of the Chalcidice peninsula (so called with reference to the colonizing efforts of Euboean Chalcis, along with Eretria and Andros). Farther eastward, the Hellespont, Propontis, the Bosporus, and the Black Sea received many colonies (and trading posts), the most prominent role being played by Miletus in Ionia and Megara, a Peloponnesian neighbor of Corinth. Milesian colonies included Cyzicus and Olbia; among Megarian settlements were numbered Chalcedon and Byzantium (later Constantinople). To the south, Cyrene on the northern coast of Africa was founded from Thera, but no known Greek colony penetrated the already densely settled and politically advanced region of Egypt or the Levantine district at the extreme eastern end of the Mediterranean. Here the Greeks were limited to establishing trading posts such as Naucratis on the Nile Delta and Poseideum at the mouth of the Orontes River near modern Al Mina.

Greek presence overseas was not, of course, without precedent. The Mycenaeans, as we saw, had extended their influence throughout the Mediterranean; and, following the Bronze Age, the Great Migrations had pushed the boundaries of the Greek world across the Aegean to the seaboard of Asia Minor. But the colonial movement was of a different nature. In contrast to the unofficial, even spasmodic movements of the prehistoric era, the new colonies were subject to formal organization under city-state leadership. Procedure was intricate and charged with significance. First, an official "founder," sometimes a man of high birth or political standing, was appointed. The founder's initial task was to seek the approval of the god Apollo at Delphi—an early example of the great political influence the oracle would exert in the archaic and classical periods. With the god's blessing, the founder assembled the colonists, led them to the site, and divided the land among them. But the procedure did not end there. A flame was transported from the sacred hearth of the mother city to the new hearth of the colony, symbolizing the original and continuing link between the two cities. The relationship might come into play later when the colony itself sent out its own secondary colony (as in the examples of Gela and Corcyra above), because the founder normally was summoned from the original mother city—an acknowledgment of the latter's traditional prerogatives. Similar cooperation extended from domestic matters to the colony's relations with other states, including warfare. These were clearly something more than haphazard responses to population pressures.

What were the causes of colonization? What motivated the mother city to dispatch a colony? The question is not easy to answer, for the movement antedates the activity of the major surviving classical historians. Some scholars, however, have suggested that trade was the driving force. Indications certainly point in this direction. Occasionally, a settlement is identified not as a colony but as an *emporium,* or "trading post." Naucratis in Egypt and the emporia along the northern coast of the Black Sea fall into this category. In a few telltale instances there are signs that the establishment of the colony was preceded by trade contacts between the future mother city and the region to be colonized, which suggests that the settlement was designed to enhance such contacts. Elsewhere, the simple fact that a colony was situated in an area of known mineral, agricultural, or other wealth constitutes a strong *prima facie* case that economic exploitation was the object. And, to be sure, whatever may have been the original motivation, commercial exchanges, especially between mother city and colony, are known to have transpired in later times. But it is one thing to conclude that colonization had an economic dimension, another to assert that the establishment of colonies was part of a deliberate program of economic imperialism. When the purpose was commercial, the term for such a settlement was *emporium*, and these were few and far between. Nor do our written sources betray awareness of any such designs—a strange circumstance if the expeditions were imperialistic from the outset.

A different kind of answer to our question is prompted by the fact that the local economies of the colonies are frequently found to have been primarily *agricultural*. Many colonies were planted in relatively unpopulated regions with access to available arable acreage. One of the duties of the founder was, as noted, to carry out the division of the new land; and, in one telltale instance, Syracuse in Sicily, the new settlers were called "sharers of the land." No less clear an indicator are the signs of land pressure in the homeland. Growth of the population was mentioned earlier in connection with the rise of the city-states. Could such population growth have reached the point of *over*population? To fully appreciate this factor, it is important to grasp the full meaning of *overpopulation* in its ancient Greek context. At one level, of course, it is a question of the ratio of arable land to numbers of mouths to feed. In Greece, the basic problem was exacerbated by the customary practice of equal inheritance of an estate by all legitimate sons. Over time, as a result, a farm would be divided to the point at which further division among two or more sons would result in plots too small to support the new owner and his family. At the same time, the inalienability of land (that is, the customary prohibition against its changing hands except by the traditional mechanisms of inheritance or dowry) precluded increasing one's holdings by purchase. So, when this point was reached, someone had to leave. At a higher level, whereas most Greeks (surely the typical case) were concerned with the life-or-death matter of securing acreage sufficient for survival, others, of elevated social rank, were concerned not with mere survival but with the luxury of maintaining an appropriate level of prestige and influence. And in this agricultural regime, land alone was a possible or worthy source thereof. Thus even an aristocrat, though his storerooms were well stocked, might be driven to join a colonial enterprise. But both sets of motivations go by the same name: land hunger.

Greek colonists relocated abroad with the goal of replicating the social and political order of the mother city. The new settlement would be a polis, complete with constitutional government, an exclusive citizen franchise, and a social hierarchy based on land ownership. Indeed, it was precisely the establishment of a city-state polity characterized by internal solidarity and by a typically Greek self-absorption that must have worked against disintegration and have contributed significantly to the long-term success of many of the new colonies. But what about the native populations in whose territories the colonists had planted themselves? The evidence presents a mixed picture. Some colonies were accompanied by the expulsion of the local populations (as at Syracuse); others, by contrast, arrived at the invitation of a native ruler (as at Megara Hyblaea). Subsequent relations also varied. Some Greek colonists reduced the indigenous people to serfdom, as happened at Syracuse and at Heracleia on the Black Sea. At the opposite extreme, there are signs of the political inferiority of Greek settlers or traders at Naucratis in Egypt and in the Scythian territories along the northern shore of the Black Sea, although, in the latter instance, archaeology has revealed that Greek culture simultaneously made deep inroads in Scythian art, religion, and lifestyle.

It would seem to follow that, in matters affecting the native peoples, the Greeks were opportunistic, adjusting their arrangements to the demands of the particular situation. The primary purpose of the typical colony was, again, to solve the problem of land hunger. Commercial opportunities, including those potentially beneficial to the mother city, could be pursued at a later time, although, if conditions in classical Greece are any indication, what economic exploitation did occur was the work of private entrepreneurs acting without prompting or direction from metropolitan or colonial governments. In political dealings, too, Greek practice was likewise opportunistic. Colonists might pursue advantages or make concessions as the strength or weakness of the local populations allowed or dictated.

Culturally, a similarly laissez-faire attitude seems to be in evidence. The colonial movement was no more a crusade of cultural conquest than it was an imperialist adventure. Naturally, an advanced alien civilization implanting itself in foreign surroundings will, simply by virtue of its presence, affect the host culture, quite apart from the attitude or intent of either guest or host. A degree of hellenization was therefore inevitable. But this was a two-way street. Classical historians acknowledge a degree of intermixture between colonists and natives, and there is no reason to doubt their judgment. While, constitutionally, a colonial citizen body may have been an exclusive group, mutual acculturation could occur in less formal circumstances, including domestic settings, since no prohibition against intermarriage is known to have existed. Archaeology and art history testify eloquently to the magnitude of the impact of Eastern traditions on Greek culture during the so-called orientalizing period. Colonization had opened the door to an era of impressive cross-fertilization. It is undeniable that foreign influences played a vital role in this "renaissance" of Greek civilization.

THE REDISCOVERY OF LITERACY

A remarkable example of Greece's benefiting from contact with foreign neighbors is provided by the rediscovery of literacy. Although this event occurred at some time during the later eighth century B.C. and involves no known colony or colonial region, it plainly belongs to the general context of Greece's overseas contacts.

Both the Minoans and the Mycenaeans had possessed the gift of literacy, as we saw in Chapter 1. The two cases, however, were somewhat different. Minoan Linear A has been found on a wide variety of objects, both official and private. This suggests two things: first, that the script was put to a comparably wide range of uses; and, second, that competency in the writing and reading of the script was not confined to a narrow class of literate specialists. Not so, however, with Mycenaean Linear B. The Mycenaean script occurs exclusively on the tablets discovered in the palace centers, and the content of the texts relates exclusively to matters of administration. If Linear B was in fact put to different uses, it is strange that no examples have survived (as is true, for example, of parallel documentary records of ancient Near Eastern civilizations). It may well be, then, that the earliest known system of symbols for the writing of Greek was merely a bureaucratic tool and that expertise in its use (reading as well as writing) was confined to a small class of professional scribes. Literacy may not even have been highly valued, or its absence lamented. Writing and reading among the Mycenaeans might have ranked no higher than other, menial skills. But we really do not know.

Whatever the status of the scribes, there is no reason to assume that Mycenaean society was generally literate. "Letters"—literature, history, and scientific or other speculative writing—might not have existed. In fact, the certainty that the Homeric poems, concerned as they are with an event of Mycenaean history, originated in the late Bronze Age suggests a powerful counterargument. Because the poems are now regarded as the products of an oral (that is, nonliterate) culture, is that not a sign that Mycenaean society, out of which the oral Homeric tradition emerged, was nonliterate or, at best, that what literacy there was did not extend to imaginative uses of the Greek language?

Not a trace of writing, in any event, has come down to us from the four or five centuries of the Dark Age. When literacy was reacquired, the new script bore no relation to the Mycenaean syllabary—another indication, incidentally, that the latter system had died out long before. Thus, strictly speaking, two innovations are in question: (1) the reacquisition of a writing system after centuries without a script of any kind; and (2) to make a new point, the acquisition of a script possessing immeasurable advantages over Linear B. Fundamentally, Linear B had combined pictographs (representations of familiar objects) and logograms (symbols or signs individually standing for a syllable). Because such a system requires the use of a great number of distinct symbols for effective communication, mastery is eventually achieved by only a small cadre of "experts." Second, it was a very imperfect and clumsy instrument, thereby limiting the possible applications for even those few experts. But the alphabet incorporated the phonetic principle, the idea that the individual symbols stand not for objects or syllables but for *sounds,* with every sound of the language (vowel, diphthong, or consonant) ideally enjoying a one-to-one correspondence with a distinct character, or letter, as is true of ancient Greek. The consequences of the difference were far-reaching. The number of different symbols needed to record the language is at once greatly reduced, simplifying learning and thereby making the script accessible to a far wider public. And, because every sound of the language can be represented by a letter or combination of letters, anything than can be spoken in the language can also be written. At the same time, expression of ideas is no longer inhibited by a system (such as Linear B) that, because each pictograph represents an already-existing (and perhaps socially or politically approved) object, is inherently incapable of breaking away from the entrenched conventions of the status quo. Thus the possibilities for the expression of new as well as old ideas became virtually limitless.

It is widely assumed that the mechanism for the transmission of the Phoenician alphabet to the Greeks was trade. The time of transmission was about the middle of the eighth century B.C. The historian conjures up images of Greek traders in some Phoenician port in the Levant (perhaps at Al Mina) noting the practical advantages of the use of an alphabet for business purposes. In any event, the system of characters was adopted lock, stock, and barrel, with only few modifications, and seemingly put to immediate use. Thus, before the eighth century was out, the epics of the Trojan War, attributed to the blind Homer of Chios (an island off the Ionian coast), were for the first time committed to written form. So, too, shortly later on the mainland, the theological and didactic poems of another traditional poet, the Boeotian Hesiod. From Athens, beginning about the same time as Hesiod's activity, crude attempts at writing are preserved on decorated pottery; and, elsewhere in Greece, about a century later, were made the first hesitant trials at inscribing texts permanently on stone. The former examples are manifestly of a private, even personal, character; the latter are expressly records of acts of governments. Such a range of uses, especially when one considers the readerships that they imply, point to a dramatic widening of the literate Greek public. Surely the economy and efficiency of the new alphabet were factors contributing to this development.

But what about the contribution of the new literacy to the Greek renaissance? It is one thing when a writing system is employed to record already-existing (orally transmitted) traditional texts or conventional ideas. It is another when that system plays a contributing or decisive role in the conception of something new. A case could be made that the alphabet, once its latent potential had been fully realized, was of indispensable importance in the reemergence of high Greek civilization.

THE RISE OF HISTORIOGRAPHY

A dramatic illustration is provided by historiography—the writing of history. Prior to the reacquisition of literacy, the oral tradition (to judge from those survivals that were at a later time committed to written form) consisted largely of epic poems; other traditional narratives variously classified as myths and legends; lists of names of kings, priests, and other notables; and local chronicles of different sorts. These compositions were generally characterized by a naive, uncritical attitude. But, by the early classical period, Hecataeus of Miletus, one of earliest and probably the most important of the so-called logographers, or writers of accounts, could write: "I write what I believe to be the truth, for the Greeks have many stories which it seems to me are absurd." Another half-century later, Herodotus and Thucydides would be investigating the causes of war and probing the nature of human behavior. In between fell the advent of literacy. Did it make the difference?

Work by modern social scientists suggests that it did. The matter turns on how the oral culture on the one hand and the literate on the other respond in different ways to change. In an oral culture, adaptation of the tradition to change is the rule. The memories of the transmitters of that tradition consciously or unconsciously alter it through admission, omission, emphasis, or rearrangement, in step with the changing conditions. Those conditions embrace not only the subject matter of the tradition but also, and equally importantly, the audience (or other recipients) of the oral performance. Again, consciously or unconsciously, the reciter may adjust subjects, attitudes, or viewpoint to suit the expectations of the audience—something like the politician who adjusts the same basic presentation to the location, social class, gender, or age of the listeners. Such behavior is frequently condemned in our society, but in ancient Greece it was an entirely expected, normal, and perhaps inevitable feature of orality. Such flexibility allowed the "text" to keep in synch with an evolving societal or cultural order. For Greek antiquity, the classic example is the Homeric poems. Although nominally an account of an event of the Mycenaean period, the "Homeric" society depicted in the poems bears little resemblance to the late Bronze Age world. As a result of four or five hundred years of the operation of the oral culture, Homeric society evolved into a likeness of Dark Age society of the tenth or ninth centuries, with very few preserved traces of its original Mycenaean setting.

Not so a culture endowed with literacy. Literacy opens up new possibilities, first through the creation of written texts, by "freezing" those texts in a permanent form. Neither wholesale change nor gradual adjustment to evolving circumstances is any longer possible under normal circumstances. The result is the gradual development of a lag between text and current reality: the text remains the same while society continues on its course of evolution. Generally put, the distinction between past and present comes into sharper relief. Another, related consequence is the possibility of skepticism. The availability of texts in permanent and easily accessible form makes feasible their scrutiny and evaluation in ways not possible in an oral culture. Inconsistencies, omissions, and other defects are more readily noticed, for the reader may at leisure study the text or compare widely separated passages. Even more seriously, the disparity between the attitudes preserved in the text and those of the readership may widen to the point at which the text's claims are finally threatened with outright refutation or rejection.

Literacy, by providing the means for *critical evaluation* of received traditions, satisfied a necessary condition for historical investigation. Now, to what uses did the early Greek practitioners of historiography put this new tool? By and large what the surviving fragments of these lost writings reveal is a *critical* reworking of traditional subjects or material, some of it passed down to the logographers by the oral tradition. Cases in point are their systematizations of myths, especially those recording the genealogies of persons or families claiming descent from a god or hero; and the so-called local histories, particularly those tracing the story of a city-state to its legendary or supernatural origins. Other writings of the logographers are less obviously traditional and probably grew out of interests promoting, and reinforced by, the Greek overseas colonial expansion, such as geographical treatises, often cast in the form of an imaginary coasting voyage (hence called the *periplus,* or "circumnavigation"), with a description of the lands and peoples appended to the mention of each port. Eventually, the description evolved into an independent work, an ethnographic account of the customs of various non-Greek peoples. Such explorations of human societies would later occupy a prominent place in the *Histories* of the classical historian Herodotus. Still another category, of essential importance to the historical enterprise, comprised the chronological works that attempted to systematize received listings of kings, priests or priestesses, and magistrates. Because historical events had been, and continued to be, dated with reference to the king, priest, or other dignitary in whose time the event occurred, the study of such material served a higher purpose than might be immediately obvious. Taken together, these early studies paved the way for historiography as the classical Greeks were to understand that intellectual discipline. And it was the advent of literacy that had made them possible.

IRON AGE SOCIETY

Strictly speaking, the "darkness" of the Dark Age that ushered in the Greek Iron Age refers not to any particular level of culture but to the relative dearth of information that has come down to us about that period. Yet even silence, especially the silence of the physical record, may tell us something. Palaces, massive fortifications, cities, if ever constructed, could not normally have perished without a trace. Perhaps the Greeks of the Dark Age, therefore, lived in primitive dwellings made of perishable materials. Perhaps they had reverted to a nomadic existence, forgoing permanent dwellings altogether. Similar inferences are prompted by the absence of remains of major engineering projects, luxurious artifacts, and (with particular relevance to the preceding section) inscriptions on stone or other durable materials. Generally speaking, compared to either the Mycenaean era or to what was to follow, the silence suggests that the Dark Age of Greece was in fact marked by a relatively low level of civilized life.

Additional, positive clues come from a perhaps unexpected source: the Homeric poems. Although concerned with an event of the Mycenaean era, the poems are, as we have seen, actually the products of nearly five centuries of oral composition, beginning (presumably) with the Trojan War itself and culminating with the writing down of the *Iliad* and the *Odyssey* soon after the adoption of the Phoenician alphabet in the eighth century B.C. In the interim, nonliterate bards continually amplified, reworked, and elaborated the steadily expanding material. Each generation, having learned the traditional material from its predecessors, reexpressed it in its own terms before transmitting it in turn to the next. In the process, the tradition was constantly being infused with the ideas, attitudes, and impressions of material culture appropriate to the circumstances of the bards active at the time. The end result was a body of poetry that, although in terms of its larger narrative structure (including plot, gross geographical and political setting, and the very idea of a violent attack on a walled town) still recognizably Mycenaean, is nevertheless fundamentally a reflection of the Iron Age, indeed with a decided emphasis on the later period of composition, the tenth and ninth centuries B.C. Thus, to put it crudely, historians may profitably treat the *Iliad* and the *Odyssey*, at the level of contextual detail, as sources of information on early Iron Age society. Particularly rich is the information provided concerning institutions, social organization, religion (including myth, ritual, and burial styles), military practices and weaponry, and so on. The one proviso is that the purposes of the Homeric bards were quite different from ours, that details about society and culture are at best extraneous to the character of an epic poem, and that for these reasons no rigid assumptions can be entertained regarding literal accuracy, exact chronology, or completeness of coverage. Indeed, some of the detail may be distorted by poetic invention; and, even if all the details were literally accurate, the very fact that the poems were in the process of composition for so long suggests strongly that those details, taken collectively, could not all belong to a single societal regime.

None of these drawbacks apply to our most important source of information, Hesiod's *Works and Days*, a work explicitly devoted to contemporary Greek society in the later eighth century B.C. Like Homer's epics, the *Works* is a poem (indeed, it is composed in the same epic style as the *Iliad* and *Odyssey*) but, unlike Homer's, the setting is the present place and time, and the author, speaking in the first person, purports to describe his own personal circumstances. His father, Hesiod tells us, had been engaged in sea trade but, failing at that, had moved from Cyme in Aeolian Asia Minor to the tiny village of Ascra in Boeotia, a region of central Greece. Hesiod presents himself in the *Works* as a poor dirt farmer. However, in another poem he reveals that it was when he was tending flocks of sheep on Mount Helicon in Boeotia that the Muses inspired him with the gift of song; and in the *Works* he boasts of a victory in song at a contest in Chalcis on Euboea. The idea that a composer and singer of epic poetry should also have been a subsistence-level farmer has struck many as odd, even impossible, and has given rise to the theory that Hesiod's self-representation as a farmer is merely a literary invention. But even if it is, the poem may nonetheless accurately record the lifestyle and attitudes of his contemporaries.

The peg on which Hesiod hangs his poem is a quarrel with his brother over their inheritance, which Hesiod believes has been unfairly divided. The brother had brought this injustice about by paying off "the bribe-eating *basileis*," the local bigwigs who had heard the case when it came to trial. Hesiod makes no effort to mask his hostility toward these men, an attitude that is probably part of his more generalized suspicion of "the smithy and its crowded lounge"—that is, of the town and its distractions. Instead of hanging out with the city folk, Hesiod's farmer, the nominal reader of his poem, might make more profitable use of his time at home. To this farmer Hesiod imparts in the *Works* a vast quantity of advice and information concerning the proper (and profitable) management of a small farm (as well as a shorter account of good navigational technique). Note, importantly for understanding the deeper purpose of Hesiod's poem, that it is not a how-to book for the raw beginner. Throughout, the emphasis is not so much on the basics as on the niceties of selection, quantity, and, above all, timing. The implication is that it is attention to details that makes or breaks a man. The farmer leads a precarious existence, constantly perched on the edge of disaster. The loss of a crop, the death of an ox, or too many (or too few) children can mean ruin. Dutiful attention to Hesiod's advice might make the difference.

The great value of Hesiod's poem resides precisely in the fact that it is presented in the form of advice, in its *didactic* orientation. Not a description of his society, it is rather *normative* in the sense that it represents the ideals of that society (at least from Hesiod's point of view), quite apart from the particularities of individual cases or even the average experience of the society as a whole. To turn to one of our specific concerns in this book, take as an example his advice on the desirable composition of the farmer's household:

> Bring a wife to your house at the right age, while you are not much short of thirty years nor much older. This is the right season of life for marriage. Let your wife be four years past puberty, and marry her in the fifth. Marry a virgin, so that you can teach her careful habits, and above all marry one who lives near you. But shop around in order that your marriage not be a joke to your neighbors. For a man can carry off nothing better than a good wife, but, by the same token, there is nothing worse than a bad one—a freeloader who roasts her husband without the benefit of a fire, strong though he may be, and delivers him to a savage old age.

> There should be only one son, to sustain his father's house, for this way wealth will increase in the home. But if you leave a second son, you'd better die old. Even so, Zeus can easily provide indescribable wealth to a greater number. The greater the industry and the more the hands, the greater the increase.

Besides the wife and children, the household will include slaves:

> First things first. Get a house, and a woman, and an ox for the plow—I mean a slave woman and not a wife, who will also drive the oxen. And make everything ready at home.

> Let a robust man of forty years drive them [the oxen], a man drawing a ration of a four-quarter loaf and eight bites for his meal, one who will attend to his work and plow a straight furrow and is beyond the age for staring at his buddies but will keep his mind on the task at hand.

Marriage, and with it children, are universally recommended for all. Age at first marriage, female virginity, and proximity of the bride's natal residence are likewise subject to specific guidelines. The assumptions and values underlying these norms will be taken up in Chapters 7 and 9 in the context of the much fuller record of the classical age. At the narrative level, the recommendation that there be only a single son may allude to Hesiod's own situation, because he and his brother had quarreled over the division of the inheritance. As we saw in our discussion of overpopulation, the practice of dividing estates equally among legitimate sons might, and certainly did, result in the excessive fragmentation of farmland. (Hesiod's statement that more hands means greater productivity is merely a grudging admission of the short-term benefits of a large family.) How much better off would Hesiod himself now be had he been the only son!

Besides, slaves, male and female, are present, in accord with both prehistoric and later ancient Greek practice (see Chapter 5). And note, too, that the purpose of owning slaves is not to create leisure for the free owner, for Hesiod's farmer is always at work. If Hesiod has an axe to grind, in fact, it is that we mortals, free as well as slave, seem to be condemned to a lifetime of unremitting toil. Slaves, complementing the small number of free children, serve, not to create leisure, but to increase productivity. All told, Hesiod's ideal farming household is a harbinger of the social arrangements of the best-understood ancient Greek society, that of classical Athens.

It is questionable, however, whether the same applies to Hesiod's specific views on the subject of women. Besides the quotation above about the greedy wife who roasts her husband without the benefit of fire, consider the following:

> Do not let a shapely woman, by wheedling and prattling, deceive you. She has an eye on your barn. The man who trusts a woman trusts thieves.

No more complimentary is his portrait of Pandora, the first mortal woman and, in Hesiod's mind, a symbolic representative of all women:

> For before this time the tribes of humans lived on earth apart from and without evils and hard work and the painful sicknesses that the Fates send upon people. For when life is hard, mortals grow old quickly. But the woman [Pandora], removing the great lid of the jar with her hands, scattered the contents. And she devised grievous troubles for humans.

> For from her [Pandora] comes the race of females. From her comes the deadly race and tribes of women who live among mortal men, a pain, no helpers in accursed poverty, but only when there is a surplus. [Hesiod goes on to compare women to the drones of a beehive who stay at home consuming the fruits of others' labors.] (from the *Theogony,* or *On the Origin of the Gods*)

No imaginable reconstruction of Hesiod's social environment, certainly none based on an analogy with the well-documented arrangements of classical Sparta and Athens, could begin to justify these outpourings of hostility toward women. The term *misogyny*—Greek for "hatred of women"—would seem applicable. But this observation still leaves unanswered one vital question. Is this the misogyny of Greek society as a whole (or even, as some would have it, the wellsprings of a long Western tradition of sexism) or is it merely one individual's personal, idiosyncratic attitude? The former alternative is supported by the generally normative nature of Hesiod's didactic presentation and, in the case of the Pandora story, by the certainty that that story enjoyed an existence and popularity among ancient Greeks entirely independent of Hesiod's treatment of it. Favoring the latter alternative is the author's general disgruntlement with the world. He sees the present Iron Age as the end product of a long decline from Gold to Silver to the Age of the Heroes to Bronze, ending in the unrelieved misery of his own day. The particular object of his disgruntlement is the necessity of work—physical manual labor—and, if we allow ourselves to believe that Hesiod was really, as he says, a poor farmer, it is not hard to imagine why. Farm labor in classical antiquity was physically debilitating to an extreme degree, not to mention the stress caused by a life poised on the brink of ruin. Human being that he was, Hesiod may have cast about for a scapegoat. We have already seen him target his brother and, beyond the family, the "bribe-eating" judges who decided the inheritance case against him. Now he targets women, a point of view already conveniently built into a popular myth of Pandora. Hesiod's misogyny is no less real, but it is questionable whether it should be generalized into a societal phenomenon.

Nonetheless, Hesiod's vision does rise above the merely personal grudge. To the contrary, he subscribes to a conception of the social order entirely in keeping with that of archaic Greek cities. This is seen most clearly in his mythical work the *Theogony* (*On the Origin of the Gods*), quoted above. In that poem Hesiod constructs a pyramidal hierarchy of gods and humans, with Zeus, the Homeric "father of gods and men," securely stationed at the apex of power. Below, and through links forged by his seven marriages (serially concluded) and the resultant children, Zeus rules the universe in conformity with the transcendent principle of Justice. Beneath the divinities, human men and women comprise a lower class of the social order, subject to the will and interventions of the gods, whom they worship and to whom they appeal for aid. Sometimes, as in the instance of the early Greeks and their divine benefactor, the giver of fire, the god Prometheus, the relationship resembles that of clients' dependence on a powerful patron. Now, what does all this mean in terms of a historical human society? An analogy is at work. Hesiod's gods and goddesses occupy a superior position relative to human beings in a single great society of "gods and men" which corresponds analogously to the superior position of an elite upper class relative to the lower classes in contemporary Greek societies. Hesiod's gods—and this may be said of Greek myth and religion generally—are cast in the mold of, and behave like, a Greek aristocratic ruling elite. They, and the entire hierarchical structure of which they are a part, are a projection onto a divine backdrop of the human society out of which their creators, including Hesiod himself, came.

Suggested Readings

For an overview of the period covered by this chapter, the best choice is the *Cambridge Ancient History,* 2nd ed., vol. 3, and 3rd ed., vol. 2 (Cambridge, various dates). J. Chadwick's revisionist account of the Dorian "invasion" mentioned in our text will not, however, be found there. Closely tied to the ancient sources is L. H. Jeffery's *Archaic Greece: The City-States c. 700–500 B.C.* (London, 1976). For an archaeologist's account of the renaissance, including the emergence of the city-state (with the findings cited in our text), see A. Snodgrass, *Archaic Greece: The Age of Experiment* (London, 1980). (Another study of the latter subject by an eminent historian is C. G. Starr, *The Rise of the Polis* [New York, 1986]). The period is also well treated by various authors in "The Expansion of the Greek World, Eighth to Sixth Centuries B.C.," *Cambridge Ancient History,* 2nd ed., vol. 3, pt. 3 (Cambridge, 1982). Chapter 37, "The

Colonial Expansion of Greece," by A. J. Graham, is a comprehensive account of the subject, including some of the details incorporated here; the same scholar's *Colony and Mother City in Ancient Greece* is now in its second edition (Chicago, 1983). The social scientists mentioned in the discussion of literacy are J. Goody and I. Watt, authors of "The Consequences of Literacy" in Goody's volume of essays by various authors entitled *Literacy in Traditional Societies* (Oxford, 1968). For the use of the Homeric poems as sources for Iron Age society, see G. S. Kirk, *The Songs of Homer* (Cambridge, 1962); and especially "The Homeric Poems as History," in the *Cambridge Ancient History*, 3rd ed., vol. 2, pt. 2, ch. 39(b) (Cambridge, 1975). The archaeological content of the poems was classically treated by H. L. Lorimer, *Homer and the Monuments* (London, 1950). For the interpretation of Hesiod's work, the authoritative commentary is M. L. West, *Hesiod: Works & Days* (Oxford, 1978). With regard to Hesiod and the relationship of his divine society to his contemporary human society, the most persuasive statement is that of W. K. C. Guthrie, *The Greeks and Their Gods* (Boston, 1950).

Chapter 3. Attica and Athens: The Built Environment

The developments and movements discussed in the preceding chapters reached their completion by the middle of the sixth century B.C. The city-state had achieved maturity; that same polity, the city-state, had been exported in the form of colonial settlements far and wide over the Mediterranean littoral; and (a development falling outside the disciplinary range of this book) high culture had been revitalized in step with groundbreaking innovations in science and philosophy. The Archaic Age now drawing to a close had proved to be truly a renaissance of Greek civilization.

Thanks to the acquisition of alphabetic writing, the rise of historiography, and eventually the practice of recording various kinds of texts on stone, the succeeding period, the Classical Age, is relatively richly documented. This fact, as explained in the Introduction, permits us to narrow our focus to a single state: Athens. Athens, as we have seen, had survived unscathed the upheavals occurring at the end of the Bronze Age and, a century later, upon the entry (or uprising) of the Dorian Greeks. By the later seventh century B.C., we can begin to speak of specific events and personalities and, by about the end of the sixth, a fairly intelligible account of Athenian state and society becomes possible. The following seven chapters, 3 through 9, will look at Athens from various vantage points over this period of two centuries—to be precise, from the foundation of the democracy in 508/7 B.C. (after we have traced its development in Chapter 4) down to the Macedonian takeover of Athens in 322 B.C. (For other landmark events of the Classical Age, see the Chronology, pages ix–x).

THE BUILT ENVIRONMENT: THE BIG PICTURE

Attica

Attica, the territory of the city of Athens, though smaller in area than the smallest state of the United States of America (Rhode Island at 1,248 square miles), was positively huge by the standards of ancient Greece. Attica comprised the southeasternmost extension of the Balkan peninsula, bordered to the north by the hills that separated Athenian territory from Boeotia and on the east, south, and west by the Aegean Sea. Very much to the point for the ancient historian, Attica embraced considerable topographic diversity. Three great plains—the Thriasian, the Attic, and the Mesogeion (or "Midland")—straddled this wedge-shaped territory from west to east. The city of Athens itself was situated near the sea to the southwest, at the lower extremity of the middle plain, and was ringed by mountain ridges to the west (Mount Aigiale), north (Mounts Parnes and Pentelikon), and east (Mount Hymettos). Beyond the urban center many lesser settlements—a major port town, several substantial villages, and a multitude of tiny hamlets—dotted the plains, hillsides, and coastal strips.

The Acropolis

The city of Athens developed under circumstances more or less corresponding to the model proposed in Chapter 2 under the heading "The Emergence of the City-State." The earliest known settlements were on the Acropolis, a high, steep, rocky outcrop rising above the surrounding farmlands (see Map 3–1). Naturally, the Acropolis' defensive properties were its chief attraction. By the Bronze Age the citadel was encircled by a massive fortification wall (called the Pelargikon), within which was enclosed the Mycenaean king's royal palace, among other structures. Also in accordance with the model, a temple in the name of the patron divinity—in Athens' case, Athena—is among the earliest known monumental erections. At the foot of the citadel were nestled the residences of the early Athenians themselves, at first farmers of the adjacent countryside and later, with increasing frequency, including a nonagricultural component of craftspeople, merchants, and laborers.

The Agora

At an early date, the development of the public infrastructure spilled over from the Acropolis itself onto the flats in the immediate vicinity. Eventually, the level area to the northwest of the Acropolis (and bordered by low hills to the south and west) was chosen as the site of the community's civic center. From an early time it was called the Agora, a term originally meaning "place of assembly" and loosely paralleled by the more familiar Roman term *forum*. Its first such development occurs prior to the classical period, perhaps during the time of Solon, a lawgiver of the early sixth century B.C. (see Chapter 4). By the time of the fully developed democracy, the Agora (and its immediate environs) had emerged as the physical seat of government. All the organs of the democratic government to be discussed in Chapter 6—the Assembly, the Council of Five Hundred, the boards of magistrates, and the courts—were housed or headquartered either in the Agora or on the nearby hillsides, the Areopagus (the seat of a predemocratic Council) and Pnyx (the principal meeting place of the Assembly). But the Agora's importance was not confined to the constitutional apparatus. As we will shortly see, the Agora was also a hub of activity embracing many aspects of Athenian public life—political, commercial, social, and intellectual as well as constitutional. This is a fact of major

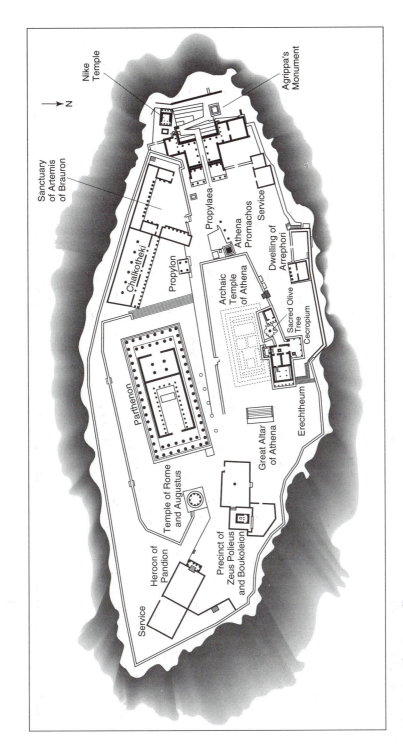

N

Nike Temple

Agrippa's Monument

Sanctuary of Artemis of Brauron

Propylaea

Athena Promachos

Service

Dwelling of Arrephori

Chalkotheki

Propylon

Archaic Temple of Athena

Sacred Olive Tree

Cecropium

Parthenon

Great Altar of Athena

Erechtheum

Temple of Rome and Augustus

Heroon of Pandion

Precinct of Zeus Polieus and Boukoleion

Service

Map 3–1. The Acropolis

significance for an understanding of ancient Athens—and of Greek civilization in general. True, the Athenian population may have been domiciled in more than a hundred communities distributed widely over the roughly one thousand square miles of Attica, but not only the democratic constitutional apparatus but virtually all of public life of the city as well was concentrated into this tiny district at the foot of the Acropolis.

The Port Town of Peiraeus

From this brief overview it will be clear that, if we scan the entire history of the city down to the founding of democracy, Athens' center was gradually displaced from the Acropolis to the Agora. The Acropolis of the classical period has been well characterized by some scholars as merely symbolic and ceremonial. To mention only the most vital factor, with the construction of the mighty circuit wall ringing the city, the Acropolis' fortifications were rendered redundant at best. And, again, not the citadel but the Agora had emerged as the seat of government. But there is one important qualification to this simple picture that has to be made. It concerns the port town called Peiraeus, situated on the Saronic Gulf about five miles to the southwest of the city center (see Map 3–2).

Early on, Athens' port had been at Phaleron, the point on the coast closest to Athens. This location eventually proved unsatisfactory. It afforded little protection from the weather; in the absence of deep anchorage, ships were simply pulled up onto the beach. Both deficiencies were rectified by the transfer of the port to Peiraeus up the coast to the west. This new site offered no fewer than three harbors, with anchorage and superior protection from the open seas. Early in the fifth century, under the guidance of the statesman Themistocles, Peiraeus was enclosed within its own fortification walls. One of the three harbors had been fortified late in the preceding century, but this was the first enclosure of the entire harbor complex with its adjacent town. A half-century later came the decisive development when two long straight walls were constructed, the more westerly linking the circuit wall of Athens to Themistocles' Peiraeus fortification; the easterly, the city wall to Phaleron. A short time later, a second Peiraeus wall, paralleling the first and creating a narrow corridor between the city and the harbor, was added. This corridor was henceforth known as the "Long Walls." Now the city was linked by defenses to its port. Indeed, the city had literally been *extended to* the port, marking a still further shift away from the original prehistoric center on the Acropolis.

This reorientation of Athens' layout was driven ultimately by concerns of military strategy. The completed system of fortifications provided protection of the harbor and, more critically, guaranteed access between city and port even in the event of enemy siege. Should a hostile army invade Attica, the Athenians could still reach the fleet at Peiraeus in order to carry out

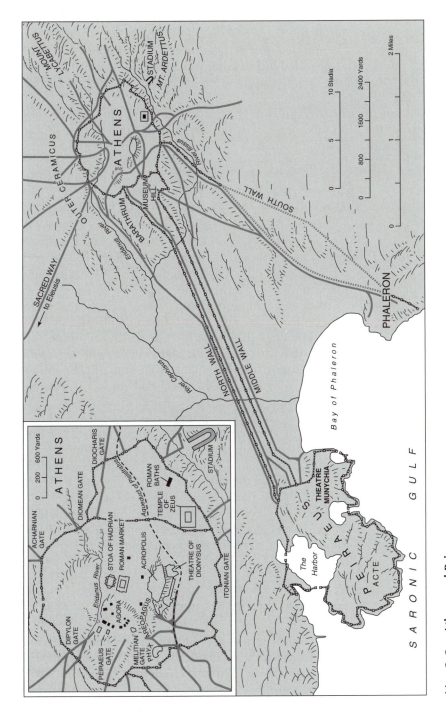

Map 3–2. Athens and Peiraeus

MOUNT LYCABETTUS

ATHENS

STADIUM

MT. ARDETTUS

OUTER CERAMICUS

MUSEUM HILL

BARATHRUM

River Ilissus

SACRED WAY
to Eleusis

River Eridanus

River Cephisus

SOUTH WALL

NORTH WALL

MIDDLE WALL

PHALERON

Bay of Phaleron

SARONIC GULF

PEIRAEUS

The Harbor

THEATRE

MUNYCHIA

ACTE

10 Stadia

2400 Yards

2 Miles

ATHENS

ACHARNIAN GATE

DIPYLON GATE

PEIRAEUS GATE

MELITIAN GATE

PNYX

AREOPAGUS

DICOMEAN GATE

DIOCHARIS GATE

Eridanus River

STOA OF HADRIAN

ROMAN MARKET

AGORA

ACROPOLIS

Aqueduct of Pisistratus

ROMAN BATHS

TEMPLE OF ZEUS

THEATRE OF DIONYSUS

STADIUM

ITONIAN GATE

0   200   600 Yards

naval operations; and, if the crops of Attica were destroyed by the enemy, vital supplies could be shipped into Peiraeus and be transported to the city through the corridor provided by the Long Walls. And just this scenario was realized during Athens' lengthy struggle against Sparta: the Peloponnesian War of 431–404 B.C.

But our present concern is to grasp the societal, not the military, significance of the built environment of the city-state of Athens. To state the obvious, Athens' decision to pursue a maritime policy and the implementation of that policy through the construction of the fortification system had the effect of bestowing enormous importance on the harbor and its town. Peiraeus became, as one archaeologist has put it, a "duplicate" city. A few particulars will illustrate the point. Predictably, the permanent population grew large, as rowers, craftspeople, and traders naturally settled near the scene of their military or commercial employment. Yet this was a planned growth, for it is recorded by Aristotle that a rectangular checkerboard grid of criss-crossing streets had been laid out by Hippodamus of Miletus, ancient Greece's most distinguished city planner. Eventually the town grew to include, besides the harbor and commercial installations, an industrial quarter, an Agora (or perhaps two) of its own, two theaters, temples and shrines, and various other public buildings. The latter included a council house and generals' office that coincided with and duplicated structures in the Agora in the city. Nor did these harbor town installations go unused. The democratic Council is recorded to have met "on the jetty," and one of the theaters served as the temporary meeting place of the Athenian Assembly. Real meaning is therefore to be attached to the phrase "duplicate city."

Although it remains true that the urban center never surrendered its dominance, it is fair to say that the Athenian city-state of the classical period was *bipolar*. The new orientation, again, reflected the decision to pursue a maritime policy. Culturally speaking, the effect was one of a decisive challenge to the land-based agrarian regime that had characterized early Athens and that remained characteristic of much of Greece throughout antiquity. The majority of Athens' citizen population may have been landowners and farmers (see Chapter 8), but the physical plant, as it were, points to a preoccupation with the sea.

THE BUILT ENVIRONMENT: STATE AND SOCIETY

With this larger picture in mind, we may now turn to a more detailed examination of the built environment with respect to the principal themes of this book—ancient Greek state and society. From the following discussion it will soon become clear that the two spheres, as manifested in the record of contemporary buildings and spaces and their attested uses, were inextricably intertwined. The Agora, in particular, will emerge as the clearest embodiment of the integration of public and private one could imagine. But, in the end, the characteristics of monumentality and permanence will indicate Athens' far higher estimation of the public, outdoor activities of the male citizen elite.

Public Architecture and the Pervasiveness of Religion

Religion is an appropriate place to begin this investigation, for three reasons. First, with the exception of the fortification walls, it is likely that altars or shrines were among the very first permanent, monumental structures to be erected in the emerging Greek civic centers. Second, besides this priority in time, shrines, and especially temples, were without a doubt the most elaborate and costly of all structures at Athens and elsewhere in Greece. Qualitatively, too, religion enjoyed some sort of privileged status within the architectural environment. The third factor is pervasiveness. Religion, monumentally speaking, was omnipresent. Within each private residence, for example, the hearth (Greek *hestia*) was, as a reflection of its great practical importance (as a source of warmth, light, and cooking heat), evidently a sacred place, for "hearth" with a capital *H*, Hestia, will eventually evolve into a Greek deity. Before many a home stood a *herm*, a pillar bearing a stylized representation of the god Hermes and serving to ward off evil from the household within. In every village, local (as well as common Greek) divinities, heroes, and heroines were represented monumentally by small temples, shrines, altars, and other sacred installations. In Athens, the area in and around the urban center was dotted with an incredible number of similar sacred fixtures. So, with respect to chronology, expenditure of effort and resources, and sheer pervasiveness, religion enjoyed a decided priority.

To a reader familiar with the principle of separation of church and state, this situation naturally prompts a question. Were not "church" and "state" separated in ancient Greece, in Athens in particular? What we have just said about religious monuments in and around Athens might suggest that they were indeed not—that sacred and secular were closely intermingled. In fact, one might be tempted to suggest that religion pervaded the Athenian public establishment to the extent that the terms *sacred* and *secular*, except for their roles as useful analytical categories, cease to be meaningful for general characterizations of the built environment of this particular city-state. Because religion was everywhere, no basis for the distinction existed.

However, the actual situation in Athens is in fact more complex. The arrangement of the civic center, at least during its classical phase, reveals no such consistent striving for integration of sacred and secular. To begin with, take the Acropolis. During the Bronze Age, the citadel combined the functions of fortified place of refuge, site of the royal palace, and probably seat of the cult of the patron divinity. But with the emergence of the city-state and the evolution of the Agora into a civic center, the defensive function was assumed by the circuit wall enclosing the wider urban area, and the powers of the now-defunct monarchy were distributed among a number of civilian officers housed in the central square. These developments left the citadel with a primarily religious—that is, ceremonial and symbolic—role to play. Thereafter, during the classical period, that role assumed major monumental proportions. The Parthenon, the temple dedicated to the Virgin Athena and the ultimate architectural glorification of the longstanding cult of the patron divinity, emerged as the centerpiece among public religious structures.

Notable lesser shrines included the Erechtheum (dedicated to a number of divinities and heroes) and the tiny but exquisite temple of Athena Nike. Naturally, of course, not every major shrine could be accommodated within the constricted confines of the summit of the citadel. From an early time and continuing into later periods, religious structures were also erected on the available areas below. One, the Olympieum dedicated to the supreme Greek divinity, Zeus, was far more massive even than the Parthenon. Boldly begun on a gigantic scale by the tyrant Pisistratus in the sixth century B.C. (see Chapter 4) but not completed until the time of the Roman emperor Hadrian about seven hundred years later, it stood on level ground to the southeast of the citadel. Another major temple, like the Parthenon a product of the Periclean building program of the mid-fifth century B.C., was the temple of Hephaestus (and Athena), the Hephaesteum. This shrine was perched on a low hill overlooking the northwestern quadrant of the Agora. But, generally speaking, it was the Acropolis that was the locus of religious architecture, to the conspicuous exclusion (as we will see) of the "secular" Agora.

Before we turn again to the Agora, a word or two more on the role of religion in Athenian public life. The temples (as well as the lesser religious fixtures) were the scenes of various cultic events, above all the ritual sacrificing of animal victims on the altars found in every shrine and located, where there was a temple, before its entrance. (Ordinarily, large gatherings did not take place within a temple, as modern worship services might suggest.) These sacrifices, whether offered as a form of praise, supplication, or thanksgiving, reflected a basically contractual understanding of the meaning of religion. Humans offered the sacrifice in the hope of a favorable reciprocation by the divinity. Reciprocity, after all, was the dynamic governing the economic, social, and political exchanges pervading ancient Greek society, so it is not surprising to find Greeks cultivating similar relations with their gods and goddesses. Nonetheless, and critically for the human worshipers, the divinities did not always receive the entire burnt offering. Unless the sacrifice was propitiatory or purificatory, the victim's cooked flesh was shared among the celebrants. For many Greeks, as is now generally accepted among historians, such public sacrifices were among the rare occasions—perhaps in some cases the only occasions—when meat was consumed. Religiously speaking, such meals have been described as a sort of "communion." This may mean a communion between worshiper and object of worship, provided one is at liberty to imagine that the flesh consumed by the celebrant symbolically embodied the very divinity of the god or goddess itself. But for the hungry participant, the theological point may have mattered less than the opportunity, offered at public expense, to sustain life.

Nor is this the only point of significance for the historian of society. Religious events—not only sacrifices, but also festivals, processions, and sacred functions of all kinds—are noteworthy for their surprisingly *inclusive* character. As we will see repeatedly, Athenian public life more or less consistently precluded participation by any but the adult male citizen ruling caste. But sponsorship by a divinity evidently justified or permitted a wider range of participation. Take, for example, the Panathenaia, an annual festival in honor of the patron divinity Athena and the premier event on the Athenian religious calendar. Participation, far from being confined to citizens, was thrown open to women, underage Athenians, and resident aliens as well. A similar inclusiveness marked another important Athenian rite: the Mysteries of Demeter and Persephone. The point is that religion served to recognize and, at least for a short time, integrate a far wider community of Athenians—the community defined not by membership in a citizen elite but rather by the social reality of shared residence in the land of Attica.

The Agora: Diversity of Function

The Acropolis had evolved, as we have just noted, into a ritually significant, but not very useful, installation. What about the Agora? As early usage of the Greek term suggests, the Agora started out as a place of assembly, but over time, as we will shortly see, it acquired (if only on a temporary basis) an astonishing variety of other functions as well. Such a development was encouraged by its central location at the foot of the Acropolis and by the extensive flat and well-drained space that it provided.

The Agora's first noticeable development into a civic center dates to the time of the magistrate and lawgiver Solon, early in the sixth century B.C. (see Chapter 4). From that time, expansion continued through a process of addition of new to already existing facilities, rather than through wholesale replacement. Older structures, though architecturally outmoded and no longer on the scale of the burgeoning city, were shielded from destruction by their nominal association with a god or hero and perhaps by sentimental attachment. The result was that, by the end of the fifth century, the square was bordered by structures some of which were more than a century old.

The Agora was laid out as a square open in the center and enclosed by inward-facing buildings. By the end of the fifth century B.C. (see Map 3–3), construction was fairly continuous along the south, west, and north; the east side would not be fully developed until later periods. The enclosure of the space was effected in significant part by a characteristically Greek architectural form: the *stoa*, or colonnade. The stoa was essentially a long one- or, later,

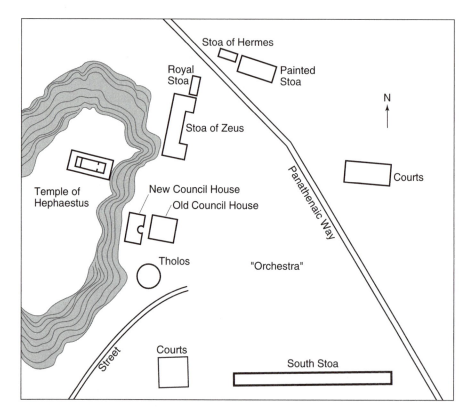

Map 3–3.   The Agora of Athens Around 400 B.C.

two-story building with a solid rear wall and a roof supported in front by a row or rows of columns. Thus a public square could be defined by arranging stoas around the perimeter with their backs to the outside and their open colonnades of columns opening onto the central space. This design was ideally suited to the sunny and temperate Mediterranean climate and to the outdoor lifestyle that climate had fostered. A visitor to a stoa, while protected from sun, rain, and wind, was still for all practical purposes outdoors. The five stoas on the Athenian Agora during the classical period therefore played a major role in shaping the distinctive character of Athenian public life.

How was this public space used? No simple answer is possible. Again, the Agora had started out as a place of assembly; and, although the formal gatherings of Athenian citizens were from an early date held beyond the Agora on a neighboring hillside to the southwest called the Pnyx, this function was not entirely lost. But the square's use for assemblies, which theoretically may have antedated any construction on the site, was eventually overwhelmed by a variety of forms of public activity. To illustrate the point and to provide the basis for the ensuing discussion, let us briefly review the evidence:

- *Place of assembly.*   In the sixth century, before the democracy, the lawgiver Solon and later the tyrant Pisistratus are recorded to have addressed crowds in the Agora. Still later, under the democracy, a form of banishment (called "ostracism") requiring a quorum of six thousand citizen voters was also conducted in the square.

- *Theatrical performances.*   Before the construction of the Theater of Dionysus on the south slope of the Acropolis, dionysiac presentations were held in the Agora, according to later witnesses. As a result, the term *orchestra*, originally denoting the circular dancing area used by the chorus in a theater, continued in the classical period to be used for the interior open space of the square.

- *Athletic competitions and related activities.*   The Panathenaic Way, which crossed the square from the northwest to the southeast, was also known as the *Dromos*, or "Runway." That the area was used specifically for running races is suggested by the remains of a possible starting line in the northwest corner, dated to around the middle of the fifth century B.C. In classical and later times, the Agora was also the scene of equestrian exhibitions.

- *Museum displays.*   Two of the five stoas, among their other functions, served as venues for public religious or patriotic exhibits. The Painted Stoa (built around 460 B.C.) housed paintings depicting the Trojan War, Theseus and the Athenians fighting the Amazons, and two historical battles involving Athenians, at Oinoe and at Marathon—the latter the scene of Athens' greatest infantry victory. Also on display here were bronze shields taken by the Athenians from the Spartans during a campaign of the Peloponnesian War (431–404 B.C.). The other stoa, of Zeus (built around 430 B.C.), was furnished with paintings of the Twelve Gods, Theseus, Democracy, Demos ("the People"), and an Athenian cavalry action in the battle of Mantinea (418 B.C.).

- *Intellectual exchange.*   Besides the ordinary socializing that naturally attends many forms of human activity, the Agora was the scene of serious intellectual exchanges. The Athenian citizen Socrates, most famous of the city's philosophers, by himself adequately illustrates the point. Plato depicts his mentor engaged in conversations with friends in the Stoa of Zeus and accosting his fellow citizens in the Agora "at the tables" (with evident reference to the temporary installations of the moneychangers). In the fourth century B.C., Diogenes, the founder of the Cynic philosophical sect, claimed to have established residence in a stoa, again the Stoa of Zeus, as well as in another public building near the Agora, the Pompeum. Another sect, the Stoics, took their name from the Painted Stoa, where their founder, Zeno, and his successors used to instruct their followers.

- *Religious activities.*   To the west, as we saw, the Hephaesteum, constructed in the middle of the fifth century B.C., looked down on the square from "the Hill of the Agora." Within the square itself there stood by the end of the fifth century B.C. an altar dedicated to the eponymous heroes of the ten tribes (see Chapter 6), a sacred hearth, an altar dedicated to the Twelve Gods, and, on a monumental scale, the Stoa of Zeus and the Stoa of the Herms (with reference to the nearby concentration of pillars representing the god Hermes), among other visible signs of cultic presence. But such fixtures fall far short of establishing the point that the Agora was in any meaningful sense, as some archaeologists have suggested, a religious space. To see that this was not the case, we return to our earlier point regarding the pervasiveness of religion. The gods and goddesses, and the physical manifestations of their cults, were literally everywhere. Indeed, it would be difficult to identify anywhere in Attica a wholly secular space, structure, organized group of people, or significant societal function. Therefore, if the Agora is to be viewed as sacred ground, its religious fixtures must exceed in scale or importance those of the general Attic environment. It plainly did not do that. There were no temples; even the Stoa of Zeus, though named in honor of a god, was in no sense a shrine. The significantly sacred ground of public Athens lay elsewhere, especially on the Acropolis.

• *Marketplace.*   Commercial activity was a major function of the Agora at Athens and in other cities, so much so that in later times the word *agora* came to mean "market." Much attention will be given in Chapter 8 to manufacture, buying, and selling in and around the Athenian square. Here it should be noted that, although most commercial activity was relegated to the periphery and side streets, the interior of the square was so used as well. Plato says in his dialogue the *Defense of Socrates*, for example, that the books of the philosopher Anaxagoras could be purchased in the "orchestra."

• *Governmental offices and venues.*   By far the most important purpose served by the Agora was governmental: in the Agora were housed the headquarters or seats of the principal organs of the democracy: the Strategeum (generals), Old and New Council Houses and the Tholos (Council of Five Hundred), and the various spaces used by the court system, as well as the mint and prison. Here, too, were the state archives (in the Metroon); innumerable stone *stelai* (or tablets) bearing official decrees and other texts; and, at the statues of the eponymous heroes of the tribes, officially posted announcements of military mobilizations and other matters of public concern. To be sure, as a result of the requirement for a large space, the Assembly met a short distance to the southwest, on the Pnyx hill, but this is the sole instance of a governmental organ permanently seated elsewhere than in the Agora itself. It is obvious that the square had gained a virtual monopoly as the physical seat of the democratic government.

The Agora, then, did indeed embody a wide range of functions and activities, as more than one archaeologist has noted. This tendency is in evidence not only over the square as a whole, but also within single buildings, in particular the stoas, which were characteristically put to a number of different, unrelated uses. This striking fact did not go unnoticed by ancient commentators, not all of whom approved. Aristotle for one, himself a resident (though not a citizen) of Athens, proposed that in an ideal state a separate agora should be established for commercial activity—a recommendation obviously (as he and his readers must have realized) in conflict with the situation prevailing in Athens. Similarly, but more consistently with Athenian practice, he claimed he would like to see a single site selected to accommodate all the dwellings of the gods, i.e., the shrines and temples. Aristotle, as we can tell from his surviving writings, was aware of conditions in many Greek cities, but even so it is hard to escape the conclusion that he was responding specifically to the diversity of function so characteristic of the civic center of his own city of residence.

At the same time it is evident that not all the various functions contributing to this diversity were on anywhere near equal footing. Two criteria appropriate to evaluation of the architectural record, *monumentality* and *permanence*, unmistakably indicate the priority of governmental functions. Everything else was, architecturally speaking, subordinate or inferior to the physical or spatial demands of the democracy. Such facilities as existed for theatrical performances or athletic contests were by comparison insignificant or temporary. Especially to the point, the commercial activity to which Aristotle objects so strongly was carried on within ramshackle stalls, booths, or tables, or entirely without the benefit of any structure whatever. The visitor arriving at the Agora just after daybreak or when bad weather had driven people under cover would have been confronted by a uniform cityscape of impressive, permanent stone governmental installations—and little else.

The same conclusion may be reached by an alternative, negative route. Three nongovernmental functions did in fact, at one time or another, acquire or gain access to major permanent facilities, but in no case was the facility in question situated within the Agora of the period of the classical democracy. Once again, temples. Eventually, no fewer than three temples (the Temple of Ares, and the "southwest" and "southeast" temples), all brought from sites elsewhere in Attica, were reassembled within the square. But all three belong to the Hellenistic or Roman periods. Secondly, the market hall. Under the democracy, no permanent stone facility for commercial activity existed. Not until the end of the first century B.C. was a great peristyle court (actually four stoas arranged in a square), about one hundred yards on each side, constructed immediately to the east of the Agora. Thirdly, the philosophical schools. As already noted, philosophers frequented the stoas, and indeed, one sect took its name from a stoa, but no dedicated physical structure worthy of being called a "school" was ever erected in the Agora or even within the urban center. Rather, it was outside (or just within) the walls, in the gymnasia, that the philosophers and their followers found their more or less permanent homes: in the Academy (Plato), the Lyceum (Aristotle), and the gymnasium at Cynosarges (Antisthenes and the Cynics).

So consistent a pattern could not have been accidental. As a matter of principle, the classical democracy had reserved the square to serve as the forum for the official business of the citizen class. The Agora was the physical embodiment of Athenian democratic institutions. Yes, great numbers flocked to the square in pursuit of a variety of purposes, but such activities were incidental to the primarily governmental functions of the civic center.

Public Architecture Outside the Urban Center: The Gymnasia

Mention has just been made of the gymnasia. These were athletic facilities, often including a separate installation for wrestling called the *palaestra*. Wrestling seems to have been the most popular of sports among Athenian, and probably all Greek, boys and men. Athens' three known gymnasia were distributed around the edge of the urban area, to the northwest (the Academy), east (the Lyceum), and south (Cynosarges). Each, in keeping with the pervasiveness of religion, was formally dedicated to a hero or divinity, although in no instance could a gymnasium be regarded as a particularly sacred space.

Besides their athletic function, the gymnasia served social and, to our present point, intellectual purposes. For, as just noted, they became the homes of the philosophical schools. Why the philosophers should have sought out these suburban locations, and gymnasia in particular, is not immediately obvious. It is not enough to wax eloquent about the harmony of the physical and the intellectual among ancient Athenian Greeks, if only because such "harmony" would still require explanation. One thing we do know is that the philosopher Socrates, who was given to accosting and interrogating his fellow citizens in the Agora, caused many of them considerable irritation. So he (and others like him) may have found the atmosphere of the gymnasia more congenial. For one thing, the young men likely to visit an athletic facility, precisely because of their youth, were perhaps more promising, and certainly more resilient, candidates for philosophical discussions. Nor is it to be forgotten that what we call "higher education" was in ancient Athens an upper-class pursuit, and that there are clear signs that the clientele of the gymnasia included boys and men of just this class. When we come to consider the habits of aristocratic society (see Chapter 4), it will be evident that the gymnasium (and its palaestra) proved ideal venues for the pursuit of their distinctive lifestyle, of which high-level intellectual exchange was one component.

In any event, it would obviously be a mistake to think of the Academy or the Lyceum as nothing more than a "gym." They would be more faithfully characterized as the haunts of a prosperous and leisured urban set, some young, others (like Socrates himself, who is said by Plato to have visited both the Academy and the Lyceum) older, some more inclined to physical exercise, others to intellectual activity, but all dedicated to the cultivation of leisured pursuits, particular of the high-class variety. It is unlikely that the hustle and bustle of the Agora would have appealed to boys and men of such background, lifestyle, and tastes.

ARCHITECTURE AND THE OUTDOOR CULTURE OF ATHENS

From the foregoing discussion it should be clear that to a great extent Athenian public life was conducted out of doors. True, some of the buildings used for governmental functions, such as the Council House and some of the judicial venues, were roofed, but the meetings of the Assembly, whether convened on the Pnyx or elsewhere, were always held under the open sky. So was the quasijudicial procedure called ostracism, mentioned earlier. The large sports arenas, the hippodrome (for equestrian events) and the stadium (for Olympic-style athletics), were too large to be roofed, even if it had occurred to anyone to do so. The numerous theaters, such as the Theater of Dionysus (and, later, of Herodes Atticus) on the Acropolis, the two in Peiraeus, and several others in some of the outlying demes, were all open-air affairs. The one exception was the relatively small Odeion constructed under the Acropolis in the time of Pericles, which had a roof supported by a multitude of interior columns (also roofed was a second Odeion built centuries later under Roman rule). Market activity, given the flimsiness (or nonexistence) of the installations reported by the sources, was certainly conducted out of doors, as it continues to be today in bazaars and produce markets throughout the Aegean region.

In the religious sphere, visitors to Greece are of course most impressed by the monumental peristyle temples, such as the Parthenon, whose columns originally encircled solid-walled and roofed interior buildings. Yet, as already noted, sacrifices were performed on the altars before (not inside) the temples, and in any case much religious activity transpired in sanctuaries or shrines that were little more than a wall with a gate enclosing an open-air altar. The gymnasia combined enclosed and open-air spaces, the latter including groves, shaded paths, and running tracks; and the palaestra, essentially an open court surrounded by colonnades, was similarly open to the sky. And the colonnades, or stoas, that served in large part to define the Agora in town were again, as we saw, a sort of compromise between the need for protection from the elements and an overriding desire to remain outside at the same time.

Since, finally, private houses lacked interior water delivery systems, their occupants were compelled to venture outside to wells or to fountain houses sometimes located in or near the civic center. Shopping expeditions, though perhaps on a less regular basis, likewise required that someone travel to and from the area of the Agora. So a hermetic, stay-at-home existence was not possible for most people. By choice or necessity, most residents of Attica regularly ventured into public spaces.

DOMESTIC ARCHITECTURE AND ATHENIAN SOCIETY

Given this pronounced trend toward outdoor activity, all the more importance attaches to domestic architecture. When we turn to the subject of the women of Athens, we will see that, in contrast with the outdoor culture just characterized, there is some reason to believe that females of all ages led relatively sequestered lives. The degree of sequestration is debated, but it is certain that women did *not* engage in the constitutional, political, military, commercial, and agricultural activities that kept many Athenian men away from their residences for much of the day. All females, and male minors, spent disproportionate periods of their lives in their homes. Are we driven, then, to accept a rather radical division of space according to gender: that the open-air public spaces, including the domain of democratic government, were the exclusive territory of adult citizen males, while women and minors were confined to the private, interior spaces of their homes? There is undoubtedly much truth to this model, but is the situation really so simple and straightforward?

At the time of the outbreak of the Peloponnesian War, the citizen population numbered about thirty thousand—all adult males—with an increasing percentage residing in the urban center. Many of these citizens were heads of households. In view of these facts, an archaeologist's estimate that about six thousand houses were situated inside the city circuit wall may not be far off the mark, although allowance must be made for the existence of an incalculable number of tenements (that is, multiple-unit dwellings) mentioned by contemporary literary and epigraphic sources. Of course, many other Athenians, perhaps a majority, still resided outside the walls in or around the many rural villages of Attica.

Regrettably, virtually no traces of this vast domestic infrastructure have been discovered. Most houses perished in antiquity, owing to their relatively flimsy construction. A typical Greek house was constructed of walls of unbaked mudbrick, or adobe, resting on a low stone *socle* (or foundation); the roof timbers carried tiles of terra cotta. Once the roof and any plaster on the exterior walls were gone, the brickwork would decompose rapidly in the rain. Besides, much of ancient residential Athens now lies inaccessible beneath the urban sprawl of the modern city.

What few examples we have of domestic architecture are confined to the excavated area of the Agora and its immediate environs. Although little of these structures survives above the foundation courses, at least some basic floor plans can be discerned. Especially thick wall socles suggest that some structures rose to a second story. Street-level floors were of hard-packed earth. Remains of drains suggest the existence of bathrooms. Terra-cotta grills and loom weights point unambiguously to cooking and weaving within the house, both activities allocated to females in this society. In the so-called Industrial Quarter to the southwest of the Agora, it is evident from fragments of craft materials, tools, and other remains that the occupants engaged in stonecutting, vase throwing, and metalworking. (Cottage industry, as will be suggested in Chapter 8, may have contributed significantly to Athenian economic productivity.) Outside some of the houses were wells and cesspools.

These are merely some particularly telltale features of the physical record. In fact, archaeologists' reconstructions of individual houses (including many from Greek sites outside Athens) reveal considerable variation in specific architectural design and layout of rooms. But amid these variations a single salient feature stands out: the interior courtyard. Two points relevant to the concerns of this book are in order. First, to attempt to answer the question posed earlier, the existence of an open-air court at least frees us from the necessity of assuming that the occupants of an Athenian house, especially women and children, spent their days confined to interior, sunless spaces. The second point concerns the orientation of the Athenian house: it faced inward, away from other houses and especially from the street. From our examination of the Athenian household in Chapter 7 it will become clear why, in the densely packed urban center, the family (or at least its nonadult male citizen members) insulated itself from contact with the outside world. Nor was such insulation limited to the existence and use of the interior courtyard. Literary evidence reveals more than excavation could regarding the internal arrangement of the rooms—bedrooms in particular. Males and females were segregated within the dwelling. Specifically, in a two-story house, females were normally relegated to the upper story, with the purpose (as we will see) of maximizing their inaccessibility from the street outside. When a stranger knocked and the door opened, the stranger would not see (or be seen by) the wife or daughter of the male citizen owner. Abstractly put, in its inward focus and interior design, the Athenian house embodied the society's estimation of the proper place and relative inaccessibility of its female (and minor) members.

The houses excavated by archaeologists and attested to by written texts were, as we have seen, dwellings of modest scale and value. Were they in fact typical of classical Athens? Demosthenes, writing in the fourth century B.C., states that the houses of prominent political figures of the preceding era (namely, Miltiades and Aristeides) were no more splendid than those of their neighbors. But Demosthenes' judgment does not go unchallenged. Beyond the city walls, more substantial dwellings seem to have existed, for Thucydides speaks of the luxuriously appointed country houses of upper-class Athenians, and excavation has revealed private houses constructed on a more impressive scale than those in the city. Nonetheless, the range of variation is not great, certainly not even approaching the orders of magnitude separating the homes of the poor and of the rich in ancient Rome. The relative uniformity in the scale and value of Athenian housing is, furthermore, paralleled by the relative uniformity of the size of Athenian farms (see Chapter 8). These two basic economic facts may suggest a material undergirding for the egalitarian tendencies of the Athenian democracy.

The modesty of Athenian private domestic architecture contrasts astonishingly with the extravagantly sumptuous public constructions that crowned the Acropolis. The mind's eye imagines an island of gleaming marble hovering amid a sea of mudbrick and terra-cotta roof tiles. Some have, perhaps rightly, found here evidence of greatly contrasting valuations of the public and private domains of Athenian society. The Acropolis (and, less magnificently, the Agora) were the concrete embodiments of the citizen regime, and the lavishness and ostentation of their appointment testifies materially and symbolically to a prioritizing of the institutions through which Athens enacted its policies and advertised its public identity: government and religion.

Suggested Readings

For a general overview of the archaeology of Athens, a good choice is R. E. Wycherley, *The Stones of Athens* (Princeton, 1978). The same author's *How the Greeks Built Cities*, 2nd ed. (New York, 1976), considers the relationship of architecture and town planning to everyday life in all of ancient Greece. The reports of the excavation of the Athenian Agora, the crown jewel of American classical archaeology, can be found in the journal *Hesperia*, the journal of the American School of Classical Studies at Athens. Ancient references to the Agora are collected and translated in Wycherley's *The Athenian Agora, Literary and Epigraphical Testimonia*, vol. 3 (Princeton, 1957); and all aspects of the public square are discussed in detail in his and Homer A. Thompson's *The Agora of Athens*, vol. 14 in the same series (Princeton, 1972). An accessible yet authoritative overview is John M. Camp, *The Athenian Agora: Excavations in the Heart of Classical Athens* (New York, 1986). For a detailed study of the port city, see R. Garland, *The Piraeus: From the Fifth to the First Century B.C.* (Ithaca, 1987).

Chapter 4. The Development of the Athenian Democracy

The concern of the present chapter is with the evolution of Greek, specifically Athenian, government down to its fully developed form in the classical period. Following the destruction of the Mycenaean state (and with it, in all but a few instances, rule by a king or monarchy), this process of evolution begins with a form of polity called aristocracy. Rule by a social elite of "the best" typified the world of the archaic poet Hesiod, the social historical content of whose writings we reviewed at the end of Chapter 2. From these beginnings the city governments matured according to a fairly uniform sequence: aristocracy to oligarchy (including its subform, timocracy), to tyranny, to democracy. Except for tyranny (a foreign word denoting rule by a single extralegal and autocratic "tyrant"), these terms reveal a change in the composition and widening scope of the enfranchised; that is, of those possessing citizenship and political rights. We see a shift from rule by "the best" (aristocracy), to "the few" (oligarchy) or "the wealthy" (timocracy), and finally to "the people" (democracy).

This is the sequence we find at Athens, and it is likely that some such pattern of events also characterized more or less the developments at other Greek cities—with one major qualification. Democracy, "rule by the people," cannot on present evidence be regarded as the typical end product of the evolution of Greek government. Many regimes remained essentially oligarchical. Sparta, however deviant in other respects, is a case in point. In the same period that Athens' "radical" democracy was flourishing, Sparta still had a dual monarchy; considerable executive powers were wielded by a small board of elected "overseers" (in contrast to the many large boards selected by lottery at Athens); and a senate staffed by the two kings and aristocratic elders controlled the agenda of the citizen assembly. But even if Athens does not represent the typical Greek experience, it claims our attention for three important reasons: (1) again, Athens is the best documented of all ancient Greek cities; (2) Athenian institutions, due to the city's transcendent political, economic, and cultural might, were exported to or voluntarily imitated by other Greek cities; and (3) surprising as it may seem (since democracy is so much a part of modern Western experience), ancient Athens provides the *sole* example of the successful adoption of direct democracy by a major independent government in Western history. In a direct democracy, unlike representative democracies, decisions are made, not through representatives, but directly by the people themselves. So, particular importance attaches to the case of Athens. By what historical processes did this unique instance of direct government by the people arise? How did it function? How did it survive as long as it did? What were its ideological underpinnings? These are some of the questions to be addressed here and in Chapter 6.

Before we undertake our investigation, a further preliminary point must be made. The subject of Athens' government only possesses significance to the extent that, during the period of the democracy, political power was expressed through governmental institutions. Negatively put, our investigation would have less significance if it were the case that, despite the existence of popular government, political power was in fact wielded by wealthy merchants or by a military force or authority or by religious figures, to pick some historically possible examples. But at Athens, the power holders, the decision makers, were in fact the elected or appointed officers or participants in the organs of government that comprised the Athenian state. When war was declared, when a treaty was concluded, when domestic policy was formulated, it was actually the result of the workings of the democratic constitution and not the product of extragovernmental forces. This is fortunate for us because, as we will see when we reach Chapter 6, sufficient evidence is available to reconstruct not only the fixtures and mechanics of the democratic government, but also the principles and ideology underlying its design and operation.

FROM ARISTOCRACY TO DEMOCRACY

The Sources

In any inquiry of this kind there is inevitably a problem with sources—"inevitably" because the period with which we are dealing, from the emergence of the archaic state down to the creation of the democracy in 508/7 B.C., is not documented by surviving reports of contemporary witnesses. Stone inscriptions, on which ancient historians rely for much of our knowledge of the detailed workings of ancient Greek government, did not come into regular use until about the middle of the fifth century—over a half-century into the new democracy. Nor is it even likely that the earlier stages of the development of the constitution were chronicled in any form, inscribed or not, for as late as Solon (traditional date of archonship, 594 B.C.), poetry remained the preferred mode of expression. As a result, the historian is dependent on the reconstructions and speculations of writers of the classical period: notably, Herodotus and Thucydides, writers on fifth-century history who in several flashback digressions preserve valuable information about the earlier period; and a work attributed to the fourth-century polymath and philosopher Aristotle entitled *The Constitution of the Athenians*. The derivative nature of these accounts means that their authority is no more trustworthy than their (now mostly lost) source materials. Thucydides cites an inscription from the period of the tyrants (miraculously preserved and now on exhibit in Athens), and it is assumed that all writers exploited for chronological guidance a list of chief magistrates (the archons) possibly extending as far back as 683 B.C. Otherwise the historians were probably largely dependent on oral traditions (preserved, for example, by leading aristocratic families) or on their own inferences from contemporary survivals, especially institutional ones. Additionally, Aristotle is believed to have been dependent on the now-lost works of the so-called Atthidographers, the first local historians of Athens. But these writers are known to have been given to political bias; so Aristotle's reconstructions must be approached with more than the usual caution. Nonetheless, sufficient trust-worthy evidence is available to piece together a more or less continuous narrative and to support speculation about the underlying historical dynamics.

Competing Models of Political Conflict

Not surprisingly in light of these limitations of the evidence, alternative types of explanation for the sequence of events we are about to trace have been advanced by ancient Greek historians. These may be schematically portrayed in the form of three distinct models:

1. Class conflict.   According to classic Marxist (and neo-Marxist) formulations, historical change results from conflict between essentially economic classes labeled "patricians" (nobles), "plebeians" (poor free people), "slaves," and so on. This model has superficial appropriateness to a society, like the Athenian, so internally divided by differences in wealth. Moreover, the ancient Greeks themselves tended to view civil strife as a struggle between the rich and the poor. But, as we will see when we describe the principal components of Attic society (Chapter 5), not economic classes but rather constitutional "orders" (citizen, resident alien, slave) provide a more realistic and analytically power-ful tool for understanding the internal dynamics of this society.

2. Regional conflict.   Some scholars believe that the physical and demograph-ic fragmentation of Attica gave rise to and fostered a corresponding political fragmentation. Some of the revolutionary upheavals we are about to review were plausibly attributed by the ancient sources to just such localized con-centrations of power, with ideology (reactionary, moderate, or radical) expressly claimed to vary correspondingly from region to region. The ques-tion is how far this model, unquestionably supported by a few good cases, can be taken as the key to the understanding of the entire evolutionary process.

3. Aristocratic infighting.   That upper-class (wealthy or aristocratic) Athenians and other Greeks competed with one another for political dominance is a well-established historical fact. What is not so evident is whether those con-flicts that appear to pit against each other competing ideologies (oligarchic versus democratic) or competing class interests (rich versus poor) were no less, on closer inspection and analysis, actually contests between rival individual aristocrats and their factions. (Ancient Republican Rome provides a classic and well-documented illustration of this phenomenon.)

Methodologically, it is important to emphasize that none of these three models is offered here as a freestanding theory that, in isolation from the two others, might supply a sufficient explanation for the entire process of development. From the narrative of events it will soon become apparent that no such exclusive application of any of the three models in its pure form can account for our record in all its complexity. Rather, our purpose is to identify the principal factors or dynamics that *in combination with one another* played a role in the unfolding of the Athenian constitution. It will be for the reader to judge in what ways, and to what extent, any of the three was operative in the several historical episodes that now follow.

THE ARISTOCRACY

Athens reemerges into the light of history under the domination of an aristocracy called the Eupatridai or "Well Born." By this term later historians seemed to point to the preeminence of familial or quasifamilial groupings of one kind or another. What were these groupings? Scholars once believed in the existence of powerful "clans" (Greek *genos,* plural *gene*), which, like the well-known Roman *gentes,* allegedly monopolized early Athenian political life, but this belief has now been exploded and the Athenian clans relegated to the role of apolitical cult associations. Another, better candidate, the *phratry,* or "brotherhood," was certainly in existence at this early time (for one thing, references to it are found in the Homeric poems), and its importance in classical society may have been an outgrowth of an earlier, vital role under the aristocracy. Still other upper-class groupings, not identifiable by any collective term such as clan or brotherhood, were regional in orientation, concentrated in a village or cluster of contiguous villages and with a cultic focus. (An example would be the Tetrapolis, or Four Towns, at Marathon in northeastern Attica.) Local bigwigs, comfortably situated at the apex of the social hierarchy, dominated these agrarian communities. Proponents of the second model above (regional conflict) make much of the political roles played by these regional organizations. According to one well-received theory, the democratic order that would eventually emerge acquired some of its distinctive characteristics *in response to* just such localized concentrations of aristocratic power.

Of institutions under the aristocracy little is known. The king of Mycenaean Athens was gone, replaced by a board of officers called *archons* (Greek for "rulers"), among whom the sweeping powers of the former king were apportioned. Eventually they numbered nine: the archon *basileus* ("king" archon), polemarch ("war archon"), the archon eponymous (after whom, when the office became annual, the year was named), and six *thesmothetai* ("dispensers of judgments"). Upon completing their term of office, the archons automatically became lifetime members of a deliberative consultative body, the Council of the Areopagus (so called with reference to a low hill near the Acropolis on which its meetings were held). The Council's functions were not, like those of later democratic bodies, legislative. It did not pass decrees or formulate laws. Rather, the archons probably came before it to seek advice or for approval of their official actions. Because its membership represented the accumulated experience and wisdom of the Athenian political community, its recommendations tended to be followed. Thus the Council's authority and influence far exceeded those of a second body of citizens, the Ekklesia, the Assembly of all free Athenians. The Assembly's powers probably included deciding questions of war and peace, for the Homeric poems show that even a king could not undertake a military venture without the approval of his soldiers. (*Soldiers* and *citizens* are in fact two words denoting the same people.) The Ekklesia also reportedly elected the archons, but because in later times only the wealthy were eligible to hold the office, it is likely that under the aristocracy only Eupatridai could be nominated.

CYLON'S FAILED COUP D'ÉTAT (632 B.C.)

The first recorded challenge to the aristocratic order is associated with an Athenian named Cylon. Only a few facts about him are preserved, but they are highly suggestive. He was a Eupatrid noble. He had scored a victory in a running race in the Olympic Games of 640 B.C. He had married the daughter of the tyrant of Megara, a neighboring city-state to the west of Athens. During a subsequent Olympic festival (perhaps two Olympiads, or eight years, after his own victory), backed by his father-in-law's army, Cylon marched on Athens and occupied the Acropolis. According to Thucydides' account, the Athenian people, once they perceived what was happening, came in from the countryside and besieged the rebels on the citadel. After the escape of Cylon and his brother, the remaining Cylonians were forced to come to terms with the chief executive officers, the archons, whose chief was Megacles, a member of the Alcmeonid family. The archons promised safe escort down from the Acropolis, with a trial to follow. But the magistrates reneged on the agreement, killing the Cylonians as they descended. The Alcmeonids were held responsible for the fiasco, placed under a curse, and driven into exile.

Cylon's attempted *coup d'état* had ended in failure, but the sources of his power had not been inconsiderable. According to one ancient writer, his Olympic victory may have led Cylon to believe, superstitiously, that a subsequent Olympic festival would be an auspicious time to launch his revolution. Perhaps so, but Cylon may also be our earliest Greek example of a popular celebrity—in this case, a successful and highly visible athlete—attempting to convert that popularity into political power. After all, Athenian Olympic victors in later times would be rewarded with a seat of honor and free meals in the town hall for life. Cylon's marriage to the daughter of the man who was to furnish his army is, similarly, a very early Greek example of a dynastic marriage, with all its considerations of material, social, or political advantages. But the vital detail is Cylon's Eupatrid status, a clear hint that the attempted coup was not ideologically motivated by class differences. If, in any case, his goal had been to advance the cause of lower-class Athenians, they should have joined in the attempt; instead, they appear to have cooperated with a board of magistrates headed by an upper-class aristocrat. The episode more closely resembles infighting among the elite. The membership of Megacles, the man responsible for the treacherous slaying of the conspirators, in the powerful Alcmeonids, and the fact that not only Megacles but his entire family as well was cursed and exiled, perhaps reveals the identity of Cylon's aristocratic adversary. It is evident that, of our three models, the event conforms most closely to that of aristocratic infighting.

THE LEGISLATION OF DRACO (621 B.C.)

In 621 B.C., about a decade after the probable date of Cylon's abortive revolution, occurs the second stage of the march toward democracy, the promulgation of a legal code by an Athenian named Draco. Although ancient writers credit the lawgiver with codification of existing law, it turned out that, within a short time, nearly all of the new code had been superseded by the laws of Solon, with the result that only one of Draco's statutes, the one on homicide, remained in force in the classical period. By a happy accident, part of its text has survived in a later (but still ancient) copy. According to the prevailing modern reconstruction, Draco's law modified the existing practice that allowed the relatives of a homicide victim to take vengeance unless a pardon had been obtained by payment of blood money. The modification, while otherwise leaving intact the principle of self-help, prescribed separate treatment if the homicide was *involuntary*. A special court was established to rule on the question of presence or absence of intention; and if the accused was found to have acted involuntarily, the new law called for his exile. (Exile would be a mild penalty in comparison with the fate he might otherwise suffer at the hands of a victim's relatives.)

The significance of this law has been much discussed. It was only natural that historians would attempt to link a law on homicide with the bloodletting precipitated by Cylon's march on Athens only a few years before. The interpretation of that event just offered, that the episode was essentially a violent conflict between competing aristocratic factions, prompts the assumption that further, retaliatory outbreaks of violence soon followed. Draco's law could then be viewed as the state's attempt to stop or at least contain the carnage. But according to the view sketched in the preceding paragraph, *premed-*

itated murder—the very type of homicide characteristic of vendettas carried out by rival factions—was not addressed. The old practice of compensation by payment of blood money, or, failing that, retaliation, would continue as before.

A second, more wide-ranging, interpretation, is that Draco's laws were progressive in that they updated, or otherwise improved upon, whatever laws had been in force previously. This theory would fit the view that Draco innovated by distinguishing between voluntary and involuntary homicide, while permitting more lenient treatment in the latter case. Against the theory, however, is the fact that, as stated above, virtually all of the Draconian code was superseded by that of Solon; if the earlier laws were progressive, they were not progressive enough. Against it also is the unanimous verdict of antiquity that Draco's work was unnaturally severe. To mention only one picturesque piece of ancient imagery, his laws were said to have been written in blood. At best, the Athenian's contribution to the legal system was to bring together, and perhaps to systematize or render self-consistent, a hodgepodge of miscellaneous isolated statutes. Liberalization of that system was another matter altogether.

A third possible dimension of Draco's work remains: the fact of publication itself. The new code was a written code, very possibly the first such written code at Athens. If the laws had already been in existence in unwritten form, with Draco's work (excepting perhaps the law on homicide) confined to their compilation and publication, we could understand both their unusual severity (that is, the laws were archaic to begin with) and their rapid demise (in the face of the truly progressive legislation of Solon). But publication, even of outmoded laws, would represent a major advance. No longer could aristocratic lords, the sole repositories of the law, interpret or recast the law at their whim and to suit their own interests. The reader will also recall the remarks in Chapter 2 about the consequences of literacy's being introduced into an oral culture. Once a text (including a law) is published, it is fixed, and, once fixed, it can be examined, studied, and criticized at leisure by the literate readership. Written or inscribed texts would have allowed the Athenian public to learn just what the law said or did not say. Perhaps more importantly, it provided a platform for their modification in years to come. It may be no accident, then, that Draco's initial codification and publication of a written legal code were so soon thereafter followed by the new legislation of Solon. Draco's legacy was not progressive change, but rather the establishment of one of the key conditions necessary to make such change possible.

THE REFORMS OF SOLON (594 B.C.)

Ancient sources provide no reason to believe that Draco's work, except for the law on homicide, went beyond codification, or at best minor modification of existing Athenian law. But Athens had been facing, and continued to face, severe societal problems unrelated to the legal system, particularly in the economic sphere. Indebtedness, the most pressing of Athens' ills, had reached crisis proportions. Among the indebted were the "sixth parters" who, as their unusual name suggests, worked the land in exchange for one-sixth of their gross production. Whether these Athenians owned the land (which they had mortgaged to rich lenders) or as tenants worked land owned by their creditors is disputed. But Aristotle is explicit on the point that, if the poor failed to make their payments, both they and their children were subject to seizure; "for," he adds, "all loans—among which are presumably included the rents—were made on the security of the person." Scholars disagree about the reconstruction of events referred to by this (and related) texts. Possibly, to mention one likely scenario, many Athenian farms had reached the subsistence level, such that in an average year just enough foodstuffs were produced to sustain the owner and his family. But deforestation and its consequences, overuse leading to a decline of fertility, or climatic changes might have reduced productivity to the point at which farmers were forced to borrow in order to see themselves through to the next harvest. If the borrower did not own land to use as collateral or if the land he did own was already encumbered with debt, the one major possession he had to offer as security was his person (that is, his personal freedom). Such loans had been made and when, as the crisis continued, the debtors defaulted, the creditors assumed ownership of the collateral by enslaving their debtors, in some cases literally selling them abroad as slaves.

The crisis reached such alarming levels that the still-aristocratic power structure, apparently including the large landholders themselves, was forced to take action. A major upheaval, perhaps a revolution, could have been among the possible outcomes if nothing had been done. It was decided to appoint a lawgiver, the Eupatrid Solon. Solon was formally elected archon eponymous for the year 594 B.C., and it was apparently in this capacity that he introduced a sweeping series of reforms. That portion of the reforms dealing with the debt crisis was called in Greek "the Shaking Off of Burdens," with specific reference to the cancellation of existing debts. Henceforth, too, borrowing on the security of the person of the borrower was to be prohibited, and, presumably at public expense, those Athenians who had been sold abroad were redeemed and reestablished on their farms. Thus the immediate situation had been addressed, and from this time forth no Athenian, by reason of default on a debt, would suffer enslavement.

But it is also important to note what Solon did *not* do. Most importantly, he did not, as revolutionary programs were typically to demand, confiscate and redistribute the land, even though it must have been obvious that it was precisely the precariously small size of the subsistence plots that had rendered their owners so vulnerable to indebtedness. Furthermore, Solon shut the door on any future confiscations by requiring that, from his time on, the archon proclaim upon entry into office that he would maintain the existing distribution of property. No fundamental, lasting change had been brought about. To save the state from self-destruction, existing debt had been wiped out (admittedly, by ancient standards, a revolutionary measure), but, except for the merely humanitarian prohibition on future loans on the security of the borrower, little had been done to ease the plight of the poor—above all, the landless poor.

The System of Income Classes and the Constitution

The inference that Solon, despite the cancellation of debts (with the resulting losses suffered by wealthy creditors), did *not* in fact aim at a revolutionary overthrow of the existing order is confirmed by an examination of the second major component of his reforms: the income-class system. Solon divided Athenian citizens into a hierarchy of four groups, each defined by annual income measured in terms of agricultural produce. (The unit of measure, the *medimnos*, corresponds more or less to an English bushel.) The classes were:

Pentakosiomedimnoi	"500-bushel men"	500 bushels or more
Hippeis	"Knights"	300 bushels or more
Zeugitai	"Owners of two oxen"?	200 bushels or more
Thetes	Meaning unknown	Under 200 bushels

The names Solon chose for his classes reveal something of his purpose. To begin with the one straightforward item, *hippeis* are equestrians or "knights," a term reflecting the importance of the horse in aristocratic society and a suitable title for men of relatively substantial wealth. *Zeugitai* may mean literally "the yoked ones," that is, men prosperous enough to plow with (two) yoked oxen, although some have associated the term with the "yoking" of the hoplite phalanx—another possible indication of a modest degree of prosperity (see Chapter 8). *Thetes* is a word of uncertain etymology, but in Homer's poems the *thetes* are hired laborers, landless and poor, and on this basis the word would be a suitable designation for Solon's lowest income class. Thus far the titles are more or less traditional, although the use to which Solon put them was new. But "500-bushel men" has correctly been recognized as an entirely novel formation. It was new because it embraced not only rich Eupatrids but also men of great wealth from outside the aristocratic elite and for whom, consequently, no old-fashioned traditional term existed. The Athenians of the topmost tier, the principal beneficiaries of the reform, included, to borrow from the French, the "new rich." Some, as has long been suspected, may have been traders. Some, as has been more recently argued, may have been farmers who, unable to succeed by growing cereal grains on the rocky soil of Attica, switched to new "cash crops" that thrived in such conditions: olives (for oil) and grapes (for wine). But had the aristocratic families of the elite, often owners of large cereal-producing estates in the great plains of Attica, welcomed the new rich to their privileged circle? Certainly not. Although now enriched through nontraditional forms of commercial activity, the newly wealthy had been excluded from holding positions of influence in the Athenian government (above all, the archonships and hence membership in the Council of the Areopagus) by reason of their not having been born into Eupatrid families.

Solon's purpose in creating the income-class system was to use it as the criterion for determining a citizen's access to the various departments of Athenian government and his level of participation in public life generally. Specific areas of application included the military organization, the composition of colonial populations, and, most to the point here, the boards and legislative bodies of the constitutional apparatus. To mention but two explicitly documented examples, the archonship was to be open only to members of the two topmost classes (pentakosiomedimnoi and hippeis), whereas the thetes were to be excluded from all offices (though they were presumably still eligible to participate in the Assembly of the People). The effect was to substitute wealth for birth as the principle governing the degree or level of a citizen's participation and political power. To express the change in traditional Greek terminology, aristocracy ("rule of the best") had been replaced by oligarchy ("rule of the few") or, more specifically, by the form of oligarchy called *timocracy* ("rule according to wealth"). But it is vital to remember that Eupatrids, if wealthy (and most probably were at this time), continued to maintain positions of prominence under the new regime. What they had been forced to surrender was an exclusive monopoly on higher office and hence a similar monopoly on membership in the still-influential Council of the Areopagus.

Measures to Strengthen the Economy

Recognition and empowerment of the nonnoble wealthy was only one element of Solon's attention to the economic life of Athens. Our source materials, however fragmentary or questionable their authenticity, seem to reveal a consistent interest in fostering domestic productivity through various mechanisms.

• The offer of citizenship was extended to foreigners who settled in Attica with their families in order to pursue a trade. Two points should be emphasized. First, by bringing with them a skill, these immigrants would contribute to nonagricultural productivity—that sector of the economy now being served, as we have just seen, by the income-class system. Second, the fact that the immigrants were required to bring their families with them would mean that the earnings of an immigrant domiciled in Athens would not be "exported" to a wife and children still residing in some foreign land.

• Solon required the Council of the Areopagus to investigate every man's source of livelihood and to punish those who were found not to be working.

• A law of Solon mandated that a father could not claim support from his son if he, the father, had not taught that son a trade. This law would have had two predictable effects. In the absence of institutionalized care for the old, a citizen, provided he had satisfied the conditions imposed by the law, could count on maintenance in his old age (see further on this, Chapter 7). More to the point for the present discussion, the law, by imposing so heavy a penalty for noncompliance, ensured the regular transmission of trade skills from generation to generation. No other means for such training, such as formal schools, existed.

• Solon is credited with changes in the Athenian systems of weights, measures, and coinages. Legislation by the lawgiver on weights and measures is probable. Coinage, however, did not exist as early as the traditional date for Solon's archonship (594 B.C.), but later writers (such as the Atthidographers) may have retrojected from later times an interest in the monetary system, on the theory, supported by their superior record of evidence, that Solon was indeed keenly concerned with the Athenian economy.

Plainly Solon saw his role as requiring intervention in the economy of Athens and the creation of mechanisms for its continued maintenance by the state in the future. From the specific content of these measures it is obvious that his immediate purpose was to increase domestic productivity. The beneficiaries of such increase, furthermore, were to be the Athenian people, for another law explicitly forbade export of any agricultural produce other than olive oil. But the exception, olive oil, is a major item: a product produced in quantity in Attica and much in demand elsewhere. Perhaps he intended the oil to be exchanged for cereals, abundant abroad but increasingly scarce in Athens as the growing population continued to outstrip the capacity of the neighboring farmland. If so, such a plan would have been a farsighted and enlightened departure from the generally introverted character of his economic policy. Whatever the detailed interpretation of that policy, we must remember that the increased productivity at which Solon aimed was not only fostered by the legal sanctions just mentioned. It was also to be rewarded under the new Solonian political regime, for the big winners in this revitalized marketplace, once they had reached the level of the 500-bushel men, would become eligible to play an enhanced public role, possibly including election to the board of archons, the chief executives of the Athenian state.

The Administration of Justice

At this point it might well be wondered whether, or in what ways, Solon's legislation positively benefited citizens of the lower economic and social orders. At best, the Shaking Off of Burdens had returned the indebted or enslaved to square one. What, beyond that, did Solon do to improve their condition?

First, Solon is said to have established a people's court called the Heliaia. Every party to any lawsuit tried in any Athenian court was granted the right of appeal to the Heliaia against the judgment of the presiding magistrates. Simply put, if an Athenian citizen lost a judicial decision, he was given by Solon the right of appeal to the People. Because magistrates, even after the introduction of the income classes determining eligibility to higher office, would tend to be aristocrats, what the enactment amounted to was that an ordinary citizen now had the right to have such an aristocrat's adverse decision undergo reconsideration by a body of his peers.

A second judicial measure is less clearly related to social standing. Solon enlarged the body of those citizens legally qualified to initiate a legal accusation. Previously, only the injured party could launch a judicial action. Solon gave to every citizen the right to initiate a "third-party" suit either on behalf of the injured party or more generally on behalf of the public interest. All citizens, however humble, were now potential litigants. Solon had placed a powerful weapon in the hands of citizens eager to check the activity or ambitions of their upper-class fellow Athenians. But the long-term effect was a rising tide of litigiousness that by the classical period would sweep over the Athenian judicial system.

The impact of Solon's work, as represented here, was probably most keenly felt in the economic sphere. The problem of indebtedness had been solved, at least for the time being. Measures had been taken to invigorate Athenian domestic productivity, including in nontraditional agricultural or commercial pursuits. Those entrepreneurs outside the entrenched Eupatrid aristocracy who were fortunate enough to become wealthy were now, alongside their aristocratic competitors, granted access to the higher echelons of government through the new income-class system. But despite all this activity involving the marketplace, later Athenians remembered Solon—not Clisthenes, who was to come along nearly a century later—as the founder of the *democracy*. This claim was true to the extent that Solon, in his capacity as lawgiver, created a code of laws that, with a single major revision between 410 and 399 B.C., would remain more or less intact throughout the lifetime of that government. It was for this that his memory was cherished by his fellow countrymen. But it should not be forgotten that his role as lawgiver had grown out of the crisis of indebtedness, and that he remained preoccupied with the problem of finding ways to strengthen the Athenian economy.

THE TYRANNY OF PISISTRATUS AND HIS SONS

Background: Regions, Ideology, and Personal Ambition

Solon's reforms, so far as the ancient sources inform us, were addressed primarily to problems created or exacerbated by differences in wealth. But the next phase would be further complicated by another dimension: region.

By the middle decades of the sixth century B.C., the political landscape of Attica had coalesced into three principal factions (a term to be preferred to *party*, as the latter implies an inappropriate degree of organization): the Men of the Plain, the Men of the Shore, and the Men from Beyond the Hills. The "plain" in question is the central plain of Attica. This faction's leader was Lycurgus, a member of a noble family based in or near the city center of Athens. The "shore" is certainly the strip of coast extending from the old port of Phaleron southeastward toward the Sounion promontory, since it was here that the homes of the Alcmeonids (the noble family of the faction's leader, Megacles) were primarily located (other holdings extended northward from the shore into the city). The "hills" are the low range separating the extreme eastern coastal strip from the interior of Attica. The hill people were led by the eventual tyrant, Pisistratus, from a family claiming Pylian (that is, Mycenaean) descent and whose name is shared with an archon of the early seventh century—therefore, inferentially, a family of importance and influence. Their base was at Brauron, a town centrally located on the coastal plain due east of Athens.

To anticipate our account of the events, the rise of the tyranny was the end product of a series of conflicts among these three factions. Historians have given much attention to the question of the nature of those conflicts. Regional rivalry is certainly part of the answer, but the problem is complicated by the fact that Aristotle's *Constitution of the Athenians* ascribes a distinct ideological outlook to each of the factions:

• The Men of the Plain represented the traditional landed aristocracy. The plain was a center of cereal production and thus the heartland of Blue Blood aristocrats, among whom were many who had lost heavily as a result of Solon's cancellation of debts. Furthermore, they now had to share political preeminence with the new rich among Solon's class of pentakosiomedimnoi. Their goal was to overturn the Solonian reforms.

• The Men of the Shore, led by the noble Alcmeonids, are described by Aristotle as "moderates," not without plausibility. On the one hand, these renegade aristocrats had long been at loggerheads with the traditional aristocracy (we recall the role played by the family and its ancestor, an earlier Megacles, in the Cylonian fiasco) and would continue to be so. On the other hand, no aristocrat of any description, certainly not large landholders like these, would have favored the radical agenda of the Men from Beyond the Hills.

• The Men from Beyond the Hills occupied land that was generally less productive than that of the other two regions. They were not sharing in the general prosperity of Attica. Furthermore, cut off as they were from a city dominated by urban aristocrats, geographic isolation probably increased their discontent. These were Aristotle's "most democratic" faction; we would call them "radicals." Their program would have included a call to confiscate and redistribute the farmlands of Attica.

To these regional and ideological differences must be added still another factor (corresponding to our third model): personal rivalry in the form of aristocratic infighting. Each of the leaders came from a powerful noble family; not even the spokesman of the "radicals" could claim to be a grassroots politician. The sources certainly leave the impression that the goal of each of the three leaders was to establish a personal political ascendancy over the entire state of Athens. And that is precisely what the eventual winner of the lengthy struggle in fact did. But it is important to note that, in the context of the ancient Greco-Roman world, the goals of the leadership and those of the followers need not correspond or even be compatible with one another. All Athenian leaders, until the emergence of popular demagogues in the later fifth century (and even they were typically industrialists of substantial means), were from upper-class families. What made them different was the peculiar composition of the clientele—old-line Eupatrid, renegade aristocrat, or landless poor—they chose to represent in the arena of political conflict. The student, most importantly of all, is to be on guard against the reductive fallacy. All three dimensions—region, ideology, and personal ambition—are real, and none can be reduced to any of the others.

The Rise of Pisistratus and the Three Periods of the Tyranny

For the story of Pisistratus' rise to power the most trustworthy narrative is provided by the fifth-century historian Herodotus. Around 560 B.C. the budding politician, says Herodotus, resorting to trickery, purposely wounded himself and appeared before the Assembly in Athens, claiming that he had been attacked by his enemies. With the bodyguard provided by the Assembly, he seized the Acropolis and took control of Athens. But not long afterwards, the two other leaders, Lycurgus and Megacles, joined forces to drive Pisistratus out. Some time later, Megacles, falling out with Lycurgus, approached the exile and promised to restore him to power if he would agree to marry his daughter. He agreed, and the two again resorted to trickery. They dressed up a statuesque country woman in armor to look like the goddess Athena, and she and the would-be tyrant, mounted on a chariot and preceded by messengers exclaiming that the goddess was bringing Pisistratus back, entered Athens, where the Athenian was received with open arms.

Thus was the second tyranny established. But the marriage of the tyrant and Megacles' daughter, now concluded, did not flourish. Pisistratus, put off by the report that Megacles' family, the Alcmeonids, had a curse upon it (see above, on Cylon) and because he already had grown sons of his own and so wished no new children with his new wife, refused to engage in normal sexual relations with her. Such action was not only a personal insult to the wife and her family. It was also a denial of the purpose implicit in any ancient Greek marriage—the production of children—and, still more seriously, probably a violation of the agreement with Megacles, for in a dynastic marriage of this kind, children would serve to strengthen the link between the two families. So, when Pisistratus' wife told her mother, and her mother told Megacles, he patched up his quarrel with the Men of the Plain. The tyrant was forced to withdraw from Athens once again. This time more elaborate preparations were made. Pisistratus spent the next decade building a power base by drawing on the resources of foreign peoples—Thracians, Thebans, Argives, and the people of Eretria, off the eastern coast of Attica, who allowed him use of their territory as a base of operations. In 546 B.C., the exile and his followers landed at Marathon in northeastern Attica and, marching toward Athens, met and defeated an Athenian army at Pallene. The leader of the Men from Beyond the Hills was now undisputed ruler of Athens.

There is little trace here of the regional rivalries, and their attendant ideologies, discussed earlier. What Herodotus offers is the interpersonal dimension, with a consistent focus on the relations among the leaders of the factions. Embellishment is to be suspected, particularly in the earlier stages of the story. The repetition of the trickery motif suggests a folktale element, and the entire account of the first two tyrannies bears the stamp of dependence on oral tradition (after all, what other sources might Herodotus have had?). But the formation and undoing of personal alliances and the dynastic marriage have the ring of authenticity; if nothing else, they fit the pattern of political wheeling and dealing in the solidly documented classical era. The story of Pisistratus' appeals to foreign powers is plausible, too, for the international character of the final tyranny's policies is one of its most salient features. Embellished, perhaps, but the core of the narratives looks authentic and as such provides an insight into the mechanics of the political interactions among these regionally based and ideologically distinct factions.

The Third Tyranny at Athens (546–510 B.C.)

Pisistratus had been brought to power at the head of a radical following that had been left unsatisfied by the reforms of Solon a half-century before. Solon, while canceling debts, had stopped short of fulfilling a second radical ambition: the confiscation and redistribution of the land. It is impossible to overestimate the potential significance of such a measure. Despite the growing urban population and an emerging industrial sector, Athens remained a fundamentally agricultural society. Land was the sole source of most citizens' livelihood. Land was the source of prestige defining the citizen class (since noncitizens in the classical period were debarred from ownership of "land and house"). From land emanated powerful nostalgic associations rooted in myth, religion, and family traditions. To pass from a landless or marginally landed condition to possession of a farm capable of permanently sustaining a family would be a very great step indeed. But Pisistratus, whatever his original intentions may have been, did not disturb the existing regime of ownership. At best he indirectly taxed existing holdings in farmland by taxing production (at the rate of 5 or 10 percent). If the proceeds went to fund the loans to struggling farmers reported by Aristotle, the net effect would have been a minor redistribution of wealth, but certainly not on the scale hoped for by the Men from Beyond the Hills.

Pisistratus, long a combatant in the struggle for power among factions representing, and ultimately produced by, regional divisions of Attica, knew, if anyone did, the need for the unification of Attica. The tyrant strove to achieve such a unification, certainly in a physical sense, but above all by symbolic means. Athens would become, if it was not already, the physical and spiritual center of the Athenian state. There, on or near the Acropolis, was undertaken the construction of monumental temples in the names of the pan-Greek divinities Zeus and Athena. Public festivals on a large scale were inaugurated or popularized. Dionysus, a popular god appealing to a wider public, was introduced to Athens by the tyrant; eventually, the god's festivals, the City and the Rural Dionysia, would be officially observed throughout Attica. Under the tyranny, Athena's festivals, the Greater and Lesser Panathenaia, underwent expansion, and they, too, eventually acquired the status of "national" celebrations. Temples and festivals thus symbolized the regime's program of eradicating the sectionalism that had disrupted Attica after Solon.

But a deeper insight into Pisistratus' purposes is suggested by Aristotle's report that the tyrant instituted "deme justices"; that is judicial officers who were to administer justice in the villages (or *demes*) of the countryside outside the urban center. The tyrant himself, Aristotle adds, journeyed into the rural districts to conduct inspections and to reconcile disputants, "so that they should not come down to the city and neglect their work." The same reason—to keep the citizens at work in their fields and out of public affairs—is given for the abovementioned subsidies for struggling farmers. By unification, in other words, Pisistratus did *not* intend to promote widespread involvement of the rural population in the politics of the city. The obliteration of regional loyalties by the popularization of pan-Attic cults and festivals would not be obtained at the cost of destabilizing the state by inviting increased participation of those regional interests in the new government. Abstractly put, unification was to be counterbalanced by a degree of decentralization.

A private army had brought Pisistratus to power, but there is little reason to believe that his (and his sons') continuing ascendancy depended on military force. In fact, a visitor to Athens would probably hardly have realized a tyranny existed. Herodotus' assessment sums up the situation: "Pisistratus did not alter the existing positions of honor and did not change the laws, but he governed the city in accordance with established principles, ruling well and with distinction." Thucydides echoes the point about the laws but adds that the tyrants always ensured that there would be one of their men among the magistrates. Thucydides' point is strikingly confirmed by an inscribed list of the eponymous archons (that is, the chief archons whose names were used to designate the year in the official Athenian calendar). It shows the archon of 526/5 B.C. to have been the tyrant's son Hippias and that of 522/1 B.C. to have been Pisistratus, his grandson. No less significantly, the list gives an additional name, Miltiades, a powerful ally on whom the tyrants would rely in extending their interests overseas. The office, in other words, could be filled by friends as well as by family members. Still more tellingly, the archon for 525/4 B.C. is given as Clisthenes, who can only be the Alcmeonid who would later found the democracy. Surprisingly, Herodotus says in a famous passage that the Alcmeonids remained in exile throughout the duration of the tyranny. Either he was misinformed by his source or, equally likely, he made an incorrect inference from an anecdotal tradition that portrayed the two families as hostile to one another. The fact is, hostility or not, the presence of Clisthenes' name on the list proves that an accommodation had been made between the tyrants and the future democratic politician. Again, we are cautioned by their example not to view these Athenian political leaders in excessively ideological terms. Clisthenes, a member of the noble Alcmeonids, was fundamentally no different from other high-born political leaders, and it was only under the press of circumstances that, as we will shortly see, his political agenda took the radically democratic turn that it later did.

Whatever brokering underlay the maintenance of their position, the tyrants cultivated the good will of the masses. The new temples and festivals, to which all citizens had access, have been mentioned. Add to this the patronage of famous poets and the promotion of rhapsodic competitions at the Greater Panathenaia. By such acts the tyrants could represent themselves as sustainers of the cultural and public lives of the Athenian people. For a while, their strategy appears to have been successful. The tyrants enjoyed great popularity. But eventually their grip began to loosen. To be sure, Pisistratus' death in 527 B.C. did not disrupt the regime, for the succession by his sons, of whom the eldest was Hippias, went smoothly. Beginning in the 520s B.C., however, the tyranny experienced a series of setbacks in foreign policy. A turning point came in 514 B.C. when two Athenians, Harmodius and Aristogeiton, angered by a personal slight, attempted to overthrow the tyranny, choosing a festival, the Panathenaia, for the attempt. Due to a miscue, only the younger brother, Hipparchus, was assassinated, and Hippias, the eldest son, survived to institute a pogrom of the conspirators, real or imagined. The Reign of Terror lasted until 510 B.C. In that year the tyranny was finally overthrown with the aid of foreign intervention. Herodotus tells how the Alcmeonids, now in exile, undertook the contract for rebuilding the temple of Apollo at Delphi, which had been destroyed by fire. By completing the project with exceptional lavishness, the family put the Delphic priests under obligation to them, with the result that, whenever Spartans came to consult the oracle, the response (regardless of the nature of the question) included a plea to free Athens from the tyranny. The Alcmeonids, in simpler terms, had bribed the oracle of Apollo. Accordingly, Sparta sent first an expedition by sea, later another by land under King Cleomenes. The land force succeeded in besieging the tyrants' family on the Acropolis. When the tyrants attempted to sneak their children through the lines and they were captured and held hostage, the tyrants agreed to depart from Athens. Thus ended the tyranny.

THE CREATION OF THE DEMOCRACY

The departure of the tyrants resulted in a power struggle at Athens between two aristocratic factions. One had remained in Athens under the tyranny; it was led by Isagoras, who was elected archon for the year 508/7 B.C. The other was headed by Clisthenes the Alcmeonid who, from some time following his own archonship in 522/1 B.C., had been in exile. On his return to Athens, however, he discovered that he could not prevail against Isagoras, and then (and only then), to quote Herodotus' words, "he took the Demos into his faction." Thus the wealthy aristocrat, under the force of circumstances and without discernible ideological purpose, committed himself to representing the interests of the people, should he, with their support, emerge victorious from the struggle. But Isagoras had invited the intervention of King Cleomenes, and when, with the arrival of a Spartan army, Clisthenes and his supporters withdrew into exile once again, the Athenian people rose up, ejected the Spartans, condemned Isagoras, and recalled Clisthenes. Thus, in 508/7 B.C., the stage had been set for the creation by the Alcmeonid aristocrat of a new form of government—the *demokratia*, "rule by the Demos."

Suggested Readings

The story of the unfolding of the Athenian constitution is told in the first half of the ancient treatise mentioned at the beginning of this chapter: the *Constitution of the Athenians* traditionally attributed to the philosopher Aristotle. Although not an Athenian citizen, Aristotle, whose school was housed in the gymnasium called the Lyceum (see Chapter 3), was a permanent resident of the city. An accurate translation with brief commentary is that of P. J. Rhodes, in the Penguin series (London, 1984); for the definitive analysis, see the same scholar's *A Commentary on the Aristotelian Athenaion Politeia* (Oxford, 1981). Two accessible but opinionated interpretations are W. G. Forrest, *The Emergence of Greek Democracy 800–400 B.C.* (London, 1966); and Raphael Sealey, *A History of the Greek City States ca. 700–338 B.C.* (Berkeley, 1976), ch. 4–6. Now somewhat dated is the classic treatment of the subject in English by C. Hignett, *A History of the Athenian Constitution to the End of the Fifth Century B.C.* (Oxford, 1952). For a speculative exploration of the origins of Athenian popular ideology, see C. Farrar, *The Origin of Democratic Thinking: The Invention of Politics in Classical Athens* (Cambridge, 1988).

Chapter 5. Citizens, Resident Aliens, and Slaves

With the development of Athens' government in mind, we may now embark upon an in-depth examination of the state and society of ancient Athens in the classical period. The immediate goal is to grasp the "big picture," the gross segmentation of the human population of Athens and Attica according to citizen, resident alien, or slave status. At this point we are dealing in generalities: legal definitions and categories; differences in wealth and status; and the place of the citizen, resident alien, or slave within the Athenian state. Only once this preliminary task has been carried out will it be possible to proceed to a more detailed examination of the democratic government (Chapter 6); of the family, specifically women, children, and the old (Chapter 7); and of workers—farmers, artisans, and soldiers (Chapter 8). At the end of the discussion, by way of bringing out the distinctive character of the Athenian societal regime, we will cast a glance in the direction of the society of Athens' military, political, and ideological rival, Sparta.

CLASSICAL ATHENIAN SOCIETY: "CLASSES" OR "ORDERS"?

At once we are confronted with a tough methodological question. How are we to divide up this society for the purposes of describing and analyzing it? Part of the problem is that the Athenians (like other Greeks) had multiple schemes, or at least multiple systems of nomenclature, for just such a division. Modern critiques have added still others. Which of them, if any, should we adopt?

The notion of *class*, especially where the term refers to wealth, is an obvious, and at first attractive, possibility. To ancient Greek historians the presence or absence of wealth seems to have been a decisive factor, for the frequently occurring civil wars in the city-states were often depicted in terms of a two-sided contest between "the rich" and "the poor." Naturally, no one could seriously deny the importance of property and of the power and influence it bestowed. Indeed, the criterion of wealth had already been built into the Athenian constitutional apparatus. The timocratic basis for determining access to government was formalized, as we just saw (Chapter 4), in Solon's income-class system, instituted early in the sixth century B.C. and still on the books, if not fully operational, in the time of Aristotle near the end of the democracy. According to its terms, interpreted strictly, annual income (expressed in bushels of produce) determined the level of a citizen's participation in government, so, to that extent, differences in wealth really meant something, constitutionally speaking.

But it is questionable whether wealth was the ultimate criterion defining a person's position in the social, as opposed to the constitutional, hierarchy. Alternatively, we may look, as the Athenians themselves looked, to the principal legal categories: citizen, metic (or resident alien), and slave. For these categories, not *class*, but *order* (or sometimes *rank*) seems to have become the generally accepted term. The orders (as we will now call them), although significantly correlated with wealth, were at the same time approximate indicators of gradations of social status which bore no fixed relationship to property holding or wealth in any form. A talented and enterprising metic, or even a slave, might accumulate greater wealth than that possessed by the great majority of citizens, but the latter could take consolation in their incomparably higher status. Only a citizen could hold office or vote, represent himself as a litigant in an Athenian court, own land and buildings, occupy an honorable position in the military organization, or participate through a legitimate marriage in the propagation of the next generation of citizens. Because such privileges were played out in public and were constantly validated and reaffirmed in the acts and symbols by which the state advertised itself, it is easy to see how they, or their absence, decided the question of others', and one's own, estimation of oneself—that is, status. What good was wealth if it was obtained in less than praiseworthy pursuits or if it assumed a form incompatible with universally accepted ideals?

These, then, were the categories of Athenian society that mattered the most. But we must be careful about any additional significance we may be tempted to ascribe to citizens, resident aliens, or slaves *as groups*. To be sure, each of the orders is something more than a mere statistical category, a set of members meeting some legal, economic, or other definition but otherwise not connected with one another in any meaningful way. But how much more than this were they? Discussions of political behavior in postclassical societies, to consider two distinct but closely linked possibilities, sometimes assume the presence (or absence) of *consciousness* and *solidarity* as features of the sorts of groups with which we are dealing. Accordingly, we may ask in the present case: Did Athenian citizens (or resident aliens, or slaves) cultivate a strong sense of their identity, isolating qualities or attainments that set them apart from the other inhabitants of Attica? That is, had they developed a group consciousness? And, if so, did they behave as a more or less tightly knit group? And, when threatened, did they set aside any differences they may have had in order to present a united front to that threat? That is, did they manifest solidarity? For the citizens at least, the answer in both cases is, generally speaking, yes. The metics, too, must, in response to the disabilities we will discuss, have seen themselves, if only negatively, as distinct from citizens, but whether their subordinate condition fostered a group solidarity is not determinable. Slaves, for reasons to be seen, almost certainly lacked any significant degree of cor-porate self-identity or cohesion. These differences should be kept in mind as we proceed through our examination of the components of Athenian society.

CITIZENS

The Athenian Citizenship Law

The question of who was or was not a citizen was settled at Athens by a straightforward legal definition. In earlier times, Athenian law had declared a man to be a citizen if his father was a citizen. But later, beginning in the year 451/0 B.C., when a new law was instituted under the guidance of Pericles, the definition of citizenship was narrowed. According to Pericles' law, only those who were the legitimate offspring of *two* citizen parents (that is, of a citizen father and mother who, though not herself a citizen in any substantial sense, was the legitimate daughter of citizen parents) could be citizens. The possible reasons for the new law have been much discussed. One popular theory is that the aim was to discourage Athenian citizens from marrying foreign women (say, the daughter of a foreign head of state), since dynastic marriages of this kind might have had unwelcome political consequences at home. Another is that the law was designed to compensate for the heavy loss of eligible males in war. Under the old law, daughters of citizens would have had to compete with foreign women for the diminished pool of eligible Athenian bachelors, but the new law would have eliminated that competition. The underlying assump-tion of both theories is the same. No Athenian man, certainly not one with political or social aspirations, would marry a woman if, as a consequence of her non-Athenian status, any children would be disqualified from joining the citizen body. But the point bearing on the present discussion is that, given an Athenian father and a duly betrothed Athenian mother, no further demon-stration of qualifications was required.

This definition of citizenship gains significance when one considers it in the light of other possible definitions. Alternative criteria by which "in-group" status could be determined—residence, property holding, and mili-tary status, for example—were at hand and in some instances actually adopt-ed elsewhere, but in the end Athens settled on the least controversial option, descent. Any male meeting the minimal standard established by Pericles' law, once this fact was validated by his father's deme and the Council of Five Hundred, automatically became an Athenian. Negatively, no outsider, how-ever well qualified by native talent, wealth, high (but non-Athenian) birth, or contributions to the Athenian state, could under normal circumstances break into the closed circle of the citizen elite.

Exclusivity thus became one of the hallmarks of the Athenian democ-racy. Occasionally, it is true, the government did confer citizenship on foreigners, either singly or en masse. A modern scholarly collection of the texts of the surviving decrees of enfranchisement yielded a total of something over a hundred such grants spread over the entire history of the Athenian government. Some of the newly enfranchised were already residing in Attica. For example, Lysias and Pasion, the former a resident alien, the latter originally an Athenian slave, were both naturalized by state decrees. But Lysias' grant was soon revoked, and the accomplishments of both men were so extraordinary that their cases provide scant basis for supposing that there were many other such enfranchisements which have by accident escaped our detection. Nonresidents might be enfranchised too: either individuals such as heads of state or dynasts who had materially benefited Athens, or an entire population, such as the People of the island of Samos who, late in the fifth century, played a critical role in the restoration of the democracy. But in neither instance would the recipient of the grant be expected to physically and permanently relocate to Athens in order to reap the benefits, material or otherwise, of Athenian citizenship. The numbers of the "naturalized" Athenians were therefore at any given time very small. The citizen body, in sum, had come to approximate an exclusive and self-perpetuating closed caste. Since membership in that caste conferred access to substantial and coveted material and intangible rewards, while denying them to outsiders, we are entitled to suppose, as suggested earlier, the development over time of a high degree of class consciousness and solidarity among the citizenry.

Diversity of Wealth

It has already been made clear in Chapter 4 how diverse a group of people the Athenian citizen body was. That diversity can be measured on a number of different scales: region, urban versus rural orientation, occupation or lifestyle, social class, and, of course, wealth. Throughout the next three chapters, considerable attention will be given to each of these points of difference among citizens. Here, now that we have narrowed the discussion to people (namely, citizens) of the same order (or rank), our attention will focus on differences of wealth. Wealth is, after all, the factor on which many other distinguishing features of citizens depended. But on what basis may such a categorization proceed? Solon's four classes, again, ranked citizens according to annual income. To each corresponded a level of income expressed in terms of bushels of produce. This might seem a convenient system of categories on which to base our discussion. But, unfortunately, contemporary classical writers have little to say about Solon's classes; and, in any event, only very few Athenians are identifiable as to Solonian class, including, surprisingly, the topmost category of pentakosiomedimnoi—the very citizens who, if anyone, one would expect to find mentioned in the ancient sources.

Holders of the Liturgy

If, to begin our discussion, we want to isolate the rich, we need an alternative to the "500-bushel men." An English scholar has suggested the holding of a liturgy as a more satisfactory indication of substantial wealth. The *liturgy* was a compulsory public service performed at the personal expense of an Athenian designated by the state. Although the term (which has been preserved in modern times in the sense of "religious service") had for the ancient Greeks the innocuous meaning "service to the people," the liturgy was in fact a form of taxation aimed at the resources of the wealthiest Athenians. What made the liturgy different from other taxes was the expectation that certain benefits, tangible or intangible, would be reaped by the performer of the liturgy.

To understand how this worked, one need only consider the highly visible and highly valued uses to which the funds were put: for example, to outfit and maintain for one year a warship; to recruit, costume, and train a chorus of twenty-four men or boys for a performance in a musical or dramatic festival (such as the City Dionysia); or even to wine and dine the members of one's tribe (one-tenth of the citizen population!) in a public celebration. Such enormous expenses were not, as with the systems of taxation to which we are accustomed, borne anonymously by a faceless (and usually unwilling) contributor. Rather, reciprocation in some form or another was normally expected. Not infrequently, for example, wealthy litigants reminded popular juries— which, we can be sure from a purely statistical standpoint, included some actual recipients of their "generosity"—of their past liturgies in the hope, expressed with barefaced frankness, that they will be commensurably rewarded with a favorable verdict. Such statements are not to be dismissed as self-serving opportunism out of keeping with the intent of the liturgy system and generally condemned by Athenian public values. To do so would be to anachronistically import values characteristic of later ethical systems, which are entirely out of place in a classical Greek setting.

The liturgical class, as a whole and in terms of individual Athenians, is comparatively well known. At any given time, according to our English authority, approximately six hundred citizens were eligible for nomination to a liturgy. This works out to between 2 and 3 percent of the citizen population, depending on the period in question. Furthermore, several hundred Athenians known to have held a liturgy are identifiable by name. It is primarily to these men we refer when we speak of the Athenian rich.

The Aristocracy

By the very nature of the institution, any holder of a liturgy was, pure and simple, a rich man. But it was noted at the beginning of the chapter that wealth alone did not determine a man's place in this society, even within the

privileged circle of the citizen body. Again, there is the matter of status. To put
the point in abstract terms, if we were to attempt to describe the Athenian
"upper classes," we would have to make a further distinction between a
wealthy social elite and those who merely have lots of money or property. The
two groups in question are the aristocracy and the new rich.

Aristocrats, their preeminence based on generally uncontested claims to
high birth, had once, as we saw (Chapter 4), dominated Athenian government, politics, and society. That preeminence, however, had been first
impaired, then overthrown through a long and gradual process of challenge
and response culminating in the creation of the democracy under Clisthenes.
But by no means had the aristocracy disappeared, or even necessarily been
discredited, with the rise of democracy. Many of the old families remained on
the scene, as evidenced by the record of a wide range of public activity: the
continuing custody of private (and even public) priesthoods; the erection
(and dedication in their names) of public buildings, victory monuments com-
memorating successes in dramatic or athletic competitions, gravestones, and
other structures; the authorship of, and occasional appearances in, widely
read and influential works of literature; and so on. By such means the old families kept their names before the public and maintained a continuing presence in civic affairs.

Even within the context of the democratic constitution itself, it was to
the scions of the noble houses, too, that the radical egalitarian people looked
for political leadership and for holders of sensitive elective financial and military posts. It would be wrong, however, to view this as a cynical and calculated exploitation of the old families, a reversal of the latter's earlier "use" of
democratic clienteles. Rather, Athenian voters, despite everything, seem to
have continued to hold the aristocracy in awe. Meanwhile, the aristocrats
themselves, possibly as an expression of a superior or condescending attitude,
and perhaps also as part of a strategy to hold onto whatever remained of their
previous preeminence (not to mention their wealth), regarded "public service" as an appropriate, even mandatory, element of their lifestyle. It is only
with the loss of the Peloponnesian War, when the democracy was a full century old, that we can first detect a significant movement of the aristocrats away
from Athenian public, and especially political, life. Apparently by that time
the leading families no longer desired to be part of or even associated with a
defeated and, in the eyes of many, discredited form of government.

Nonetheless, it is perhaps surprising that these inheritors of elite society had held out as long as they did. The assault on their privileged position
had been unremitting and devastating. Mention will be made in Chapter 8 of
the leveling effects produced by the introduction of hoplite armor and tactics,
which substituted for the individual heroics of the aristocratic few the mandatory cooperation of a large number of citizen soldiers, identically equipped
and dedicated to upholding a uniform code of conduct. With the emergence
of the powerful Athenian navy, the democracy was strengthened by the ener-

gizing and uplifting impact of the democratically designed and executed sea victory at Salamis during the Persian Wars. In Chapter 6 we will examine in detail the egalitarian features of the developed Athenian democracy and note the extent to which they acknowledged the capacity of all citizens to participate in the operation of government. In the area of religion, a symbolic acknowledgment of the supremacy of the people was signaled by the democratization of cults that had been traditionally monopolized by an exclusive minority of aristocratic families.

Despite this withering onslaught, it remains paradoxically true that the cultural style of the aristocracy was energetically emulated at the lower levels of free Athenian society. Perhaps this was a consequence of a time lag between inherited popular attitudes and the new populist reality represented by the democracy, in combination with the successful efforts of the aristocrats to keep themselves before the public eye. (In any event, it is difficult to isolate, as one can with some other human societies, a distinctively "low-class" Athenian culture.) And it was this fact, following on the heels of the erosion of aristocratic supremacy, that posed the greatest threat to the further survival of aristocratic society. If, in other words, aristocrats could no longer maintain a distinctive style that separated them from others, from whom they in fact differed in no substantial way, they would run the risk of absorption into the great mass of the Athenian free population.

The aristocratic response was to refashion their lifestyle in such a way that it became *inimitable*, that is, literally incapable of imitation. An American ancient historian has written convincingly in this connection of the "defensive standard" of the Athenian aristocrats. A few examples will illustrate the point. Externally, aristocrats' clothing was distinguished by its exotic origin and costliness, which put it out of the reach of the great mass of Athenian consumers. Similarly leisure activities and entertainments. The horse, whether used for hunting, for participation in races (such as Alcibiades' famous entry of seven four-horse chariots in the Olympic games), or for other forms of conspicuous display, entailed enormous initial and ongoing expense. Witness in Aristophanes' comedy *The Clouds* the plight of the hapless Strepsiades whose prodigal son's uncontrolled purchases of horses (and dogs) had landed the family hopelessly in debt. Athletics, too, were conditioned by class to the extent that, at the level of "international" competition (such as, for example, any of the panhellenic festival games), only the prosperous and leisured could afford the expense of travel and lodging over a lengthy number of days, not to mention the havoc wrought upon agricultural and domestic schedules. Aristocrats, needless to say, maintained exclusive social calendars, most distinctively represented by the symposium, the all-male upper-class drinking party. Such a party might achieve the elevated heights of conversation immortalized in Plato's dialogue *The Symposium,* such conversation itself being an inimitable activity attainable only by those wealthy enough to obtain the appropriate private education. Or, probably more commonly, the party featured exotic foods and expensive imported wines served in costly decorated vessels by slaves, with entertainment provided by a *hetaera*, or "escort" (a euphemism for female prostitute). All such manifestations of high culture served a common purpose—to insulate the aristocrat from the larger citizen society.

Aristocratic values, also, to judge from classical vase paintings, more generally celebrated the ideal of youthful beauty, an ideal that might be more readily approached by a leisured class immune from the debilitating effects of backbreaking agricultural and domestic labor. Even sexual roles acquired an inimitable aspect. Adult, married upper-class men are commonly portrayed pursuing pubescent (upper-class) teenage boys in accordance with a highly stylized—and so, for outsiders, difficult to replicate—ritual of courtship involving gifts, gestures, and niceties of timing and location. But most effective of all was the aristocratic claim to a monopoly on the possession of internal qualities attainable only by inheritance from an aristocratic parent. The boast of descent from a god or hero spoke for itself in this regard, but the same effect could be achieved by the cultivation from birth of inimitable values of "inner worth," such as "excellence" (*arete*) or "moderation" (*sophrosyne*). These were tough acts to pull off for an untutored low-class outsider trying to break into a social elite. Plainly, the farmer suddenly made wealthy by the change from cereal cultivation to the production of cash crops, or the successful merchant who had benefited politically from Solon's income-class system, or the unscrupulous sycophant enriched by opportunistic litigation faced many formidable barriers to social acceptance by the aristocratic elite.

The New Rich

The newly wealthy Athenians just mentioned emerge so distinctly in classical Athenian society that they deserve separate categorization. Indeed, it was on their behalf (or on the behalf of Athenians like them) that Solon had to invent the newfangled word *pentakosiomedimnoi*, which lacked any traditional associations, in order to bring them into his new constitutional order. Despite this great advance, however, it is fair to say that the new rich never quite achieved full acceptance within Athenian society, at least upper-class society. Even late in the fifth century B.C., when, following the death of the aristocratic popular leader Pericles, industrial entrepreneurs like Cleon and Hyperbolus assumed positions of political leadership, vestiges of the old snobbish attitude were still in evidence. The comedies of Aristophanes provide a humorous insight into this traditionalist, reactionary attitude. "New politicians" like Cleon are unfairly put down as petty retailers (see further on this point, Chapter 8), accused of being the offspring of slaves or foreign ancestors, and so on. Such treatment affords additional evidence of the old aristocratic families' success in upholding their old-fashioned, elitist system of values.

"Middle" and "Low" Classes

With the "upper" classes now accounted for, it will be possible to address the great bulk of the citizen population. Some crude categorizations and rough estimates of numbers would be helpful. According to one standard analysis of the Athenian democracy, a general picture of this kind is obtainable. The analysis is based on the record of an official census—the only such record preserved—taken late in the fourth century B.C. Twenty-one thousand citizens (down from about thirty thousand before the Peloponnesian War) were counted. The following subgroups (with their approximate numbers and percentages) are posited:

1. Hoplite soldiers (including the 2 or 3 percent
   identified above as constituting the liturgical
   class)   9,000   43%
2. Smallholders (with less than five acres);
   skilled craftsmen or shopkeepers (with five
   or fewer slave assistants); and casual laborers   12,000   57%

Hoplites.   Hoplites, the heavy-armed infantry, come as close as any group to constituting a "middle" class. Their relative prosperity (estimated at thirty *minae* or one-half talent, the equivalent of three thousand days' wages; see Chapter 9) is shown by their ability to provide themselves with their own expensive bronze armor. Many hoplites, probably the great majority, were landowners and farmers. These Athenians will receive more attention in a later chapter (Chapter 8), first in their capacity as farmers, then again in their military role.

The "low" class.   By this term we mean the majority of citizens identified above as smallholder farmers, craftsmen, and shopkeepers, as well as "casual" (that is, temporary) workers. (Again, as with the hoplites, these Athenians will be discussed in detail in Chapter 8.) To relate these categories to Solon's system, the "low" class more or less corresponded to his bottommost tier of thetes. These Athenians were, in comparison with their more fortunate fellow citizens, poor. But the English word *poor* as used here, as well as its ancient Greek equivalents, are relative terms; all they mean is that this majority of twelve thousand was less well off than the hoplites, not to mention the upper classes among them.

Support for the poor.   Abject, crushing poverty, such as the modern world has witnessed so dramatically in recent years, did not exist in classical Athens. Some of the factors accounting for this important fact will crop up in various contexts in the remaining chapters of this book. But a short summary of these factors, ending in a discussion of the vital role played by the central government, is appropriate at this juncture:

- Support of elderly or infirm parents by their adult children (see Chapter 7, under "Old Age").

- State pensions (of one obol, later two obols—possibly enough to support a single person) for citizens physically unable to earn a living for themselves.

- The exportation of excess (probably poor) population to colonies or special settlements of citizens called *cleruchies,* or "allotments." Under the cleruchy arrangement, the participating citizen received a plot of agricultural land, hence a means to earn his livelihood.

- The voluntary relocation of rural poor or landless citizens to the urban center, where additional sources of income were available.

- Finally, and most importantly, opportunities for gainful employment of various kinds in the service of the central government.

In terms of the numbers affected, the last-mentioned item, employment by the central government (in combination with the previous item, relocation from rural areas to the urban center), was unquestionably the primary reason why classical Athens knew no real poverty. In view of this fact, it will repay our efforts to briefly survey the types of such employment and to comment on their rather profound social and political consequences.

Public works projects in the urban center were a major, and conspicuous, source of government employment. Many of these were undertaken during the zenith of the democracy in the fifth century. Construction of the city walls and other fortifications, the building of triremes, and of course the government-funded erection of monumental temples and other structures on or near the Acropolis are prime examples. But such work was intermittent, subject to the availability of public moneys and to the willingness of the Assembly to pass an appropriation. Even then, a project on a massive scale might run for only a few years. The Parthenon, the centerpiece of the Periclean building program, was begun in 447 and less than a decade later, in 438, the temple with the cult statute was dedicated (work, involving only sculptors, continued on the pedimental decoration until 432).

No less important was payment for government service, to be discussed in Chapter 6. Such payments could support a citizen and conceivably other members of his family at the subsistence level, provided that he resided in the city near the seat of government and was not seriously encumbered by agricultural or other commitments.

Still another source of public money—the military organization—was available, although again on an intermittent basis contingent on legislative action. Virtually all military personnel received some form of financial assistance, if only in the form of a per diem allowance for provisions while on campaign. But to the thetic rowers in the fleet, for whom no other employment was probably available, the small wage meant the difference between starvation and survival. They, like the others, were recruited primarily from the urban population, notably from the port town of Peiraeus. Again, the availability of work was contingent in this case on Athenian military engagement with war or empire. But the empire, unlike warfare, made possible more or less *continuous* employment for not a few Athenians. According to Aristotle, seven hundred individuals served "overseas"—that is, as officers, agents, or other imperial personnel.

Taken together, this is an impressive array of opportunities. Such employment must have put food on many a citizen's table. At the same time, it must have exerted a powerful pull on the poorer rural population to relocate to the city, and on foreigners to migrate to Athens to seek whatever opportunities were open to noncitizens—if not through direct payment, then by capitalizing on the spinoff of government spending.

Social and political consequences. So complex a web of factors defies neat generalization, but two general observations are nonetheless appropriate. First, although historians attempting to assess the economic impact of government spending on the citizen body seem to assume that a given Athenian would restrict his activity to a single form of employment, it is evident that a more opportunistic individual could easily juggle a combination of governmental, public construction, and military employment in addition to any gainful employment in the private sector. Thus a citizen entrepreneur might leave his shop in the care of a trusted slave or his wife to attend a half-day meeting of the Assembly or to spend a full day in the courts. An adult son still living at home could add to the household income by rowing in the fleet. An elderly grandfather, likewise in the care of his son, could, true to Aristophanes' portrayal, pick up two or three obols by spending a day in the courts. That a resourceful citizen could have sustained himself throughout his working life by various forms of government service is not, despite the absence of appropriate documentation, beyond the realm of possibility.

But the pay is not the only aspect of the situation that interests us here. There is also the matter of the impact of continuous government employment on prevailing attitudes about gainful employment. Opportunism of the kind just described could only have worked against the male head of household's association with a specific, more or less constant and identifiable trade. Farmers, certainly, had traditionally transmitted an occupational identity in step with the transmission of their land by inheritance from father to son. Now, in the place of that orderly and predictable replication of occupational identity had been substituted an expedient exploitation of opportunities of varying character but united by a single fact: that the source of payment was the state treasury. To this we may add the second observation: the massive scale of this government employment. Aristotle's count of Athenians supported in the early days of the Empire by "tribute, taxes, and allies" (including jurors, archers, cavalry, the Council of Five Hundred, guards, and magistrates) came to twenty thousand, a very appreciable fraction of the citizen population at that time. What are we to make of so massive a dependency of the Athenian free workforce on government spending? Some of today's commentators are fond of speaking of "big government" and of its allegedly calculated attempts to promote allegiance to itself by deliberately fostering dependency. Do such notions have any place here?

Ancient Greek oligarchic critics might look at the situation rather differently. For them, the enemy was not a gargantuan bureaucracy that had acquired a life of its own and run amok, but rather the radical democratic politicians who, by sponsoring legislation enabling government employment and other spending, stood to reap (and in fact did reap) the political benefits that naturally accrued. For them, it was a question not of big versus small government, but rather, within the context of a single government with generally agreed-upon dimensions, of which side, democratic or oligarchic, was to play the coveted role of political leadership. Either way, crudely put, a government had to be staffed, an army and navy manned and paid, public buildings erected, and, in bad times, a poor population rescued from starvation. Above all, stability, continually threatened by the very uneven distribution of wealth, had to be maintained. But nothing posed a greater threat to stability than the prospect of a sudden decline of the poor population. Such a decline could be forestalled, and the public needs met, by government spending on the poor, by the provision of what historians have called "subsistence crisis insurance" (see the detailed discussion of this topic in Chapter 9). And it was partly over the privilege of sponsoring the appropriate legislation that Athenian politicians, like their Roman counterparts centuries later, engaged in combative struggles.

METICS (OR RESIDENT ALIENS)

Free, but legally, politically, and perhaps sometimes socially segregated from the citizens were the metics or resident aliens. Metics were former free citizens of other Greek states (or their descendants) who had established permanent and officially approved residence in Athens. Immigrants had probably always found their way to Athens, but it was Solon who adopted a policy of granting citizenship to those relocating with their families to Athens for the purpose of pursuing a trade. Although by the time of the democracy the path to citizenship for immigrants had been barred, according to the census of the late fourth century B.C., the metics (male heads of households?) numbered a full 10,000 to the citizens' (certainly heads of households) 21,000. That nearly one-third of the free population should have endured the stigma of noncitizen status amid a sea of visible citizen privilege points to some compelling attraction or payoff. What was it?

Athens' geographic situation, climate, and natural resources had marked the city out for success in cash crop production, certain industries, and trade, among other nontraditional commercial enterprises (see Chapter 8). The problem for Athens was that the prevailing value system precluded the full development of these potentialities by the citizen workforce. Aristocratic wealth had traditionally taken the form of land and the kinds of income generated by that land, and—the crucial point—this ideal similarly characterized the aspirations of the lower social strata. Even the poorest land-owning citizen could believe that his lifestyle differed only quantitatively, not qualitatively, from that of the elite. The result was a strong aversion to nonagricultural employment which pervaded all levels of the citizen class. Thus a set of niches was opened up for noncitizens. The metics, already debarred from citizenship and, as a consequence of the prohibition against their owning land (or buildings), already condemned to social inferiority, seized on this opportunity and did so (as far as we are informed) with notable success. Take, for example, the case of the metic Lysias, who, besides his activity as a professional writer of courtroom speeches, owned with his family a shield factory in the port town of Peiraeus. It was factories like this that provided arms for Athenian soldiers. If his case is typical (and, admittedly, given the ancient habit of noting only the successful, it may well not be), Athens' economy had by the late fifth century B.C. become significantly dependent on the talents, skills, and business sense of these marginalized immigrant residents.

Official maintenance of the metics' subordinate status was determined and multifaceted. Mention has been made of the prohibition on ownership of "land and house," one of the privileges extended to non-Athenians in grants of citizenship. If such ownership was granted to new citizens, then it follows that it was denied to metics. Resident aliens were also required to be sponsored by a citizen patron, to serve in the military in segregated units, and to pay a poll, or personal "head," tax. All these measures marked the metic out as distinct from and inferior to an Athenian citizen. (Interestingly, the poll tax was imposed not only on males but also on any metic woman not dependent on a husband or son. This amounted to recognition of the legal possibility of an independent female, a status denied citizen women: see Chapter 7).

Economically, their legal incapacity to own property sometimes reduced metics running business enterprises to the condition of rent payers to citizen landlords. But metics could, and occasionally did, lease mines and purchase slaves for industrial use. Another citizen privilege regularly extended to metics was the liturgy, or compulsory public service. Although liturgies were exceedingly burdensome, the metic who assumed that burden enjoyed the same opportunity as the citizen to reap the social, if not the political, benefits. Indeed, the liturgy is but one sign among several of a limited acceptance of metics by the citizen class. Metics took part in public religious festivities, and a famous dialogue of Plato, the *Republic*, depicts a metic socializing with eminent citizens. Perhaps their shared free status, usually in combination with a common Greek background, tended to unite citizens and metics against the unquestionably inferior slave population.

Nonetheless, the disabilities depressing the resident alien remained. Given these and the absence of any opportunity for upward mobility, one can only assume the compelling attraction of compensating advantages. Among these were a higher standard of living than was attainable in the place of origin, lucrative (and wide open) opportunities for business activity, the relative security afforded by Athenian military might, and perhaps the pleasure of vicarious identification with the high cultural glories of Greece's first city.

SLAVES

Where slaves are concerned, it is clear that their far more extreme exploitation was utterly without similar compensating advantages. The idea that such exploitation might not have been morally justifiable seems not, even amid continuous public discussion about the rights of various segments within free society, to have occurred to anyone, to judge from our surviving sources. Silence of this kind is not difficult to comprehend. After all, the Mycenaeans, ancestors of the Athenians and much honored exemplars of Greek civilization in general, had, as the Linear B tablets show, maintained a servile labor force (see Chapter 1). Furthermore, the seeming appropriateness of slavery to civilized life had been upheld by the literary representation of that society, Homer's epics, and by much intervening literature, including Hesiod's didactic *Works and Days*. Nor did Athens' practice differ noticeably from that of her contemporaries. No Greek city-state is known *not* to have practiced slavery, and involuntary servitude was a fixture of some neighboring civilizations, such as the Egyptian, for which the Greeks expressed much admiration. A modern historian might, of course, be able to cite or posit an individual Athenian (or a small class of Athenians) without slaves (or without the means to acquire or maintain slaves), but mere evidence of practice unaccompanied by any indication of attitude is obviously valueless. What matters is the societal ideal irrespective of capacity, or lack of same, to realize that ideal. The wealthy owned slaves, and there is reason to think that less prosperous citizens (or metics), whatever their actual financial situation, aspired to similar ownership and to the "self-sufficiency" that it made possible. It is no wonder, since its existence was apparently taken for granted, that slavery was neither questioned nor known to have figured as the subject of any ancient Greek historical or other account.

Where did slaves come from? Since the passage of Solon's Shaking off of Burdens (see Chapter 4), Athenians could no longer be reduced to servitude by reason of indebtedness. Nor is there evidence for the use of enslavement of citizens as punishment for a crime. No more likely a source is the breeding of already-existing slaves, in view of the considerable expense and inconvenience involved in raising the house-born infant to the age of productivity, with the added and very real possibility that the slave might die or fall seriously ill before that time was reached. It was rather to commercial slave markets that the prospective master turned for the purchase of already-mature and perhaps appropriately trained individuals. But from what sources did the markets acquire their stocks? Many slaves were supplied by distant "barbarian" kingdoms, especially those of the Thracians and Scythians to the northeast of the Greek orbit, where native traders, through conquest and capture in intertribal warfare, came into possession of, and sold to Greeks, large numbers of their own conationals. For example, Scythian archers, purchased and owned by the state (in contrast with the "chattel" slave owned by a private individual), comprised the public police force of classical Athens. Besides these large groups, the place of origin of many others can be inferred from their surviving "ethnic" given names, which reveal a wide range of nationalities.

Some slaves were taken prisoner by pirates, endemic predators of the Mediterranean whose raids often had as their object the seizure of innocent victims for sale into servitude. Still others were the survivors of defeat in interstate warfare. When, for example, in 416 B.C. the Athenians overwhelmed the tiny Greek island of Melos in reprisal for its refusal to join the Empire, the Melian men, Thucydides tells us, were executed and the women and children enslaved. Nor was this an isolated episode. Inevitably, then, Greeks, themselves formerly full citizens of an autonomous city-state, might become the slaves of other Greeks. This point is important for our estimation of the Greek ideological perspective on enslavement. Slavery was evidently not held to be a function or natural consequence of civic affiliation, ethnic identity, or race. Instead, the condition of the slave was predicated on the facts of capture, sale, and ownership as defined by an increasingly elaborate body of legal statutes. It was not, as far as Greek practice informs us (the formulations of the philosophers, Aristotle in particular, were another matter), a question of qualities alleged to be inherent in the person of the slave himself or herself. Greek slaves were made, not born.

This conclusion may make more comprehensible some striking points of similarity between the enslaved and the free. Work, to consider the most important category of evidence, did not correspond closely in kind to the legal status of the worker. Slaves routinely performed domestic tasks and engaged in agricultural labor alongside, or paralleling the work of, free persons. Other slaves, organized in crews under a private entrepreneur, toiled on public works projects under contract with the state at pay scales comparable to those of the free labor assigned to the same task. Even the monopoly on military service, normally the exclusive prerogative of the citizen class, could be relaxed when, under pressing circumstances, slaves were recruited to row in the fleet. Work in the mines, however, might appear to be an exception. The rich veins of silver in and around Laurium in southern Attica were exploited throughout the classical period by contracting the work out to privately held companies of slave laborers. As far as we are informed, free persons were not normally employed as miners. When we come in Chapter 8 to discuss the attitudes underlying work, free or servile, we will see that the crucial point was whether a person labored independently or under the direction of a foreman, bailiff, or other supervisor. Free Greeks, certainly Athenians, abhorred the notion of dependency on another person; it conflicted with their high valuation of "self-sufficiency." Miners, unlike smallholder farmers or cottage industry crafters, commonly worked in crews under direct supervision. Servility is therefore best viewed as a condition of employment rather than as a specific set of tasks or behaviors. Away from the workplace, free and slave probably differed little, nor did Athenian custom prescribe rules of dress, speech, etiquette, or other behavior whereby the two could readily be distinguished when in public. Thus a Greek writing at a later time complained that on the streets of Athens one could not tell the slaves from the free and that slaves failed to show the courtesy of giving way to free men.

Thinkers since Marx have speculated about the impact of slavery on Greek civilization. Was it as a consequence of slavery that the citizen populations of Athens and other cities were set free to engage in the high cultural pursuits by which the Greeks so distinguished themselves? Or, to put the question in more general terms, was slavery a necessary condition of the Greek achievement? No definitive answer is possible, but an approach to an answer may be sketched out.

First off, were slaves available in sufficient numbers to render feasible the supposition of such an impact? Absent any hard data, one can adduce once again the much-discussed literary account of a census conducted late in the fourth century B.C. According to this text, the citizens numbered 21,000, the metics 10,000, and the slaves 400,000! The last figure is patently wrong and is probably the result of the corruption of the medieval manuscripts. Even if we assume a wife and two children for each citizen and metic counted (thus 84,000 citizens and 40,000 metics, yielding a total of 124,000 free persons) and assume further that the number of slaves represents the grand total, we still get about 3.25 slaves per free person, an intolerably high ratio. Where would the Athenians have put so many slaves? Large slave workforces are only rarely mentioned. Plantation-style slave gangs are not recorded (despite the certain existence of large estates presumably worked by tenants or other free labor); industrial establishments employing slaves are seldom mentioned (the largest known in any case is the shield factory with its 120 slaves owned by the family of the metic Lysias); and no domestic staff even approaching the dimensions of those of the Roman elite ever existed. This leaves only the companies of slaves employed in public works projects and in the mines. For this reason, the great bulk of slaves, whatever the size of the total servile population, can probably be accounted for by the one or two owned by a multitude of smallholders and urban crafts and trading people.

If so, it is questionable to what extent ownership on this small scale could actually set the master free for leisured activity, governmental, literary, philosophic, artistic, or whatever. Two basic options were opened up by the acquisition of a slave. Either the owner used the slave to perform the labor formerly done by himself with no change in productivity except for the cost (a loss) of purchasing and maintaining the slave; or, alternatively, the slave's labor was added to his own, with a possible dramatic increase in productivity. The former model afforded leisure, the latter a better life for the owner and his family. For the farmer, fisherman, craftsman, or other worker living at the subsistence level and perpetually on the brink of ruin, this would not have been a difficult choice to make. Slavery certainly had an impact, but that impact probably did not take the form of the creation of significant amounts of work-free time for large numbers of citizens. The truly rich (again, a tiny numerical minority) were already leisured (if they so chose), and the "poor" (that is, people who worked for a living) might well have opted for increased productivity and a higher standard of living.

What was it like to be a slave? Certainly many, like the Laurium and agricultural workers, suffered great physical hardship. Slaves, male or female, adults and probably the young as well, were subject to bodily, sexual, verbal, and psychological abuse from their owners without possibility of legal redress. Indeed, Athenian law, far from protecting the slave's person, required, if a slave's testimony was to be admissible in court, that that testimony be obtained under torture. To take a hint from the Roman experience, emotional pain, or at least its threat, might and probably often did occur when an owner sought to separate by relocation or sale slaves of a single household who had formed a close attachment, possibly involving the birth of children. And one can easily imagine the humiliation regularly experienced by slaves in every social situation involving a free person, especially by those who had formerly enjoyed the dignity of freedom in their native communities.

Why, then, it has been asked, did the slaves not rise up in revolt? Several attractive answers are at hand. Again on the Roman model, the prospect of upward mobility (whereby the slave or his or her children might obtain full or partial freedom) was undoubtedly dangled before the enslaved as an inducement to good behavior. No rational person (if, under such conditions, rationality may be assumed) would risk capture and probable death as long as emancipation remained a possibility. Besides, to mention a logistical factor, most slaves (except for the gangs working in the mines, etc.) were physically separated at a multitude of domestic, agricultural, and commercial work sites and thus unable to congregate in order to plan collective action. And even if they had been able to congregate, differences of language or culture (reflecting their varying places of origin) would have impeded communication and agreement about strategic or ideological objectives. But the psychological factor may have been the most potent impediment, if slaves, once removed by a generation or two from the memory of their former lives, accepted and internalized the assumptions, values, and self-estimation imposed on them by their servitude. Under such conditions, even the will to revolt may not have materialized.

SPARTA

With the completion of our account of the gross structure of Athenian society, we turn to the one other ancient Greek city-state about which detailed information survives: Sparta. Brief consideration of the Spartan case is necessary for two reasons. Sparta, throughout most of the archaic and classical periods the preeminent land power of Greece, is of course a worthy subject in its own right. But the second, more pertinent point is that, where Athens is concerned, Sparta provides a valuable standard for comparison. Some similarities will at once be evident: in particular, the multitiered social structure, the absence of social mobility, and the exclusivity of the citizen class. Yet it is the fundamental underlying differences that are most instructive.

Sparta's early history was one of unparalleled military achievement. From a small cluster of villages on the Eurotas River, the Dorian city-state grew through conquest, first of neighboring Laconia, then of Messenia to the west, into the dominant power of the Peloponnese. But this success proved a two-edged sword. Sparta found itself perpetually saddled with the task of controlling a huge population of subject peoples. These were, first, the free citizen residents of up to a hundred towns of Laconia and Messenia called *perioikoi*, or "dwellers around." More dangerous, however, were the *helots*, or "captives," probably descendants of the earlier Mycenaean population, held in subjection as state-owned slaves. Sparta relied on these subject peoples for agricultural and industrial production and, in the case of the periokoi, for service as armed soldiers in its powerful military organization. But they and particularly the helots were most unwilling subjects.

Possible approaches to the solution of the problem were few. Inclusion of the subjects within the fold of citizen privilege, though imaginable, was clearly contrary to the Spartans' own interests. For one thing, it would have meant an end to the citizen monopoly on ownership of land, to which citizenship was intimately tied. That left one other option—militarism. Sparta would build an army strong enough to withstand even the most determined attempts at insurrection. On numerical grounds alone, this was a tall order. Herodotus, in his account of a fifth-century military campaign, gives the ratio of Spartan soldiers to the helots attending them as baggage carriers as *one to seven*. On those same campaigns, the perioikoi were consistently able to provide soldiers equal in number to those of the Spartans. Plainly, the military solution to Sparta's predicament would require extraordinary dedication and unanimity of purpose on the part of the Spartan people.

This decision seems to have set into motion a major reorientation of Spartan society. Early archaic Sparta is represented by a budding literature, fine decorated pottery, and even a few public inscriptions not qualitatively different from the records of contemporary Greek cities. Afterward, the literary impulse is extinguished, decoration (ceramic or otherwise) disappears, and documentation of public acts ceases altogether. More significantly, the energies of Spartan society were redirected away from the ideals we will see at work in the contemporary Athenian society. Given the pervasiveness of these changes, in any event, it is likely that they were the result of a lengthy period of gradual readjustment to the evolving new order. In typical fashion, however, Greek historians telescoped the process down to a single act of innovation ascribed to the quasilegendary lawgiver Lycurgus. Lycurgus was reported to have called this new order "the Discipline."

Sadly, virtually no contemporary documentation of the Discipline has survived. Instead, we are forced to fall back on later, literary sources, among them the writings of the Greek scholar and priest Plutarch, who wrote during the late first and early second centuries A.D. under the Roman Empire—perhaps eight hundred years or more after the events he sought to describe and at a time when the institutions of contemporary Sparta were centuries removed from the classical city, not to mention the era of Lycurgus himself. Even so, substantially accurate representation of the distant past by such a source is not inconceivable. Attempts had been made in Hellenistic and Roman times to restore the antique order; and however artificial or contrived such archaizing might have been, it at least served the historically valuable function of recovering whatever had survived in oral tradition or private, nondocumentary written sources.

What does Plutarch tell us? Take, as a representative series of examples, his detailed account of the typical career of a Spartan male. A male newborn, he says, was examined by "the elders of the tribes." If it was well formed, the father was permitted to raise it; if not, it was exposed—to die—in a chasm at the foot of Mount Taygetus. Quaintly, Plutarch adds that Spartan mothers used to bathe their babies, not in water, but in wine, in order to test their constitutions. At seven, boys were taken from their parents and thereafter, until they established their own households, lived in all-male barracks. Heads closely clipped, barefoot, and nearly naked most of the time, from age twelve they received a single cloak each year, rarely bathed, and slept on pallets made from rushes that they had collected themselves. Meanwhile, the boys received the attentions of "lovers" from among "the reputable young men," while the elderly males played a supervisory role, imagining that they were "the fathers and tutors and governors of all the boys." By this Plutarch means, perhaps rightly, that the customary bonds between parent and child had been dissolved in favor of the communal parentage of the state. At all ages, reading and writing were mostly ignored. Instead, what training they received was designed "to make them obey commands well, endure hardships, and conquer in battle."

Plutarch illustrates the point about enduring hardships with the famous story of the young Spartan who, caught with a stolen fox concealed under his cloak, allowed the animal to rip out his intestines with its teeth and claws rather than be detected. (Theft, incidentally, Plutarch comments, was encouraged as a device to promote resourcefulness in the young citizens.)

Upon reaching the age of marriage, the typical young Spartan is reported to have carried his chosen bride off by force. For her wedding night, the woman would have her hair cut off, be dressed in a man's cloak and sandals, and lie down in total darkness. In such condition she would be visited by her husband, who would continue these secretive rendezvous for some time while maintaining his residence in the barracks. A child might even be born, Plutarch says, before the man had looked on his wife in broad daylight. Within marriage, the exchange of women for childbearing purposes was practiced with full social approbation. An elderly Spartan might make his young wife available to some younger Spartan whom he admired and thought worthy of fathering his wife's child.

Such were some of the more bizarre stages of the male Spartan career, as transmitted by the later literary tradition. Can we believe it? It is not sufficient simply to dismiss Plutarch's information as deriving from some undependable later source, for that would leave unknown the identity of such a source and, if its claims are invented, the inspirations or purposes of such invention. Perhaps we may, then, take Plutarch's information more seriously.

Students of comparative anthropology, for example, have found parallels for some of our material in various primitive nonclassical societies. The practice of carrying off a bride by force looks like "marriage by capture." The male's secret visits to his wife while continuing to reside in the barracks resemble a "trial marriage" (with the original purpose of establishing the woman's fertility prior to finalizing the union). And the older male–younger male homosexual relationship might recall an "initiation rite" practiced in certain primitive cultures. Additional parallels could undoubtedly be found, if a determined search were made. But to what end? Just what does a parallel practice from another society, even an exact one, really tell us? To take the obvious line of approach, the historian might attempt to reconstruct a path of transmission from the society providing the parallel (or from some other point of diffusion). But one may say with confidence that none of the societies concerned lies anywhere within the range of conceivable routes of migration or of later commercial, political, or other contact.

Alternatively, survival of these practices as vestiges of a more primitive stage of development is a possible model. But, if this were true, it is difficult to imagine how such a societal regime could have survived the Bronze Age, by which time a high level of civilization had been attained and at which time, to judge from Homer's evidence, Spartan society appears fundamentally similar to that of the other Mycenaean centers. So, neither the hypothesis of survival from a distant Greek past, nor that of difussion from a foreign source seems particularly tenable.

A third and final alternative remains: that the distinctive Spartan institutions arose out of, and were thereafter maintained by, what was suggested above to have been the overriding thrust of Spartan citizen society: namely, its all-encompassing and unremitting militarism. Inspection of the stages of the male career yields a set of interpretations that converge on just this principle: the production of superior male offspring through selective eugenic practices (exposure of defective newborns, selective breeding through exchange of women); the removal of family obligations that could compete with the desired sense of total loyalty to the state; and the fostering of male solidarity through the institution of all-male living arrangements, all-male team competition, and male homosexuality. What counts here is the acknowledgment of these basic underlying purposes; it is less important to understand or be able to explain each practice in precise detail. Admittedly, some of Plutarch's information may be fanciful elaboration of a core of truth. Some of the details may be due to the influence of, or assimilation to, superficially similar but very differently motivated practices in other states (such as the aristocratic male pederasty practiced at Athens). But if the general perception that these (for the ancient Greek) bizarre behaviors evolved out of Spartan militarism is correct, then we as historians learn something of great importance about a society's behavior: the degree to which even deeply embedded, inherited institutions (such as heterosexual courtship, the nuclear family of parents and offspring, an agricultural lifestyle) may be transformed in response to an alteration of the goals of that society. People cannot be thought of as unwilling and helpless slaves to inherited societal norms. The Spartans had chosen to go down the road of militarism, and that militarism was, to put it mechanistically, the engine that drove the future development of Spartan society.

Suggested Readings

Several comprehensive works in English deal in detail with the topics broached in this chapter. The "standard analysis" referred to is that of A. H. M. Jones, *Athenian Democracy* (New York, 1958). C. Patterson's *Pericles' Citizenship Law of 451–450 B.C.* (New York, 1981) is concerned with the narrower and larger aspects of what it meant to be an "Athenian." J. K. Davies's *Wealth and the Power of Wealth in Classical Athens* (New York, 1981) is a groundbreaking fundamental work based on the same author's *Athenian Propertied Families 600–300 B.C.* (Oxford, 1971), to which reference was made in the discussion of the liturgy. W. Donlan, *The Aristocratic Ideal in Ancient Greece* (Lawrence, 1980), persuasively makes the case for the "defensive standard" of Athenian aristocratic society. On the new rich, the definitive study is W. R. Connor, *The New Politicians of Fifth-Century Athens* (Princeton, 1971). Resident aliens are exhaustively and insightfully examined by D. Whitehead, *The Ideology of the Athenian Metic* (Cambridge, 1977). On slavery, see the still-valuable collection of essays edited by M. I. Finley, *Slavery in Classical Antiquity: Views and Controversies* (Cambridge, 1960), and the same scholar's *Ancient Slavery and Modern Ideology* (Cambridge, 1983).

Sparta has received many treatments in English. Three especially discerning ones are W. G. Forrest, *A History of Sparta 950–192 B.C.* (London, 1968); P. Cartledge, *Sparta and Lakonia: A Regional History, 1300–362 B.C.* (London, 1979); and A. Powell, *Athens and Sparta: Constructing Greek Political and Social History from 478 B.C.* (Portland, Ore., 1988).

Chapter 6. The Democracy
of Classical Athens

The new form of government created by Clisthenes was a curious blend of the old and the new. Even after its full development by about the middle of the fifth century, the democracy continued to incorporate some of the cardinal principles of its earlier, more restrictive predecessors. These, as we will see, included *hereditary affiliation* in the sociopolitical segments of the state; the continuing occasional observance of *wealth* as a criterion determining eligibility for participation in the government; and selection of certain key officials by *election*. Such traits withstood even the most radically egalitarian tendencies of the democracy's proponents. At the same time, of course, there was much that was new. To illustrate the point, let us begin by considering the most striking innovation of Clisthenes' *demokratia*—the framework for the entire administrative edifice of government, the territorial organization of Attica.

THE CLISTHENIC ORGANIZATION OF ATTICA

The Pre-Clisthenic Organization

Before the creation of the democracy, even from the time before Solon, the city-state of Athens had been divided into segments for the purpose of allocating the duties and privileges of citizenship equitably. These segments comprised three tiers or levels of organization, which went by the Greek technical terms *phylai, trittyes,* and *naukrariai.* In order to set the stage for Clisthenes' transformation of this earlier, predemocratic apparatus, it will be useful to summarize briefly what little we know about each of the three tiers:

Phylai, or "tribes." At the uppermost tier of organization, the citizens of Athens were apportioned into four large groupings called *phylai* (usually misleadingly translated as "tribes"). Two fundamental features of these units are crucial to the present discussion. First, membership passed from father to son; that is, it was transmitted hereditarily by the same principle that governed the replication of the family and the larger units of the social organization. Second, as is true of a family or familial organization, the principle of arrangement was *personal*—with reference, that is, to descent and not to place of residence, the chief competing type of arrangement. A phyle, in other words, was not a place, but a group of persons.

More about these groups can be deduced from their proper names: Geleontes, Argadeis, Aigikoreis, and Hopletes. Despite the linguistic obscurity of the names, scholars have plausibly guessed their meanings to be something like "Nobles," "Workers," "Goatherds," and "Craftsmen," respectively. If so, the organization (possibly a relic of the Mycenaean Bronze Age, when the population was highly differentiated according to profession; see Chapter 1) was, at least in its original form, based on class, specifically on occupation. Since, furthermore, Geleontes always stands first in lists of the phylai, the pre-Clisthenic order had presumably at one time recognized the primacy of the nobility.

Trittyes, or "thirds."   Each of the phylai was divided into three "thirds." They, too, like the phylai, were personal in disposition and possibly reflected differences in economic and social status.

Naukrariai.   Ancient sources report the existence before Clisthenes of forty-eight or fifty such units, but their original function and significance are unknown. Possibly they were connected with ships, temples, or tax collection.

These three tiers had provided the administrative apparatus for conducting the business of the Athenian government. Boards of officers had been selected according to the phylai, with one treasurer, for example, from each phyle. The phylai were the states, counties, boroughs, or townships of early Athens—except, again, that they were not territorial. Before Clisthenes the system had evidently aroused little controversy because it seems to have endured the upheavals and reforms reviewed earlier in this chapter. But, with the creation of the democracy in 507 B.C., it would undergo a violent transformation.

The Clisthenic Organization

The reformer's organization superficially resembled its predecessor—probably deliberately so, in order to satisfy the typical Athenian's expected resistance to change. (Actually, it is misleading to speak of its "predecessor," for Clisthenes was prudent enough not to abolish the old units, though they did become obsolete.) But beneath the surface, the differences were profound.

The most fundamental change was the substitution of a territorial for the earlier personal disposition. Underlying the new organization, arranged (like the older one) in three tiers, was a threefold partition of the land of Attica. The partition created three regions, more or less geographically and topographically distinct, called the City, Coast, and Inland, although (a point not to be forgotten) the large farming sector was not confined to any one of them. Each region, though varying widely in total area, embraced more or less equal fractions of the Athenian citizen population.

Demes.   Within each region were situated at random the already-existing villages of Attica. Most of these were now institutionalized by Clisthenes as *demes* (from *demos*, the same word that, in the singular, designates "the people"). Numbering 139, the demes varied greatly in population—by a ratio of at least sixteen to one. Most were rural villages, but in the densely packed town a number of urban demes were created, probably with reference to streets or other manmade features. (Clisthenes' demes more or less corresponded to, and to all intents and purposes replaced, the pre-Clisthenic naukrariai, according to the ancient sources.)

Trittyes.   For the intermediate tier above the demes Clisthenes borrowed a unit from the old organization: the *trittys*, or "third" (more exactly, "one of three"). To create a single territorial trittys, the reformer grouped together varying numbers of demes situated within one of the three regional zones. Since each trittys was to be approximately equal in terms of population, the fact that the demes differed greatly in size meant that the number of demes per trittys ranged from one to as many as ten. But the number of trittyes per region, ten, was constant. Thus there were thirty trittyes in the whole organization.

Phylai.   The meaning of *trittys*, "one of three," alludes to the final stage of the construction of the new organization, the creation of the ten new *phylai* (or "tribes"). Each of the phylai was constructed of three trittyes, one from each of the three regions: a trittys of demes from the City, a trittys of demes from the Coast, and a trittys of demes from the Inland. Since the trittyes were roughly equal in population, the ten phylai incorporating the trittyes were roughly equal as well. In contrast to the occupational designations of the old system, the names of the new phylai were based on the names of Athenian heroes and thus were socially and politically neutral: Erechtheis, Aegeis, Pandionis, and so on. But the most striking feature of Clisthenes' system—a feature that set it apart not only from the old Attic organization but also from the known organizations of all other Greek states—was its internal integration of populations from the urban, maritime, and interior districts. This effect was produced by the intermediate distribution of the units (the demes) among the phylai through the medium of the innovating trittyes. More simply stated, a tribe of Athenian citizens now comprised roughly equal numbers of men from the three distinct regional zones of Attica.

The Purposes of Clisthenes' Organization

The new organization was unique in its complexity and in the specific form—regional integration—that complexity took. Why so complex? Why not something simpler, something more like the straightforward partitions characteristic of nearly all other Greek cities? Scholars have favored three principal lines of interpretation: antiaristocracy, gerrymandering, and mixing of population.

Antiaristocracy. Before Clisthenes, Athenian society had been dominated by social entities—families, clans, and factions—which in many cases had a strongly regional orientation. Clisthenes himself, of course, was an aristocrat, but the Alcmeonid's rivalry with the more conservative Isagoras and his faction had split the aristocracy, and once the reformer had declared himself a "democrat," he would have persisted in his efforts to weaken his opponents. Some scholars have suggested that Clisthenes designed his new organization in such a way as to cripple the regional power bases of his aristocratic and other rivals. Take, as a characteristic example, the cult center called the Tetrapolis, or "Four Towns"—the demes Trikorynthos, Probalinthos, Oinoe, and Marathon—in northeastern Attica. The Tetrapolis had supported the tyrant Pisistratus earlier in the century. Clisthenes split up this combine by placing the deme Probalinthos in a distant trittys of the phyle Pandionis, while the other three were assigned to another trittys in the phyle Aiantis. So, by splitting the regional bases of his opponents among different trittyes and phylai, the new organization, according to this interpretation, served an essentially political purpose.

Gerrymandering. This nineteenth-century Americanism derives from the name of Governor Elbridge Gerry of Massachusetts, during whose tenure election districts were redrawn in such a way as to benefit his own political party. The same has been alleged of the Athenian Clisthenes. Specifically, he has been accused of favoritism in his allocation of the trittyes to the phylai, despite the ancient tradition that the allocation be conducted by a random lottery. The accusation concerns the Alcmeonids, the family of Clisthenes, whose strongholds were located in certain demes within the urban center and along the coast south and east of Phaleron. With disturbing precision, the four urban trittyes including Alcmeonid demes were paired with the four coastal trittyes including Alcmeonid demes in the same four phylai. This is unlikely to have happened by chance. The result was the dominance of the reformer's kinsmen and supporters in as many as four of the principal administrative segments of the state (rather than their random scattering over all ten). Dominance within 40 percent of a government represents a large step toward ascendancy.

Ideal mixture of population. Even in antiquity, the "mixing up" of city, coast, and inland regions was noted as an outstanding feature of Clisthenes' work. But why? Integration of the population as a means of reducing factional rivalry and stabilizing the political scene is certainly one attractive answer to this question. The pre-Pisistratid factions (Men of the Plain, Shore, and Beyond the Hill)—although not corresponding exactly to Clisthenes' three regions—illustrate the problem as graphically as any example could. By combining trittyes from City, Coast, and Inland in a single phyle, the democratic politician could force citizens to interact and cooperate with each other—thereby perhaps lessening the tensions and leveling out the differences that perpetuated regional fragmentation. A pertinent case is the army. After Clisthenes, the infantry was divided among ten regiments, each consisting of the citizen soldiers of a single phyle. Thus soldiers from City, Coast, and Inland demes (and trittyes) would train and fight alongside one another. The same went for civilian functions, and for the many boards constituted of one man from each of the ten phylai. Can we take these as typical illustrations of a general integrative effect that Clisthenes hoped to realize in his new democratic order?

It is unlikely that we can, at least without serious qualification. Two features of the new order are in question. One is the principle that, despite the original territorial definition of the units (demes, trittyes, and phylai), the affiliations with those units were to be portable regardless of actual place of domicile. Furthermore, *in subsequent generations,* membership in the units would be determined by heredity, that is, by a son's acquiring the affiliations of his father. The operation of this principle assumes great significance as a result of the increasing trend toward urbanization, whereby citizens belonging to coastal or inland demes migrated to the urban center and established permanent residence there. Thus a demesman of, say, Marathon, a coastal deme in remote northeastern Attica, though now resident in town, still counted as a member of his ancestral village; and his sons and grandsons, though born in town, would also be officially designated "Marathonians." Consider the effect of these facts on the regional composition of the Council of Five Hundred, a body based on proportional representation of all 139 demes in accordance with a system of quotas based on population. Ideally, on paper, the Council was the ultimate embodiment of the integrative principle in that not only the regions but even the trittyes and individual demes within them were represented by a uniform numerical ratio. But, in practice, where in fact were the residences of the ten councilors from Marathon? In Marathon, in the urban center, or in still another location?

The notion of regional integration is also undercut by a second feature: the general absence of a requirement for regional representation in the boards of magistrates. These boards (which were very numerous) typically comprised ten citizens, one from each of the ten phylai. But no known rule required equal representation of City, Coast, and Inland *within a given board.* So, in a given year, an entire board could be selected from demes of a single— and, in particular, the City—region. This would be true even if affiliation with a deme (and trittys) were *not* hereditary. That is, it would be true even if everyone actually lived in the deme of his affiliation.

So, if "mixing up" or integration was one of Clisthenes' objectives, that objective was not consistently carried out through the new constitution. In fact, this is the first, but by no means the last, evidence we will see that this government, whatever Clisthenes' intentions may have been, was to come under the domination of the *urban* citizen population.

THE ORGANS OF GOVERNMENT

The Assembly

The Assembly (Greek *ekklesia*) was the meeting of the Demos of all Athenian citizens. All citizens who had reached the age of majority were eligible to attend, to address the body of the assembled, and to vote.

The principal activity of the Assembly was the passage of decrees. From the over six hundred surviving intelligible decrees from the period of the democracy an idea of the range of the body's competence can be gained. According to a recent scholar's count, about half the decrees are concerned with the conferral of citizenship and honors; about two hundred others deal with military matters and foreign policy; and the remainder are mainly about religious festivals and cults, finances (including those pertaining to public works projects), the administration of justice, and the procedures of the Assembly itself. Down to the mid-fourth century, the Assembly occasionally sat as a court of law (notably for the impeachment of political leaders and generals for alleged misconduct). Finally, those magistrates subject to election (rather than to allotment) were so elected each year in a special meeting of the Assembly. The comprehensive scope of the body is evident. For this reason there is substantial meaning in the characterization of the *ekklesia* as the embodiment of the classical democracy.

Closer inspection, however, will again require us to qualify the meaning of the term *democracy* in that characterization. Recent scholarly study proves that only a minority of the citizen body was in attendance at any given time. The key reason given is the size of the meeting place—a low, sloping hillside near the Agora called the Pnyx. Its seating capacity under the democracy was no greater than six thousand. Because this number corresponds to the number given by written sources for the Assembly's quorum (that is, the minimum number of citizens required to be in attendance in order to do business), one scholar has plausibly suggested that seating capacity and quorum were meant to coincide—that when the Pnyx was full the quorum had been attained. The point is that, once six thousand were seated in the auditorium, no others were needed—or permitted—to enter. But what was the citizen population of Athens at this time? About thirty thousand. Thus decisions taken in the name of the entire citizen body were actually made by no more than one-fifth of those citizens.

The principle of full democracy could be saved if it could be shown that, even though only six thousand voters were present on a given occasion, it was not always the *same* six thousand; that this was full democracy based on the principle of *rotation*. But this is highly unlikely. Many citizens lived at a great distance from the seat of government, and the realities of ancient modes of transportation (especially walking, the most common mode) would have made travel to town prohibitively burdensome. Farmers were already fatigued enough by their agricultural labors. True, family members and slaves were available as supplementary sources of labor, but it would be risky to assume that the head of the household could easily be absent for a full day or two. Besides, an overnight stay in town might entail unwelcome expenses. At all events, what few literary witnesses address the topic suggest an urban composition of the citizens in attendance in the Assembly. Plato, for example, mentions blacksmiths, shoemakers, merchants, shippers, rich, poor, the elite, and the humble. No farmers here, unless they are included in the "poor" and the "humble." We are driven to the conclusion that, from one meeting of the Assembly to the next, the six thousand in attendance were largely the same six thousand. Again, the urban bias of this government continues to emerge, with the added wrinkle that in this instance it appears that we are looking at an urban *minority*.

The Council of Five Hundred

Mention has already been made of Clisthenes' Council. It was the eventual successor to the aristocratic Council of the Areopagus and to the Solonian Council of Four Hundred (the existence of which has been questioned). As noted, its membership, which was selected entirely anew each year, was determined by a system of quotas based on the population of the demes. A deme sent councilors in proportion to the number of its members, with a range between one and sixteen. Ideally, therefore, the Council was truly representative of all Attica, but the reasons for doubting that the ideal was always realized in practice have already been stated. It, too, like the Assembly, may at any given time have been staffed by demesmen who, although bearers of deme affiliations from all over Attica, were in fact residents of the town.

Nonetheless, in other respects the Council supremely embodies the egalitarian impulses of Athenian democracy. This is seen in the internal organization of the Council. Evidently a body as large as five hundred was considered too large to expect *all* the business of the Council to be acted upon by the *entire* membership. So, an executive or steering committee was instituted. The committee consisted of the fifty councilors selected from the demes of a single phyle. Each of the ten phylai took turns providing the committee (called the *prytaneis,* or "presidents") in an order determined by chance over the course of the Council's year. The prytaneis probably met every day throughout the year; and a third of the committee (namely, the members from one of the phyle's three trittyes) were housed continuously in a special building designed for their use: the Tholos, on the western edge of the Agora. Now, each committee was chaired by a foreman, who was chosen by lot and who held office for a night and a day. Among other duties, the foreman presided over the entire Council and over any meeting of the Assembly taking place during his day in office. But that was not all. Athenian law permitted a citizen to be foreman only once in his lifetime. A likely demographic profile of the Athenian population yields the implication that fully one-quarter of the citizen population held this critically important post at some point in their lifetimes. And how were these foremen selected from among the membership of the Council? By a lottery—a device that, as we will shortly note, typified the "radical" qualities of the democracy.

Much the same conclusion is appropriate with regard to the Council as a whole. Its numerical strength, five hundred, was very large in comparison with the probable total citizen population of no more than thirty thousand during our period. Given, again, the likely demographic profile of the population, this meant that the usual nonrepeat rule—that no citizen could hold an allotted office more than once in his lifetime—had to be relaxed, with allowance made for a maximum of *two* tenures, though not in consecutive years. Even so, a very high percentage of citizens must have sat on the Council at least once, notwithstanding the difficulties of travel and other inconveniences experienced by many.

Accordingly, special significance is to be attached to the unusually wide range of powers exercised by the Council. The Five Hundred, since they officially received envoys from foreign states, played a vital role in foreign policy. The Council oversaw financial administration. The Council monitored the boards of magistrates. But, generally speaking, the body's decision-making powers were subordinated to its so-called probouleutic function, whereby, through a process called *probouleusis*, the Council prepared the "bills," which then moved on to the Assembly for acceptance, modification, or rejection. The Council was the source of the legislature's agenda, but its decisions were not final. This fact marks an essential difference between a democracy and an oligarchic government. In an oligarchy, a senate or Areopagus enjoys supreme authority. In the Athenian democracy, such discretionary powers were suppressed in favor of a subordinate, ancillary relationship with the sovereign Assembly. Nonetheless, the Council's authority was enormous, and the fact that most, if not all, citizens were at some point members attests, as does the random selection of the foreman, to the Athenians' deep commitment to an egalitarian ideology.

The Magistrates

The decisions of the Athenian people, expressed in the form of decrees issued by the Assembly, were implemented by various boards of magistrates. Boards existed corresponding to the various areas of competence of the legislature: the military, finance, the public infrastructure (markets, roads, buildings, and so on), the judiciary, and religion. Because each board numbered at least ten (one member from each phyle), the total number of magistrates active at any given time was large in comparison to the citizen population (and especially in comparison to that segment domiciled in the city where the magistrates were most active). Four hundred fifty can be counted (and

Aristotle attests a total of seven hundred) at a time when the number of citizens stood at no more than about thirty thousand. By any standard, when one remembers that five hundred additional citizens were sitting in the Council and that many others were serving on juries (see below), this was a big government with a sizable bureaucracy of administrative personnel.

Candidates for the magistracies were subject to certain qualifications and requirements. A minimum age of thirty was imposed. At one time, as we saw above, extent of eligibility was determined by one's membership in a Solonian income class, but by the time of Aristotle late in the fourth century B.C., these affiliations were ignored. Once selected, the magistrate-designate had to undergo a preliminary examination to determine his fitness for office; and, like jurors (see below), he was required to swear an oath that he would perform his duties suitably and lawfully. Upon completion of the annual term of office, each magistrate had to submit to an accounting, a procedure acquiring special importance when the handling of funds had been involved.

The methods for the selection of magistrates illustrate well the contrary and conflicting tendencies of the democratic government. By far the greatest number were selected by a lottery system from among a pool of volunteers. Allotment (or "sortition," an often-used synonym) represents the egalitarian impulse expressed or implicit elsewhere in the constitutional apparatus. But a certain minority of boards continued, as before the democracy and during the democracy's early decades, to be subject to election. Because all of these boards were military or financial, it is obvious that the democracy had conceded that egalitarian ideology could be entrusted only so far; the outcome of a battle or the handling of state funds would not be entrusted to volunteers selected at random. But a landmark episode in the development of the democracy cautions against any assumption that that ideology had not been taken seriously. In 487/6 B.C. the mode of selecting the board of nine archons, up until that point the chief executives and *de facto* leaders of the Athenian state, was changed from election to allotment. From that year on, the factors of experience, ability, and ambition could not—any more than one's political connections—play a role in the selection of the members of this board. At the same time, the fact that after 487/6 B.C. the known holders of the archonship were no longer the "big names" of Athenian politics (suggesting the decline of the political importance of the board) may have demonstrated to the Athenians the advantages of selection according to merit. At all events, the military and financial boards remained elective until the end of the democracy.

The Courts and Ostracism

The Athenian court system, like the Assembly, was intended to represent all the people, even though, in any given legal action, only a tiny fraction of the citizen body actually participated. Each year a pool of six thousand potential jurors—significantly, the same number as the quorum of the Assembly—was selected by lot from all who volunteered for court duty. Because the minimum age for eligibility was set at thirty, as for the magistrates, only two-thirds of a total population of about thirty thousand—or twenty thousand—were available. Thus the pool may have approached a full third of all those qualified to volunteer. As with the Council of Five Hundred and the boards of magistrates, the level of participation is astonishing.

Having sworn an oath at the beginning of the year to cast their vote in accordance with the laws and decrees, in a just manner, and without bias, the jurors, again on a purely voluntary basis, presented themselves in the Agora the morning of each day the courts were to be open. At all times, jurors were apportioned by lot to particular magistrates (and hence to the courtroom over which each of those magistrates presided) by the use of lot, but with the maturing of the democracy the procedure became increasingly complex. By the time of Aristotle the process of assignment had grown bewilderingly intricate. The underlying purpose is easy to guess. Because no potential juror—nor anyone else—could possibly, as a result of the convoluted procedure, know in advance to which magistrate, courtroom, or case he would be assigned until the very last minute, the threat of interference or tampering was virtually eliminated. No wealthy litigant or other party would now be able to secure a favorable outcome by bribing the jury. (The same purpose, incidentally, may partly account for the large size of the juries, usually in the hundreds and sometimes a thousand or more.) Fear of tampering may also have prompted the application of random allotment elsewhere among constitutional organs, though not so obviously as in the present case.

A judicial system may, of course, harbor sources of injustice other than tampering. These days much attention is given to the social composition of a jury as a factor affecting its potential for rendering a just verdict. What about ancient Athenian courts? The indicators are conflicting. For reasons already given, the jurors disproportionately represented the urban districts in close proximity to the seat of government. The minimum age requirement of thirty already, as noted, excluded a very sizable younger cohort of the citizen body. But social and economic status is the real problem. A comedy of the Athenian dramatist Aristophanes features a chorus of jurors who are old and impoverished citizens. The point about poverty is confirmed by other literary, though nonforensic, contemporary texts. By contrast, in a number of preserved courtroom speeches the litigant speaker addresses the jurors as though they were men of relative prosperity (as well as elevated social standing). But recent scholars have justly observed that such speakers may be engaging in a calculated attempt to get on the jurors' good side by addressing them in flattering terms, ascribing to them a level of wealth and social status that they in fact did not possess. Finally, there is the matter of the payment made to each juror for each day's service. Because the level of compensation was very low, only two classes of Athenians would have found jury service attractive: the very poor (to whom even a small payment was sufficient inducement) and the rich (for whom money was not a factor in any event). But service probably did not appeal to the "middle class" of Athenian society, for such men could not voluntarily leave more profitable employment in exchange for the near-starvation compensation the jury system provided.

Thus far no mention has been made of a "judge." That is because there was no judge, only a presiding magistrate. This is perhaps the most startling difference between the ancient Athenian and a modern Western court system. All was left to the litigants and jurors. No legal authority was present to rule on admissibility of evidence, to settle points of law, to oversee the sentencing procedure, or to perform any of the manifold functions that we associate with the duties of a judge. Nor were attorneys present. Instead, the litigants represented themselves, although they might, and often did, retain professional speechwriters to compose briefs for them. (Such famous figures as Demosthenes and Lysias are among the known such "logographers.") It was up to the litigant to look up laws and decrees, to assemble the appropriate documentation (wills, contracts, and so forth), to line up witnesses, and in general to ready his presentation. After two sets of alternating speeches by plaintiff and defendant, the jurors cast their votes in secret, with the majority ruling. If a conviction was obtained, the two sides proposed alternative penalties, and the jurors voted again, choosing by majority vote between the two proposals. A famous example of this legal process (although not, like our forensic texts, an authentic brief) is the dialogue of Plato called the *Apology*—a literary adaptation of the speech delivered by the Athenian court system's most illustrious defendant, the philosopher Socrates.

Athens was famous among ancient Greeks not so much for the Parthenon or the plays of the dramatic stage as for its litigiousness. Solon, we recall, had given litigiousness an initial boost by introducing the appeals process and, most of all, by creating the third-party suit. Because monetary damages were awarded in certain types of actions, and because a percentage of those damages went to the successful prosecutor, unscrupulous Athenians (called "sycophants") soon made a practice of filing suits, sometimes on trumped-up charges, in the hope of enriching themselves. To reduce the incidence of such frivolous litigation, the Athenian people instituted mandatory fines if the prosecutor failed to achieve a certain minimum number of votes. But even so, the Athenian citizen body persisted in its litigious ways, and by the time of the developed democracy, the number of legal venues in or around the Agora had grown to about a dozen.

Superficially resembling the workings of the court system but fundamentally distinct from it was the procedure called *ostracism,* instituted by Clisthenes. Ostracism was a form of banishment. The procedure resembled a decision in the court system in that the outcome was determined by the vote of a theoretically representative segment of the citizen body and in that the outcome was, given a sufficient number of votes, the taking of negative action against an individual citizen. It was distinct from a trial, however, in that no charge of criminality was involved and the banishment did not constitute a form of punishment. A brief rehearsal of the procedure will illustrate these points. Every year the Assembly voted on whether to hold an ostracism procedure; if the vote was affirmative, the ostracism was conducted some time later in the Agora. Each citizen who elected to participate scratched on a fragment of pottery (Greek *ostrakon,* hence "ostracism") the name of an Athenian he would like to see banished. The *ostraka* were counted. If a quorum of six thousand was attained, that citizen whose name appeared on the greatest number (but not necessarily on a majority) of the ballots was required, within ten days, to leave Athens for a period of ten years. Again, note that the banishment was not equivalent to the criminal penalty of exile and that, in line with this, the ostracized citizen retained his citizenship and ownership of his property.

What was the purpose of this bizarre "negative election" (as it has been called)? The simplest explanation is that it was a means of defusing a potentially explosive political situation. If two or more factions were locked in struggle without hope of peaceful resolution, ostracism could remove one (but only one) of the leaders of those factions each year. The record of the names of the banished includes Hipparchus (a relative of the tyrant of that name), Megacles (an Alcmeonid), Xanthippus (the father of the eminent democratic politician Pericles), and Aristeides (another leading political figure)—clear evidence that ostracism, whatever its intended purpose, was in fact used against politicians. But the procedure, as described above, was obviously open to abuse. Surviving ostraka preserve the names of a large number of "nobodies," recorded on only a single ballot or two. It is likely that some of these were not public figures, but rather the objects of purely personal enmity. Because the vote was conducted in secret, nothing prevented a citizen from submitting the name of a man who had, for example, failed to repay a loan or insulted his daughter. Even worse, ostracism was subject to tampering. A cache of 191 ostraka was discovered in a well in the Agora all but one bearing the same name, Themistocles (a prominent democratic politician of the Persian Wars period), and study of the writing style proves that the ballots were inscribed by only 14 different persons. Plainly these ballots had been prepared in advance by an organized group of Themistocles' opponents, but by some mischance were discarded before being distributed to voters. It is no wonder that ostracism disappears from the record without a trace in the final decades of the fifth century B.C.

QUALITIES OF THE ATHENIAN DEMOCRACY

Assembly, Council of Five Hundred, magistrates, courts, and (in the fifth century B.C.) ostracism—these were the principal operative components of the Athenian democracy. What is needed now is a characterization of that government in terms of the ideological principles implicit in those components and their functions. To accomplish this, we focus upon the democracy in its fifth century B.C. form. At the same time, we will acknowledge that it was not until some time after Clisthenes that the constitution's more distinctive features were fully to emerge and that the fourth-century democracy (down to its suppression in 322 B.C.) underwent some significant structural changes and power shifts among the principal organs of the government. What follows applies to the democracy during Athens' "golden age."

Voluntary Participation

Although every citizen was qualified to engage in governmental activity at nearly every level, no one was *required* to participate. Nor is there any trace of an ideal that encouraged or rewarded such participation, with the signal exception of an isolated remark ascribed by Thucydides to Pericles' *Funeral Oration*—a text of notoriously dubious fidelity to the subject it describes: Athens in the fifth century B.C. To the contrary, nonparticipation was sometimes praised as "minding your own business," and after the loss of the Peloponnesian War, some leading aristocrats literally withdrew from political life rather than continue to be associated with the democratic government. At the same time, the purpose of pay for government service (see below, under "High Level of Participation") was in part to encourage attendance in the assemblies and courts in times of declining citizen population. As noted in Chapter 4, the third-party suit introduced by Solon also had the effect of rewarding participation, albeit sometimes dishonorable participation, in the legal system. Admittedly, it is a mixed picture, but on the whole Athenians upheld the ideal that a citizen could choose to participate or not as he saw fit.

Opposition to One-Man Rule

Two qualities characterized a king or tyrant: (1) his authority was individual and unchecked; and (2) because he might hold power as long as he lived and could transmit that power dynastically to a son or other person of his choosing, his authority was unlimited over time. Both these features of one-man rule were opposed by Athens' democratic institutions. All political power was divided (and thereby potentially checked) by the extension of the principle of collegiality to all organs of government: the legislature, magistracies, and courts. No single officer existed. To prevent continuity of an officer's authority over time, the tenure in all offices was limited to a single term of one year. No citizen could hold the same post twice; and in the one exception to this rule, the Council, the second tenure could not be consecutive with the first. All the members of the boards of magistrates and of the Council began and ended their tenure at the same time; no members remained to afford continuity of personnel or outlook by being carried over into the following year.

The one glaring exception to all this was afforded by the board of generals. Although there is no evidence that any single member of the board enjoyed greater authority than his colleagues, consecutive reelection and therefrom continuity of power was permitted. During the mid-fifth century, one man, Pericles, held this elective office at least a score of times, including consecutive tenures from the late 440s to his death in 429 B.C. Although Athens under Pericles was in name a democracy, Thucydides referred to it (with good reason) as actually "the regime of its first citizen." In short, it was through the office of general that the Athenian people were able to counteract any undesirable effects created by the otherwise general observance of an egalitarian ideology.

Egalitarianism

From our description of the various elements of the constitution, it is evident that in some very substantial sense Athenians regarded all citizens as "equals" and thus equally capable of performing governmental functions. Egalitarianism, furthermore, was reflected in practice as well as in ideology, for the very high level of participation had the inevitable result that the Assembly, boards, Council, and courts were in large part staffed from the *lower* echelons of citizen society. If many of those serving turned out to be uneducated or lacking in experience, such a deficiency could be transformed into a virtue, as more than one litigant's brief, delivered before a popular court, reminds us. But the ideology's most visible manifestation was the use of the lottery nearly everywhere a selection had to be made (with the exception, once again, of the election of the military and financial boards). True, the *purpose* of the lottery (to mention one attractive suggestion) may have been to eliminate the element of conflict occasioned by elections. Even so, the underlying assumption remained that all citizens were regarded as sufficiently qualified to carry out the duties of government.

High Level of Participation

The involvement of a very large percentage of Athenian citizens in government was required by (1) the multitude of large boards of magistrates subject to the nonrepeat rule; (2) the need to fill the Council of Five Hundred each year (with only one repetition permitted); and (3) the application of the high quorum of six thousand to the Assembly, to ostracism, and to the pool of jurors (from which panels numbering in the hundreds were to be drawn). How was such a high level of participation made possible? The following factors are relevant:

• *The absence of a property qualification to determine eligibility.* By Aristotle's day, we saw, the Solonian income classes, though still on the books, were no longer enforced. No citizen, however poor, was legally disqualified from service.

• *The availability of free time for government service.* Leisure time was created to an indeterminable degree by the ownership of slaves among even the less prosperous segments of citizen society and, also to an unknown degree, by the alternative free labor provided by family members, tenants, or hired laborers. However, as noted in Chapter 5, not every citizen would have used such labor sources to create leisure time for himself.

• *Pay for government service.* Attendance in the Assembly, tenure on the Council, each day's participation as a juror in the court system, and certain other forms of service were compensated by the state treasury. The payments, though low, were sufficient to make government service possible for, and even attractive to, citizens otherwise unable to participate for financial reasons.

Nonetheless, as high as the level of participation was, the full exercise of the franchise at any one time was limited to a small fraction of the citizen population by the seating capacity of the meeting place of the Assembly. The device of rotating the entire citizen body through the Assembly over time is not, as we saw, applicable in the Athenian case. Since the Assembly expressed the will of the sovereign People, this was a serious limitation on the workings of the direct democracy.

Promulgation of the Acts of Government

Because every citizen was potentially qualified to play a part in government, and because the decisions of the Assembly and Council were expressed in the name of the People, it was only natural that those acts be made available in "published" form to the Athenian public. The People had a right of access to the record of the People's acts. Papyrus texts were placed on file in an archive called the Metroon on the west side of the Agora. Texts inscribed in permanent form on bronze or stone were placed in public areas in and around the civic center. Such practices seem to imply a literate public, and obviously *some* competent readers were expected to be on hand to justify the existence of these records. But it would be a mistake to think in terms of a generally educated citizen body. Educational opportunities, as we will see in Chapter 7, were few and in any case open only to the well-to-do. Nor is there reason to suppose that even a minimum of competence was required as a prerequisite to citizenship at any time.

The Urban Bias

Mention has been made of the fact that the seat of the democratic government was physically situated in and around the Agora at the foot of the Acropolis. The inevitable effect was that those many citizens who lived in demes located outside the urban center were at a great disadvantage should they wish to exercise their civic rights. Proportionate representation by region or deme *appears* to have been built into the Council of Five Hundred and the boards of ten, but our earlier discussion showed how residents of the city could have dominated in both cases. If, as in the instance of the Assembly, the democracy at any given time was being run by a minority, it was also probably an *urban* minority.

THE URBAN MINORITY AND THE DEMES

The conclusion just reached is a disturbing one, above all because the extension of full rights to all citizens, the various expressions of egalitarian ideology, and the wide publicity that the acts of the government received could only have made each and every Athenian aware of his own potential role as a citizen. The citizen farmer residing in the distant demes of Rhamnous or Oinoe was certainly quite aware that only by the accident of his physical location was he not able to play his role in the decision making and other processes of the democracy. But all was not lost. There existed an alternative venue for the exercise of his political rights as a citizen: his deme. Besides their roles as segments of the central government (the demes, for example, as we saw, provided the basis, according to a quota system, for the selection of the Council of Five Hundred), the demes were internally organized as more or less self-sufficient village associations. They possessed a political structure of their own which operated independently of other demes and, especially, of the urban center. It was in the deme organization that the *de facto* disfranchised, excluded by the accident of distance from the seat of government, were able to express and to live out, admittedly on a lower scale, whatever political aspirations had been awakened by the ideology of a participatory direct democracy. Thus, as had been true since the tyrants, the state of Athens, though now united ideologically, remained in actual practice significantly decentralized and politically fragmented.

Suggested Readings

For the classical Athenian democracy, the fullest continuous ancient source is the second half of the treatise *The Athenian Constitution,* traditionally attributed to Aristotle. A good translation with introduction and notes is, as noted at the end of Chapter 4, the Penguin Books edition of P. J. Rhodes (London, 1984), to be supplemented by the same author's *Commentary* (Oxford, 1981). The best modern description and interpretation in English, to which the above account is in several places indebted, is M. H. Hansen, *The Athenian Democracy in the Age of Demosthenes: Structure, Principles and Ideology* (Oxford, 1991). Another overview is D. Stockton, *The Classical Athenian Democracy* (Oxford, 1990). Dated, though still useful, is A. H. M. Jones, *Athenian Democracy* (Baltimore, 1986; originally published in 1957). An excellent study of the various aspects of an Athenian citizen's engagement in public life, particularly in the organs of the democratic government, is R. K. Sinclair, *Democracy and Participation in Athens* (Cambridge, 1988). For a comparative study by a leading authority, there is M. I. Finley, *Democracy Ancient and Modern* (New Brunswick, N.J., 1973).

Chapter 7. The Family, Women, Children, and the Old

THE FAMILY

Family or Household?

We all know what a family is: a group of closely related persons. We all know what a household is: all the people, not necessarily related to each other, dwelling under the same roof. But which of these two terms should the social historian use as the basis for analyzing ancient Athenian private life? The concept of the household has a distinct advantage in including the slaves attached to many, perhaps most, Athenian families. Without question, slaves played important roles in the production, consumption, and interpersonal dynamics of Athenian domestic life. Even so, for present purposes, we will orient our discussion around the family. Its members, and their interrelations, are well known (in contrast with the sources' near silence on domestic slavery), and it was the citizen family, to the exclusion of other members of the household, that was the focus of much Athenian policy and law.

Nuclear or Extended Family?

The family, though a constant fixture of human society, may assume a variety of different forms. One fundamental distinction, among others, is that made between nuclear (or conjugal) and extended families. The nuclear form, familiar from its widespread occurrence in modern Western societies, nominally comprises father, mother, and their children. More remote blood or affinal relatives, such as grandparents and in-laws, are separately domiciled in other households or institutions. By contrast, the extended family (and household), while incorporating within it the nuclear unit, also includes some of the more distant relations. It is found in many premodern societies, ancient Athens among them. Its nuclear component, in Athens' case, comprised the citizen father, his wife, sons, and unmarried daughters. Daughters, upon marriage, migrated to their husband's household. Sons, too, could, before or after marriage, establish a new residence, but in many cases they assumed control of their father's property upon reaching full social maturity (typically around thirty), sometimes before his death (see Chapter 8). In the latter case, the senior patriarch and his wife (who very often survived him) continued to live with their son, his wife, and their children. Supplementing this three-generation household were slaves; any hired help, such as a wet nurse; and possibly more distant kin, consanguineal or affinal.

Size of the Athenian Family

Athenian families were relatively small, with a total of four children only rarely exceeded in a citizen household. The determinants limiting family size may be conjectured with confidence. Production of a legitimate son (and heir) was an absolute necessity, with an additional son (or sons) a good idea as a hedge against the untimely loss of the first. But a low limit on the number of sons was imposed by the law requiring the equal division of a father's estate among legitimate sons; the Greeks did not, in other words, observe a rule of primogeniture whereby the eldest son inherited everything. If a farm or other income-producing property had already reached the subsistence level, further division among multiple heirs may no longer have been a viable possibility. A daughter, too, might be an economic liability, because a female's purpose in life in this society, to marry and bear children, could not normally be accomplished unless she was provided with a dowry—often a substantial amount of cash or property. A large number of children was plainly out of the question. Indeed, given these inhibiting factors, a single adulthood or childless marriage might appear (to us) attractive alternative life style choices. But neither option lay open for members of citizen society. Marriage was universally upheld by the Greeks as a goal of adult life, regardless of an individual's orientation or inclination (for males, the ready availability of various extramarital relationships would have made an otherwise unwelcome marriage more acceptable). And marriage and childbearing were indissolubly linked. Because both assumptions may strike us as arbitrary or odd, one is moved to ask why they were so consistently upheld.

State Intervention in the Family

Among other factors, an important, perhaps decisive, one was the intrusive role played by the Athenian state. The state—that is, the democratic body of citizens, the ultimate source of law—adopted and continually reaffirmed the maintenance of Athenian families as a strategy for the realization of certain of its administrative objectives. To that end, marriage for the purpose of producing legitimate children was an indispensable requirement. Some specific illustrations of the state's interventions in this area, regarded by many of us to be quintessentially "private," will help clarify the point.

• *Legitimacy.*   After Pericles' law of 451/0, to be "legitimate" meant to be the offspring of a marriage between an Athenian citizen and a duly betrothed Athenian woman. Only the legitimate could become citizens or inherit from a citizen father. Thus a citizen hoping to produce a son eligible for citizenship and legally capable of inheriting was compelled to do so through marriage to an Athenian woman (in contrast with informal unions such as concubinage). The marriage of necessity created a new family.

• *Adoption.* In the absence of his own biological son, a married citizen could adopt a son from another citizen family. The adopted son was often a close relative on the adopting father's side of the family; for example, his brother's son. By providing an heir to the adoptive father's name and estate, adoption prevented the extinction of the family.

• *Epiklerate.* If a citizen had a daughter (or daughters) but no son, the state allowed for the daughter's marriage to a relative on her father's side of the family, his brother standing first in the pecking order. Such a daughter was called an *epikleros*, hence the term epiklerate. The eventual husband, upon his wife's father's death, assumed control (but not full legal ownership) of the estate, which subsequently passed by inheritance to his and his wife's male children; that is, to the original testator's grandsons. Again, the effect of the law was to keep the family alive, while into the bargain limiting access to the estate to the citizen's male blood relatives and descendants.

• *Orphans.* The minor sons of citizen fathers who had died in warfare were raised to majority at public expense—another "insurance policy" enhancing the survival of citizen family lines.

• *Dowries.* Daughters of families too poor to provide a dowry were dowered at public expense. On a few occasions, the treasury dowered daughters of citizens who had served Athens well. The beneficiaries here included not only the natal family of the bride but also that of the groom, who would assume custody of the dowry. The ultimate objective was probably to support the citizen class (whose daughters were in competition with the marriageable daughters of noncitizens, such as metics) by ensuring the marriage of their daughters, but the short term result was that the institution of marriage itself—and families—were sustained in the face of competing lifestyles, such as spinsterhood or informal unions.

These laws were unambiguous in their intended practical effect. The definition of legitimacy and its link to citizenship, while excluding outsiders, male or female, from penetrating the Athenian elite, indirectly encouraged marriage and the formation of new families. Within the citizen caste, only through marriage could new citizens and eligible heirs be produced. If a marriage failed to produce a son, the law of adoption and the epiklerate provided substitutes who were, in practice or by legal requirement, closely related to the father. State support of war orphans brought immature future heads of families to the age of marriage and inheritance. Females dowered at public expense could marry and, upon marriage, enrich the household of their husbands. The combined effect was to put a premium on marriage and, once a new family was established, to ensure its preservation, through the male line if at all possible.

But what is the explanation for so determined and sustained an interest on the part of the state? Several answers are possible. Concern for the orderly transmission of property was certainly a primary factor. Disputed inheritances were a staple of the Athenian court calendar as it was. Admittedly, *any* law or regulation, consistently applied, would make for orderliness, but the particular law adopted by the Athenians, by limiting inheritance to the legitimate offspring of citizen marriages, kept private property within the circle of the direct blood descendants of the deceased. Athenian society recognized the primacy of descent, beginning with the rights of legitimate sons. Second, the family's household could, if its health was maintained, perform functions that would otherwise have to be left to other institutions. In addition to providing full care for the very young, the sick, and the disabled, the family assumed the often-substantial burden of caring for the old from their "retirement" until death. (The one exception was the tiny one-or-two-obol-per-day distribution to cripples unable to earn a living.) Finally, families, again in the absence of public institutions, collectively preserved private Athenian ancestral cults and traditions and, still more broadly, provided the apparatus for the transmission of Greek, and specifically Athenian, culture. The soldiers, wives and mothers, and producers of literary, philosophical, or artistic works were not the products of compulsory schooling, mass media, and a retail marketplace. They were the products of private households determinedly sustained with the help of public governmental interventions.

Three Features of Athenian Family Life

This discussion, admittedly somewhat dry to this point, should not be allowed to leave the impression that the Athenian family was nothing but a bundle of legal definitions and governmental interventions. Nothing could be further from the truth. For an idea of the vitality of Greek domestic life and familial interaction, the student need only consult those literary and artistic creations of classical Athens which center on the family and its doings. All told, they reveal acts and passions on such a scale that even the most outrageous of today's soap operas would pale in comparison. Take a few examples. The father (Agamemnon) sacrifices his daughter (Iphigeneia) to expedite a military expedition; his wife (Clytemnestra), whose rage is further increased when her husband returns home with a young lover (Cassandra), kills him in revenge, only to be killed herself in retaliation by her own son (Orestes). A mother (Medea) murders her own children by her husband (Jason) in order to punish him for his jilting her for another woman (Creousa). A stepmother (Phaedra) falls in love with her stepson (Hippolytus), and when he rebuffs her advances, she commits suicide, leaving a letter falsely accusing him to her husband (Theseus), resulting in her stepson's untimely violent death.

Such episodes as these, though set in a distant time and possibly fictional, illustrate three important features of the historical Greek family. First was its role as a scene of *conflict*, between spouses, between parents and children, involving step relations, and so on. A second feature, a by-product of the first, is that Greek families were *dynamic*; that is, they were prone to instability and to sometimes violent and episodic change. For both of these reasons, to understand the Greek family, we must examine it over time, over the full length of its career from beginning to end; that is, *diachronically*. This is our third point. Modern families are often popularly portrayed and idealized in "snapshot" (synchronic) form, frozen at particular moments in their existence, such as, for example, young parents with small children or a retired couple in their "golden years." But the social historian is concerned with the family from its conception to its final extinction.

Kinship Beyond the Extended Family

The circle of one's blood and affinal relations did not end, of course, at the walls of a citizen's house. Forensic and other texts reveal a consciousness of relations many removes from the elementary kin of the residential unit. Among these, special legal significance was attached to the *anchisteia*, a legally defined group of relatives on both the father's and mother's side, extending to the degree of second cousins (or, on another interpretation, first cousins once removed). These were the relatives who, according to a legally specified order, stood in line to inherit in the absence of legitimate primary heirs.

Unlike the anchisteia, which, existing only on paper, possessed no organizational cohesion, the *phratry*, or brotherhood, was a well-defined and unified group of families loosely united by a probably fictive descent from a remote common ancestor. At one time the phratries had possessed important societal roles and even under the democracy were left undisturbed by Clisthenes, probably in order to allow them to continue to play their valuable role in testing majority and legitimate descent from Athenian parents. Thus the phratry, like the family, though nominally "private," was put to work by the state to accomplish goals that would otherwise have fallen to a governmental bureaucracy.

WOMEN

Betrothal and Dowry

We have seen that, as a consequence of its own constitutional and legal acts and definitions, the Athenian state depended for its continuation on the institution of marriage. The rarity of grants of citizenship demonstrates that the people did not look to recruitment of outsiders as a means of maintaining citizen numbers. That left propagation by the citizen class itself; and because after 451/0 B.C. only the male offspring of a citizen and a "duly betrothed" Athenian woman could qualify for citizenship, new citizens could not be produced except through marriage. Thus with regard to citizenship, as with inheritance, the institution of marriage served purely instrumental purposes. It was hardly, as in modern Western societies, a merely private and personal arrangement dedicated to the emotional satisfaction of husband and wife.

Not surprisingly, therefore, ancient Greek marriages assumed a definitely contractual aspect. The contract in question (the Greek word means something like "handshake" and is traditionally rendered by the archaic term "betrothal") was normally concluded between the male heads of the two families: the prospective groom and the guardian of the prospective bride (usually her father or, in the absence of the father, another male family member such as an older brother). (How the two families came into contact with one another is poorly understood, but occasional mention is made of female matchmakers.) Much was at stake: status (each family being rated according to the quality of its member's marriage partner); future cooperation between the families; possible mutually beneficial exchanges of an economic, social, or other nature; and, for the politically active, potentially valuable alliances. Despite the probably unrealistic and wishful explorations by poets of the possibility of choice of her partner by the female, it is highly unlikely that her preferences were a decisive factor in the negotiations. As young as fourteen and until this point having little, if any, experience outside her parents' home, she may well have had no preferences to express (second marriages, involving older women, were of course another matter). Modern Western societies uphold marriage "for love" as an ideal, but no such ideal operated in classical Athens, although a great many Athenian husbands and wives undoubtedly did develop deep affection for one another.

The centerpiece of the betrothal was the dowry: property or a sum of cash provided by the bride's father and, with the completion of the marriage process, placed in the custody of her husband. Dowries were substantial; the attested examples range between 5 and 20 percent of the bride's father's net worth. Naturally, a large dowry, especially in times of an oversupply of nubile women (say, after heavy loss of unmarried eligible males in a military expedition), could be used as a bargaining chip to secure the best available groom. But the dowry's principal function was to launch and sustain the new family. Given the economic realities of ancient Greece (see Chapter 9), it is probable that, in many cases, the new couple could not have established an independent household without the dowry.

Now, a gift of such magnitude is unlikely to have come without strings attached. In fact, it was not a "gift" at all. Should the marriage end with the death of the husband or by divorce (provided, in this case, that the wife had not been guilty of some immoral act), the dowry accompanied the woman back to her guardian's (normally her father's) house, to be available to dower her a second time. The provision for the return of the dowry had important consequences. For the husband, if the dowry was large, was under pressure to treat his wife decently. If he did not and she appealed to her father and a divorce was initiated, he stood to lose the use of it. Regarded from the wife's point of view, a large dowry gave her leverage over her husband. Structurally, the link forged between the two families had an element of tension built into it, in that the dowry could be used by the bride's kin to ensure her well-being, even though she had been removed to another location and was no longer under their watchful care.

Friendly cooperation, however, may more often than not have characterized relations between the bride's natal and marital families, in view of the fact that marriages between relatively close kin were not uncommon. Several marriages between first cousins and between uncles and nieces are recorded within respectable citizen society. The probable motives, suggest scholars, concern property. Previously divided farmlands might be reunited for more profitable use if the two families were joined by a marriage. The clearest example would be the marriage of first cousins, whose fathers, each other's brothers, had divided their father's estate upon inheritance. Furthermore, if there was apprehension concerning the use or preservation of the dowry, it might be allayed by the knowledge that it was in the custody of a man bound to the bride's family not only by marriage but by generally unquestioned ties of consanguinity. Again, either way you look at the situation, these are additional grounds for suspecting the predominance of instrumental over affective motives in the selection of marriage partners.

The Athenian "Wedding" Ceremony

Greek matrimonial ideals, and the place of marriage in Athenian society, were in part symbolically expressed in a series of events following the betrothal. None of these events corresponded to a modern Western wedding. Rather, the marriage ceremony was a process that began with the "handshake" and progressed through a sequence of social gatherings and religious ceremonies, culminating in the establishment of the new family in its residence. A major component of that process was the nuptial banquet hosted by the bride's father in his house. Significantly for our point, males and females were segregated, and vase paintings depict the bride's face covered by a veil. These are clear expressions of the general segregation of the genders in Athenian society and, in the case of the veil, of the insulation of citizen females from contact with, even from the gaze of, males outside their immediate household.

From the father's house the bride, mounted on a chariot with the groom and his best man, was conducted in a ceremonial procession to the couple's new residence. This journey marked the defining moment, the turning point, in an Athenian woman's life. It marked the transition from minor to adult, from child to bearer of children, and, most significantly for her future life, from the custody of her father to that of her husband. For, whereas males, as we will see, moved by successive stages from a private domestic setting to full engagement in Athenian public life, females, upon marriage, merely migrated from one citizen household to another, perpetually dependent and never to penetrate the impermeable boundary enclosing the citizen domain.

Meanwhile, the procession was accompanied by the wedding party singing the Song of Hymen and, soon thereafter, upon their arrival at the groom's house, as they stood outside the couple's bedroom, the Song at the Bedchamber. That the bride and groom, now about to consummate their marriage, should be so closely attended by the wedding party may strike us as odd. But for the Athenians these ceremonies, whatever their religious content (largely passed over here), were a public event. Marriage, and with it childbearing, adultery, and divorce, were public acts, with ramifications, duly recognized by law, for the well-being of the state. It was therefore entirely appropriate that the wedding procession, from beginning to end, be conducted in a public setting.

Age at First Marriage and Marital Ideals

The female's extremely tender age at first marriage, set by a contemporary literary witness as ideally "not yet fifteen," has been variously explained. But two factors in particular deserve mention. One was economic. For any Athenian family, but particularly a poor one, a daughter, once she had reached a marriageable age (that is, the age of reproduction), represented a continuing financial liability. Besides, why delay the receipt of the benefits that establishing a marriage link with another family would hopefully bring with it? So, the sooner she marries, the better. The other factor had to do with virginity. Female virginity was highly prized. Sexual jealousy and a sense of exclusive ownership on the part of the male were undoubtedly factors in many cases. But at a deeper level, the high valuation of virginity might have been connected with anxiety about the possibility that one's wife could be impregnated by and bear the child of a male other than her husband. A virgin bride cannot possibly be pregnant. Again, the younger the bride, the more likely that the desired condition would be obtained. The groom, by contrast, had probably (as advised by our literary witness) reached the age of thirty or so; the determining factors, not necessarily having anything to do with marriage, will be discussed in Chapter 8.

This extreme disparity in ages would have resulted in some predictable consequences, one being the essentially father-daughter character of the couple's relationship, at least in the early years of the marriage. But the domination of parent over child could not be extended indefinitely. And eventually, because in most instances considerations of physical attraction, affection, or basic compatibility had not necessarily played a part in the decision to marry, the maturation of the wife would in many households have led to serious interpersonal conflicts with her husband. Not surprisingly, therefore, we find two particular matrimonial ideals being cultivated: the wife's obedience to her husband and marital harmony. Their acceptance and internalization, in combination with considerable economic, social, and familial pressures, probably kept married couples together in the face of even the most profound estrangement.

A Married Woman's Work and Daily Routine

The house in which a married woman lived and nearly all of its contents (unless included in her dowry) belonged entirely to her husband (and his family). According to our idealizing portrait of the new bride, the teenage bride, only minimally proficient in a few basic domestic skills, received from her husband detailed instructions regarding her wifely duties in her new setting. Only within these constricting parameters is it fair to say that a married woman "ran" her household. Some of her duties were of the nurturing variety: food preparation; childrearing in all its aspects, including the education of daughters to the age of marriage and of sons until their introduction to teachers outside the home; and care of the sick. Productive activity was chiefly represented by spinning and weaving, pursuits vital to the economic health of the household because cloth goods were so prohibitively expensive (due to the great amount of labor required for their production; see Chapter 9). (Some or all of these tasks, however, could be performed by slaves, hired help, or older children under the woman's direction.) In rural environments, it is likely that women also ventured outside the house to tend to stock animals and to cultivate vegetable gardens, tasks commonly allocated to women in traditional societies. In urban contexts, however, any such traditional allocation of these or similar extramural duties by gender was overridden by a still more inflexible dichotimization between the "inside" (females) and the "outside" (males). Free women did not, for example, leave the house to draw water or go on grocery shopping expeditions (tasks given to slaves), despite their patently "nutritive" nature.

The Seclusion of Women

Social historians have given much attention to the question of the confinement of citizen women in classical Athens. Some earlier investigators favored an extreme view that was sometimes labeled "Oriental seclusion." To be sure, women did not engage in many of the public, outdoor pursuits of citizen males; and even within the house, females were relegated to segregated quarters positioned in such a way as to insulate them from contact with the world outside.

But the documented exceptions to any assumption of a general seclusion are too numerous to ignore or downplay: women engaged in retail trade in public places; women in attendance at state ceremonies (such as the public observance for the war dead) and participating in religious festivals; women present at private weddings, funerals, and so on. It will not do to try to explain these "exceptions" away as somehow excused or accounted for by the extraordinary requirements of religion, because much of this society's private and public activity was conducted directly or indirectly in the name of religion. Women simply did in fact spend considerable time outside their homes.

"Seclusion," however, need not be restricted to literal physical confinement within the four walls of a house. A recent commentator has wisely stressed that seclusion can also be accomplished through social means, whereby men and women, though in physical proximity with each other, are kept separate in the ways that count, through the observance of moral notions such as appropriateness of behavior and "respect." In line with this view, one thinks at once of the rarity with which women are mentioned *by name* in forensic texts. Instead of supplying her given name, the speaker usually refers to "the wife of so-and-so" or "the daughter of so-and-so," as though to hide the woman's identity behind a veil of anonymity. And readers of Pericles' *Funeral Oration* in Thucydides' *History* will recall the speaker's closing comment that the most praiseworthy woman is she who is least spoken of by men, for good or for ill. If women play by the rules, in other words, men would hardly be aware of their existence and so would have nothing to say about them. Should social distance of this magnitude be maintained, there would have been little need for the physical seclusion of women.

Why seclude women? Above, mention was made of anxiety (on the part of males, of course, but not necessarily only males) about the possibility that a married woman might become pregnant by a man other than her husband. Such anxiety would be understandable in the context of a society that, like this one, attached great value to the institution of marriage, to blood relationships, and to the observance of those relationships in determining constitutional and legal rights—in particular, the ability to inherit. There is also the matter of the injury to a man's pride, not to mention public humiliation, if the son or daughter he thought was his should be revealed to be the child of another man. What if the person who was to inherit his estate and carry on the family cults and name was in reality not his son? Even should a wife's extramarital affair stop short of pregnancy, a famous forensic text reminds us, the damage to the integrity of the household could be catastrophic. What to do? Female virginity at the time of marriage provided an initial safeguard. After that, seclusion, physical or social, seems to have been this society's response to the threat posed by the possibility of female extramarital sexual contact.

Women at Work Outside the Home

Within the confines of her home, an Athenian woman carried out the routine domestic tasks mentioned earlier. Additionally, as we will see in Chapter 8, any Athenian cottage industry, if it existed, probably relied on the habitual occupants of the home, including women, for its workforce. Sometimes, too, free women worked outside the home, but undoubtedly at great cost to their respectability and self-esteem. Females of the citizen class who engaged in retail trade in the marketplace were sometimes held up to ridicule—as Euripides' mother was by the comic poet Aristophanes. A forensic text mentions the fact that citizen women, driven by necessity during the trying times of the Peloponnesian War, resorted to hiring themselves out as wet nurses—obviously something they would not have done had they a choice in the matter. Athenian cultural ideals permitted women to work, but only under the controlled conditions of the domestic household.

The Economic Rights of Athenian Women

The patriarchal orientation of Athenian society, already in evidence in constitutional arrangements, in the legal system, and now in the segregation and seclusion of women, operated with a vengeance in the economic sphere. Bluntly put, women possessed virtually no economic rights. The dowry accompanying a woman into marriage at no point became her own property. For the duration of the marriage, it remained in the custody of her husband; should the marriage come to an end, under most circumstances it was returned with her to her natal household. Inheritance, too, was an affair involving only males. If a man had legitimate sons, they divided their father's property equally among them. Daughters inherited nothing.

Mention was made above of the epiklerate. In the absence of sons, if a man had a daughter, she was legally designated an *epikleros,* meaning literally "with the estate" (but often mistranslated "heiress"). The law, reduced to its essentials, allowed for a kinsman of her father (according to a strict order, beginning with his brother, her paternal uncle) to marry her; if he could or would not, the privilege devolved to the next patrilateral kinsman, and so on. Once the epikleros had married and produced a son, that son (or sons) stood to inherit their maternal grandfather's estate. Thus the law, using the epikleros as an intermediary, had the effect of keeping the ancestral property within the family as defined by the male blood line. But again, at no point did the daughter, unlike a true heiress, ever come into possession of her father's property.

Finally, Athenian law prohibited a woman from engaging in a financial transaction of a value greater than one *medimnos*—a small amount, as one scholar has calculated, roughly equivalent to a week's grocery shopping for a typical family, thereby permitting her performance of routine domestic tasks. The sole property to which a woman was entitled was her "clothing and jewelry" (a frequent phrase in forensic texts), but even they, technically speaking, if acquired after the beginning of her marriage, belonged to her husband.

Widowhood, Divorce, and Remarriage

The wide gap in ages for males and females at first marriage made frequent widowhood a statistical certainty. Many wives, some while still relatively young, were predeceased by their husbands. Add to this natural cause the occasional heavy loss of male lives in warfare. On the female side, death of the mother in childbirth made many a husband a widower. For both males and females, the onset of then-untreatable diseases, such as the plague that swept through Athens early in the Peloponnesian War, would have brought untold marriages to a premature end.

A marriage might also end in divorce—by mutual consent or at the initiation of either party. The grounds were probably often infertility (for, after all, the purpose of a marriage was to produce legitimate children, especially sons) or female infidelity, to mention two plausible but not easily document-ed possibilities. A man divorced his wife simply by ordering her from his house. The woman who wished to divorce her husband, however, seems to have needed the help of a male citizen (usually a relative) and her divorce was valid only if a written report had been submitted to the archon. To this extent, the state reserved to itself the final say regarding a woman's marital status.

No dishonor was attached to divorce *per se* (dishonorable acts leading to divorce were, of course, another matter). Nor, whether the marriage had ended by death or by divorce, was either a man or a woman expected to remain celibate thereafter. (The *yiayias* of traditional modern Greece, clothed in black and perpetually faithful to their departed husbands, had no coun-terparts in ancient Athens.) Remarriages, in fact, occurred, and in a few doc-umented cases children were produced in the second marriage. For a woman, of course, the only alternative to remarriage was returning to the custody of a male member of her natal family. In Athenian citizen society, an "indepen-dent" woman of marriageable age was both a legal and a cultural contradic-tion in terms. Positively put, the primacy of marriage and childbearing, so deeply embedded in ancient Greek culture and so staunchly supported by the Athenian state, probably overrode any sentimental notion of loyalty to the for-mer spouse, if indeed a lasting affection had ever existed or developed in the first place.

CHILDREN

Why Have Children?

Thus far, the account given of marriage and the family has identified as motives for childbearing only those issuing from the concerns of the state with reproduction of the citizen class, the orderly transmission of property, and so on. But how did an Athenian husband and wife look at the situation? What were their motives for bearing children? The question is not as easy to answer as one might suppose. The reply that modern western cultures provide to such a question typically involves emotional feelings or disinterested higher principles transcending any selfish interests or prospects of personal benefit to the parent. For ancient Athenians, emotions probably played a part, but attending them, or constituting their basis, were numerous additional practical (or, to use a technical term, *instrumental*) purposes that were anything but disinterested. For one, legitimate sons (whether natural or adopted) alone provided heirs and the means of ensuring the continuation of the family and traditional names, as well as the maintenance of ancestral cults. Adult children, as suggested in Chapter 5, were, in the absence of pension plans, retirement communities, and nursing homes, the principal means of support of their parents in old age, so failure to reproduce could have dire consequences in the later stages of one's life. As long as older sons and daughters lived with their father and mother, they also provided an invaluable addition to the labor force of the household. Children afforded companionship, particularly for a house-bound mother, grandmother, or other female relative subject to socially enforced seclusion. Upon marriage, a grown son or daughter might provide an enduring link of social, economic, or even political value with another household. And so on. That such utilitarian calculations figured in an Athenian's decision to marry and to bear children is undeniable. What is open to question is whether, and to what extent, emotional (or "sentimental") feelings were an element in the production and raising of children. Naturally, the mere cataloguing of a number of particular cases of parents with such feelings, or of other parents without such feelings, would not suffice to demonstrate that ancient Athens resembled or did not resemble a modern Western society. What we are in search of is a societal ideal. Future study, particularly of contemporary literary texts, may one day provide the answer.

Childbirth, Birth Control, Exposure, and Infant Mortality

For an adult male, the most hazardous risk to life was posed by warfare. For an adult female, it was childbirth. The playwright Euripides made his Medea (a mother who presumably knew whereof she spoke) say, "I would rather stand in a battle line three times than give birth once" (*Medea*, lines 250–251). Even though apparently only females normally attended deliveries, with the result that we have no first-hand testimony on the subject, what clues do survive would tend to support her appraisal. As we have seen, Athenian girls typically married in their early teens. Because the onset of menstruation had probably occurred by this time, and because there is no reason to doubt that brides conceived soon after marrying, these very young mothers and their babies, medical science now tells us, would have been in statistically greater danger of complications. Furthermore, no conception of hygiene yet existed, although, since births took place in the home, at least ancient Athenian women were spared the unhealthy conditions of early modern hospitals. No physician was normally present—not that it would have mattered, given the fact that Greek medicine, since it was based not on dissection or other direct observation but on analogy with animals or deductions from theoretical postulates, badly misunderstood female reproductive anatomy. Rather, the expert in attendance was the midwife. Her ministrations, though sometimes reflecting inappropriate Greek cultural norms (regarding, for example, the woman's posture during delivery) or baseless superstitions (such as using only the left hand to deliver the baby), were nonetheless grounded in actual experience.

Still, the hazards of childbirth were formidable. To mention only one glaring deficiency, the Caesarean section had not yet been developed (the first recorded surgical removal of a fetus dates to about A.D. 1500). In the event the baby could not be delivered (if, for example, the presentation was breach or transverse), the mother could be saved only by removing the fetus through the use of techniques that invariably resulted in its death, if not injury to the mother as well. Even with such measures as these, maternal mortality has been estimated to have been as high as 10 to 20 percent. It is no wonder that so many Greek female divinities were attributed with a competence in human childbirth and that, following the hoped-for successful delivery, visits were sometimes made to their sanctuaries with offerings of thanks.

Childbirth had its public as well as its purely domestic dimension. We should expect as much, in view of the foregoing discussion of the state's fostering of families. According to a late scholarly source, the birth of a boy in Athens was heralded by hanging a crown of olive leaves on the front door; that of a girl by hanging a wad of wool. The point here is not the distinction between genders (or their symbolization) but the publicizing of the birth. Medea's line—delivered before an Athenian audience—goes a step further by comparing childbirth to warfare, the latter a quintessentially public act conducted only in the name of the state. Publicly displayed funerary relief sculptures portraying a woman in position for delivery marked the graves of women who presumably had died in childbirth. These are the beginnings of the sustained process of integrating the child into the social fabric of the Athenian state. Childbirth was not, any more than marriage, conceived as a purely personal act of self-fulfillment devoid of societal meaning.

Athenian families, we saw, were to be kept small. Sons, at least one but better two, were eagerly hoped for, as long as not too many daughters were acquired in the process. But how could family size be limited in the absence of the Pill, vasectomy, and tubal ligation? How could female births be checked? Circumstantial evidence suggests that, once the desired number of children was obtained, abstinence was practiced, a strategy made feasible by the alternative sexual outlets available to married males (see Chapter 8). Other methods of birth control are documented: coitus interruptus, occlusive agents, and spermicides, although none, as practiced in antiquity, could have been effective. In the event of an unwanted pregnancy, abortion remained an option. True, the Hippocratic oath prohibited physicians from administering a certain abortifacient, but Greek law (at least at Sparta and Athens) permitted abortion (provided the father had been duly consulted), and some of the philosophers, including two active in Athens, Plato and Aristotle, approved of abortion on general principles. No ancient Greek is recorded to have upheld any rights possessed by the fetus. Nor is such likely in view of the general Greek tolerance of a more drastic measure taken in the case of the actual birth of an unwanted child—exposure.

Exposure, meaning literally "a setting out," was the practice of abandoning a newborn outside the home, in the wilds, in a public place, and so on. Two observations are at once in order. First, exposure did *not* amount to infanticide, certainly for the Greeks, for the parents had not killed the child; rather, they had left its fate to the gods or to "fortune." Another distancing maneuver was to entrust the actual "setting out" to another person, probably in many instances the midwife who had delivered the baby. The second point is that, in fact, an exposed newborn probably often did survive, picked up to be raised into slavery, or to become the child of a childless couple, or when an exposed male was deviously substituted (without the father's knowledge) for an unwanted female newborn (the so-called "supposititious" child). What we do not know with any certainty is *which* newborns were most likely to be exposed, and for what reasons. One scholar identifies four "high-risk categories": (1) girls, (2) deformed or sickly infants, (3) illegitimate offspring, and (4) the offspring of slaves. Strong circumstantial cases could be made in favor of each of these groups. What about numbers? Another scholar conjecturally put the incidence of *female* exposure at 10 percent of female births. But the fact remains that, despite the popularity of exposure as a theme in Greek myth, legend, and literature, not a single authenticated case from classical Athens has come down to us. Indeed, it is likely that, although exposure was tolerated at Athens, it was not often practiced or was practiced with great reluctance. The principal reason for thinking this is that the nondocumentary sources just mentioned do nothing to disguise the extreme repugnance awakened by exposure. Guilt feelings or denial may be reflected by the popularity of the theme of the exposed child who is rescued, grows to adulthood, and returns home to be reunited with its parents. Not surprisingly, in postclassical times certain Greek states—Athens, however, not among them—did enact legislation limiting the practice of exposure.

Repugnance, guilt, and denial there may have been, but in the final analysis exposure was permitted, even advocated by leading Athenians. Does not the practice of exposure, whatever feelings of remorse may have attended it, indicate an extraordinary lack of affection for the newly born? The same question may be posed regarding infant mortality due to natural causes, which for ancient Greece has been estimated to have occurred at a rate as high as 30 to 40 percent in the first year of life. Such deaths were only rarely commemorated by burials with inscribed tombstones and, when they were, the death is never characterized in the epitaph by the formulaic word *untimely* (as was frequently the case, say, for a young adult). Apparently little note was taken of the loss of an infant. To explain this (to us) disturbing fact, social historians sometimes invoke the theory of parental "indifference." The theory ascribes the apparent absence of emotional involvement with the newly born to the very high rate of infant mortality. Because the risk of death was so high, the argument goes, parents withheld their involvement, thereby making bearable the loss of an infant, whether by natural causes or by exposure.

Alternatively, one could explain the same facts with reference, not to high infant mortality, but to ancient Greek parenting practices. Care for the infant was commonly entrusted to others (such as slaves or wet nurses), hence decreasing parental involvement. For the first several days, moreover, because the infant had not yet received a name (see the following section), it was without a real identity and thus would be less acutely missed. Even a named child, if it died, could be "replaced" by another, provided, one would assume, the new child was given the same name as its predecessor. (The normal Greek practice of naming sons after their fathers, or particularly their paternal grandfathers, would have fit easily with such a strategy.) Any of these practices, singly or in combination with the others, would have had the effect of softening the blow even in the presence of what we would regard as "normal" affection for the newborn.

Rites of Passage

The Athenian newborn came into the world without a social, familial, or personal identity. A valid approach to the subject of childrearing at Athens is to view it as a gradual process, punctuated at intervals by ceremonial "rites of passage," of establishing such an identity. At about five days, in a ritual called the *Amphidromia* (the "Running Around"), the infant was carried around the hearth of the house (as the source of warmth, heat for cooking, and light, a place of obvious practical and, for that reason, religious significance), possibly in order to ritually mark its entry into the household. Shortly thereafter was celebrated the Tenth Day rite, when the child was named and the father, putting to rest any uncertainty on the question of paternity, acknowledged the child as his. With the establishment of the child's membership in the household, of its parentage, and of its personal identity in the form of a name (often, as just noted, that of a parent or grandparent), the child was prepared to proceed to the next stages of childhood. These were not inconsequential formalities. Had the father refused, for example, to acknowledge his paternity on the Tenth Day, the child's further progress toward acceptance into respectable Athenian society would have been forestalled. If a boy, he would never have become a citizen or have been able to inherit his father's estate. If a girl, her own chances of ever marrying a citizen would have been virtually nil, since she herself would not have been "a city woman" and so capable of producing citizen children under the terms of Pericles' law on citizenship.

The Conceptualization of Childhood

Any assessment of childhood in Athens must deal with a major theoretical issue confronting students of this and other human societies; namely, that concerning the conceptualization of childhood. Some peoples, as in modern Western societies, conceive of children in terms of distinctly childlike behaviors and attitudes which are fundamentally dissimilar from those of adults. This is the conceptualization with which we are familiar. But other peoples, according to a theory first propounded in connection with historical study of modern Europe, see children as essentially immature adults. What makes children children, in this view, is that their latent or potential adult capacities—physical, intellectual, moral—have not yet been brought to the point of full adult realization. Children differ from grownups only quantitatively, not qualitatively. A child in other words is only an incomplete, miniature man or woman. What about the ancient Athenians?

The record seems to reveal a mixture of the two conceptions. Toys, at least some of which must have been manufactured by adults (that is, by the "conceptualizers" of childhood), included hoops, tops, and rattles, all of which seem child-specific and unrelated to any future adult activity. But others—rocking horses, play carts, small-scale houses, and model ships, as well as dolls—*might* have been designed as the miniature adult's versions of the real thing. Games, more straightforward in their implications, look like pure child's play. Consider, for example, a dice game called knucklebones, and the Athenian equivalents of blindman's buff, piggyback, and duck-duck-goose. Artistic portrayals might be thought to offer decisive indications, but again their evidence is equivocal. Until the late fifth century, Attic painters depicted children as adults, only decreased in stature. Later, they begin to look more and more like real children. How to explain the change? Two explanations are possible. *Either* Athenians saw children as small adults (as reflected in the early depictions), while artists (but not the rest of Athenian society) learned in time to portray them more faithfully, as a purely technical innovation. *Or* Athenians always saw children as children, but it took time for painters to break the habit of depicting them as smaller versions of the grown-up figures they were more used to executing, and to conform to the cultural standard.

As a final court of appeal one could also look to family activities involving children in company with adults. Children joined their parents in religious observances (such as ritual sacrifices), a possible indication of shared (adult) status. But it is equally possible that the reason for the inclusion of children was to promote family solidarity and perhaps even, as one scholar has suggested, to secure the favorable acknowledgment of the children as children by the gods. Normal domestic routines were, in any case, anything but egalitarian. Minors, like citizen women, were of course absent from the aristocratic all-male adult symposia (see Chapter 5). At typical meals, children ate with their mothers and, if in the company of their fathers, sat on chairs while the adult men reclined (on couches, propped up on one elbow in the classical manner). Such evidence indicates a division of the family between adult males and all others, the ranking of minors with (disfranchised) women, and, to return to our question, the incapacity of children. If boys and girls were conceptualized as latent adults, arrangements within the house preserve little evidence of the fact.

The Education of Children

The early stages of "education" (a broad term which here will include, besides formal schooling, practical training and socialization) amounted to the child's modeling on the parent (or other adult) of the same gender. A girl entered marriage in her early teens equipped to shoulder some of the domestic routines detailed earlier in the chapter. Her teachers had been her mother, very possibly a paternal grandmother, or female slaves. She would receive no further education, formal or otherwise. Fathers were in effect required by a law of Solon to provide their sons with a trade and in the case of farmers whose sons would inherit their land, the trade in question must have been the father's trade—namely, farming. Those parents with loftier ambitions for their sons, such as higher elective office in the democracy, were compelled to go beyond the household. No teachers, fathers probably lacked the requisite skills, very possibly had no time, and were culturally disposed to spend their free time not with their children but with other males outside the family. A school or professional tutor was a necessity.

Institutionalized education as we know it, whether public or private, hardly existed in classical Athens. What "higher" educational opportunities were available were provided by freelance teachers operating on an entrepreneurial basis and without the support of public funding or subsidization of any kind. They were accessible only to those who could pay their fees. No law mandated a minimum level of education or competence, even for future citizens. From about the age of six to fourteen, boys received instruction in "grammar" (reading, writing, and study of the poets), music (singing to the lyre), and athletics. This curriculum was driven largely by practical considerations, rather than by a high valuation of the acquisition of knowledge for its own sake. Literacy was indispensable for any citizen who aspired to an active role in the democracy; music may have been cultivated for its social value in the upper echelons of citizen society; and athletics were undoubtedly regarded as good preparation for the more generally competitive nature of Athenian public life. Beyond fourteen, ability to pay (as well as inclination) became the deciding factor, limiting further opportunities to families of substantial means. Notoriously high fees were charged by the sophists, professional itinerant (and non-Athenian Greek) teachers who offered instruction in rhetoric or "the art of persuasion"—again, with obvious potential application to a public career in the democracy. Girls, since they received no education beyond the acquisition of domestic skills, probably remained, in a literal as well as a legal sense, essentially intellectual children. Not a single Athenian woman of the citizen class is known to have made even the most trifling contribution to the high culture of classical Athens. The lone woman to have made a mark in Athenian intellectual circles was, significantly, the noncitizen former slave and high-class prostitute Aspasia, the lover (and later the wife) of the politician-general Pericles. Thus the educational "system," by its specific content or (in the case of females) total absence, prepared men and women for their respective adult roles in the open-air and domestic arenas of Athenian society.

Integration of the Child into the Athenian Community

Socialization of the young and their preparation for adult roles in the Athenian community had still another dimension, in addition to the parts played by family members and formal teachers. Despite the postponement of citizenship for males until about age twenty and its outright denial to females for life, both popular ideology and institutional arrangements expressed the state's essentially parental attitude toward the children of the citizen class. That is, the state itself, like a parent or a teacher, played its own role in the maturation of Athenian boys and girls. Figuratively, the land of Attica could be portrayed as the "mother" of Athenians. Athens was also of course, anticipating practice in later ages, the "fatherland." Institutionally, under the classical democracy, the state extended its resources (as we saw earlier) to raise to adulthood the children of citizen fathers who had died in warfare and to dower the daughters of the indigent. To illustrate the point somewhat differently, in archaic times, Draco's law of homicide placed responsibility for avenging a citizen's murder on the victim's near relatives. In contrast, the government of the classical democracy, through the extension of the criminal justice system, took this role upon itself, thereby usurping what had once been a function of the private family. The government was by degrees assuming the role of parent to the state's children. It will come as no surprise, therefore, to find that the state allocated public roles to both boys and girls in official functions. Statewide public religious festivals afforded the principal opportunities, with provision made for children generally or, more pertinently for the point about socialization, for boys and girls separately.

Boys, for example, were regularly recruited for choruses which competed in the singing of lyric poems at various public festivals. (The organizers of the choruses were the wealthy holders of liturgies appointed for that purpose; see Chapter 5.) Because the chorus represented a phyle, and because each boy was selected from the phyle of his father, the competitions had the added benefit of introducing the youths to the administrative apparatus within which they would carry out their future public tasks as citizens. Equally to the point, the competitions were conducted on a public stage before a public audience seated in the principal public venues of the city. They were not, in other words, the ancient equivalent of a ballet or piano recital witnessed only by relatives and friends.

The same characterization applies to the public athletic events in which boys competed, with the difference that the competition was on an individual basis and for that reason all the more appropriate to its societal context. An emerging individualism and the *agon,* or "contest," wherein those individuals competed, were among the hallmarks of Athenian public life of the classical period.

But for girls the situation was entirely different, reflecting the contrasting socialization patterns of females. Negatively, no Athenian female singing groups existed, despite the earlier example of such assemblages at Sparta and the prominence of adult female choruses (played by males in female costume) in contemporary Athenian drama. Part of the explanation must be that girls, as we saw, were not trained in music (as was the case at Sparta), such attainments being the exclusive reserve of disreputable *hetaerae.* What few public roles were accorded to girls were of a ritual nature, but with a decidedly domestic slant. Take the Symbol Carriers, two or four in number, who, at age seven, were charged with weaving the cloak to be draped over the cult statue of Athena during the Panathenaia, with tending the sacred olive tree of Athena, and with carrying baskets (of grain?) on their heads to the shrine of Aphrodite on the slopes of the Acropolis. Two other girls called "Workers" were responsible for washing the robes that draped the wooden image of Athena of the City. No boy, nor (for that matter) a male of any age, is known to have been assigned tasks of this type. It is obvious that the domestic routines allocated to females by Athenian society were being acted out publicly and under the aegis of the official state religion. The purpose was presumably to dignify such routines; to show their vital importance to the well-being of the community; and to provide ideal exemplars of appropriate female behavior for both participants and onlookers.

Some social historians have found additional significance in the fact that these festivals and ceremonies brought out of their homes and joined together in a communal activity girls who, in view of their general confinement both before and after marriage, would see each other only rarely, if ever. These were opportunities to "compare notes," so to speak; to evaluate one's own life in the light of the experiences of one's peers; and even to develop a kind of group consciousness. Such consciousness very possibly, readers of Attic comedy may reflect, underlies the female solidarity of Aristophanes' imaginative, but probably essentially true-to-life, representations of women in his *Lysistrata, Women at the Thesmorphoria,* and *Women of the Assembly*—all plays first produced before classical Athenian audiences. Whether such an effect was actually intended by the authorities is of course another matter altogether.

Rites of Passage (continued)

Through the combination of home instruction, formal schooling, and participation in public activities, Athenian children were prepared for the roles they would play in adult society. What remained now was, resuming the process launched soon after birth with the Amphidromia and Tenth Day ceremonies, to formally and publicly mark the final stages of the passage from childhood to adulthood. The relevant ceremonies are:

• *Admission to the phratry.* At about age sixteen, boys and possibly girls were introduced to the phratry, or "brotherhood," during the festival called Apatouria. Although the brotherhoods were private organizations, it is believed that all citizens belonged to them, so to that extent admission to the phratry marked a step toward full acceptance in the citizen body. That admission required the affirmative vote of the membership of the applicant's father's phratry. The father was required to demonstrate the child's legitimacy (that is, that the child was in fact his by a duly betrothed Athenian woman). The transition to a higher level of maturity was marked ritually by a formal cutting of the child's hair.

• *Admission to the* genos, *or "clan."* Members of upper-class families, but not the great bulk of the citizen population, belonged to clans, now believed to have been elite social organizations of a fundamentally religious or cultic nature. Sons were admitted to the clan of their father.

• *Admission to the deme.* During his eighteenth year, a boy was admitted to the deme of his father provided that the father was able to demonstrate his son's majority and legitimacy. Successful passage of these tests, admission to the deme, and the entry of the boy's name on the official register of the deme marked the first official acknowledgment of his existence by the state (both the Amphidromia and Tenth Day, by contrast, had been wholly private ceremonies). Ancient texts characterize enrollment in the deme as alternately "departure from childhood" and "entry into manhood."

• *Service in the* Ephebeia, *or "Youth Corps."* Following admission to the deme, Athenian youths spent the next two years in mandatory military training and service in the *Ephebeia,* or "Youth Corps," in and around Attica (see Chapter 8). At the completion of the second year, the ephebes formally entered the citizen body. Because the second year was spent on a tour of remote border forts, commentators have noted that ephebic service taken in its entirety approximated the completion of a formal rite of passage. To wit, separation and exclusion from the community were followed by a final phase: the rite of reincorporation.

Two general observations are in order. First, these ceremonies amount to a progressive movement away from the private domestic setting toward full integration in the public community of Athenian citizens: membership in the residential household (Amphidromia); in the family as defined by descent (Tenth Day); in the genos (aristocrats only) and the phratry (Apatouria); in the village component of the state, the deme; and finally in the full citizen body itself (completion of the Ephebeia). The second observation is prompted by the process of partial duplication by the state of the tests of majority and

legitimacy, for the entrance requirements of the phratry more or less coincided with those requirements imposed by the deme a short time thereafter.
Why this duplication? Why were government officials simply not satisfied with
the verdicts of the phratries? One answer, probably sufficient in itself, is that
the central government, whatever estimation it may have had of the reliabili-
ty of the phratries, undoubtedly wished to reserve for itself final judgment on
acceptability of candidates for citizenship. But another is that the state was co-
opting the arrangements of the private sector by deliberately mimicking them
in its own bureaucratic procedures. The state, in other words, could compete
with the phratries, while compelled to leave them intact, by simply replicating
their functions within a constitutional setting. Thus the apparent duplication
of function by "state" and "society."

Girls were, with the possible exception of the phratry, excluded from
this process altogether. Beyond the initial rites associated with childbirth, the
principal transition remaining for a female was marriage. Marriage marked
her movement from the household of her birth to that of her husband, thus,
in contrast with the male's movement into the public sphere, confirming her
perpetual restriction to the private domestic world.

OLD AGE

As we will see in examining the career of the Athenian male citizen, the sixtieth year marked a landmark in a man's life. No longer liable to military call-
ups, as a fifty-nine-year-old he spent a year serving as a state-appointed arbitrator in the judicial system. At home, this was also about the time when, with the
arrival of his first-born son at full adulthood, he may have stepped down as
head of his household. Sixty is, therefore, for Athens, a reasonable point to
take as marking the onset of old age (for the details on the periodization of the
citizen career, see Chapter 8). Luckily, work done decades ago by a classics
scholar provides us, as a starting point for our discussion, a rough estimate of
the percentage of people aged sixty or older for the whole of Greece: about 10
percent. (This figure is probably on the high side, for it is based on a survey of
funerary inscriptions in which the age at death was recorded. A man or woman
who had lived to a remarkably great age is more likely to have had age at death
thus recorded than a person dying at a more ordinary age.) For Athens, surviving documents show that, later in the fourth century B.C., when a year's class
of ephebes numbered about five hundred, the same year's class of arbitrators
numbered just over one hundred—a survival rate of about 20 percent over the
years of military service. This finding is important, for it demonstrates the presence in Athens of a sizable body of more or less "retired" people among the citizen class. True, infant mortality, maternal death in childbirth, and military
casualties took a heavy toll, but once an Athenian man had reached the landmark age of thirty or thereabouts, and a woman had ceased childbearing, the

chances of survival to a ripe old age were not bad, given the relatively favorable living conditions enjoyed by the citizen class.

Public Roles of the Old

The point about "retirement" should not be overstated. Withdrawal from public life was a gradual process and, in some cases, probably never carried to completion. Thus various types and stages of engagement in affairs by the old are detectable in the sources. For example, in the Homeric poems, those revered repositories of archaic Greek traditions, the advice of an elderly Nestor or Priam was accorded great respect. Nor was this a mere literary convention, for the same deference to advanced age is manifest in archaic Greek institutions. At Sparta, the Council of Elders (all sixty or older) played important consultative and legislative roles; and, at Athens, the Council of the Areopagus, prior to its decline under the radical democracy, had wielded a similar authority. The Athenian arbitrators, all in their sixtieth year, were just mentioned. Also at Athens, the jurors are typically portrayed in Aristophanic comedy as elderly citizens; because the pool of volunteers was very large (six thousand, or up to a quarter of the citizen population), it is evident that substantial numbers of old men participated in the court system. In the military organization, although their regular active service as combatants had long ceased, old men were still employed as messengers, were posted as guards on the city's fortifications, and, in recognition of their extensive experience, were sometimes valued as advisors in matters of policy and strategy. Various religious functions were also placed in the hands of old, male and female. In the private sphere, old men frequently figure as *paedagogues* (literally "leaders of children"), conducting their charges, invariably boys, to and from their schools or tutors. They are also encountered as participants in intellectual pursuits. The elderly Athenian philosopher Socrates is but one of an extraordinarily large number of elderly "lovers of wisdom." On a less lofty level, sources depict old men engaged in story-telling, gossiping, board games, and, among the elite, as guests at aristocratic drinking parties. Women, once past menopause, seem no longer to have been subject to the confining conventions of their younger counterparts, but even so elderly females are only rarely seen in public. The one extradomestic role that has left a consistent mark on the record is that of nurse—a predictable extension into later years of a typical female domestic function. All told, the accumulation of evidence is impressive. By no means could it be said that the aged had been abandoned or forgotten by Greek society.

Popular Attitudes About the Old

Not all of these "jobs" can be dismissed as low-risk, nonconsequential leavings of the more active younger age groups. To be an arbitrator, juror, advisor, or priest or priestess signified Greek society's willingness to bestow on the old a meaningful degree of responsibility. It may come as a surprise, then, that at Athens and throughout Greece generally the old were treated with contempt and abuse. The phenomenon can only partly be explained by the human race's universal aversion to the debilitating effects of advancing age and the approach of death. The comic stage in particular held up for ridicule such figures as the dirty old man, the elderly miser, the aging drunk, the old hag chasing after a handsome young man, and so on. The stock, stereotypical caste of some of these characters, in combination with the writer's evident expectation that they would get a laugh, suggests that they represented well-known and common features of the old and that people found those features funny. Why did Athenians find so ridiculous the very class of people, among them some of their own citizens, to whom they were simultaneously entrusting positions of high responsibility and commanding considerable respect?

An answer is suggested by the specific character of some of these comic figures. What made the dirty old man funny to the Athenian audience was the spectacle of his attempting to engage in an activity (namely, sex) normally appropriate (in the Greek public's estimation) for a much younger man. Each period of life had its own appropriate patterns of conduct and attitude, and an old man could only make a fool of himself when he tried to sustain or resume the habits of his youth. Perhaps it is a universal tendency of at least some of the old not to give in gracefully to the decline of one's vital powers, but in the case of Athens there were additional, exacerbating factors. One was the prevalence of the youth culture in classical Greece. That culture is illustrated by the myths of gods and goddesses in the prime of life, who never age. It is illustrated further by the choice of subjects in contemporary artistic portrayals of human beings; the vast majority are youthful, and even old subjects are presented in an idealized form devoid of any of the undesirable marks of advancing age. Resistance to and loathing of aging must have helped to foster in the old a desire, doomed to end in laughable failure, to imitate the ways of the young.

What Athenians *did* value in older Athenians was their accumulated experience—especially so because advanced age typically rendered the old immune to the impulsiveness and emotional volatility of younger men and women. Age and appropriate behavior coincided, however, in the socially approved roles of arbitrator, juror, paedagogue, and nurse.

Legal Protection of the Old in Athens

But the abuse of the old, at least at Athens, did not end with a few laughs at their expense in the theater. Such abuse extended to neglect or even violence. The following points of Athenian law imply as much:

- It was illegal for an Athenian to strike a parent.
- A law declared that an Athenian who failed to teach his son a trade was no longer entitled to care by that son in his old age (the impli-

cation being that the old were not always cared for by their grown sons).

- A law required an Athenian to provide his parents with a proper burial.

What is the societal context of these legal measures to ensure the proper treatment of aged parents by their adult children?

It was on adult children that, in the absence of pensions and public (or private) institutions for the care of the elderly, the responsibility for the well-being of aged parents rested. True, Athens provided small payments from public funds to those who were infirm and thus unable to earn a living, and free meals for life in the Prytaneion to distinguished benefactors of the state. Some of the beneficiaries of these grants happened to be or to become old, but it was not by virtue of their old age *per se* that they received public assistance. So, the expected caretakers were one's grown children—above all, sons. Evidently, not all sons or daughters saw fit to meet the obligation society had imposed on them, or did so only in response to the coercive force of the legal system. Several factors may have contributed to this state of affairs.

Individualism, with its gradual encroachments on the traditional sacrosanctity of family-based codes of behavior, had loosened the bonds of obligation between relatives, even close relatives. The flourishing youth culture, just mentioned, guaranteed that, in a world of young and old individuals, the higher valuation would be placed on the former and younger family members would be inclined to neglect or abuse their older kin. But a more specific factor involves the handing over of family property by the older to the younger generation (see Chapter 8). Prior to the handover, the adult son, eager to launch his own household, more likely than not was champing at the bit. The control and ownership of the estate must have been a constant source of conflict, but until the actual transfer was made, the elderly parents held a powerful card. Afterward, when that card had been played and the parents had surrendered what remained of their leverage over their children—then, one would guess, the Athenian laws became especially applicable and necessary for the protection of the aged. Without an external source of retirement income or institutions to which the old might flee, elderly parents found themselves in a very vulnerable position indeed. What remains quite unknown is the severity of the situation addressed by these laws. Were they, given the generally decent treatment of the old, designed to keep in line only a small minority of abusive or neglectful children? Or were Athenians generally disrespectful of their elderly parents?

The natural effects of aging, in combination with the absence of effective medical treatments, inevitably resulted in varying degrees of misery for the elderly. At the pessimistic extreme, the inhabitants of the island of Chios were said to have regularly practiced suicide on reaching the age of sixty. Even the philosophers, themselves typically old men, though bestowing praise upon a long life, freely admitted the drawbacks of advanced age. Yes, a famous exception is provided by an aged speaker in Plato's *Republic*, a rich man named Cephalus. Discounting the benefits afforded by his great wealth, Cephalus finds compensation in the fact that old age confers on him freedom from the passions of youth and thus enables him to participate in intellectual activities. He insists that an upright man, suitably raised in sound values, will actually experience happiness in his final years. But such a Pollyanna view was probably less typical than that of Plato's own teacher, Socrates, who, on the eve of his own execution, welcomed death because it would permit him to avoid the torments of old age.

Nor did contemporary ideological systems offer much consolation. Beliefs in an afterlife anything like a Greek's life on earth are not encountered. And the secular ideal that immortality resided in the permanence of one's achievements would certainly not have appealed to the ordinary Greeks whose accomplishments did not approach the standard normally required for such lasting recognition. Ultimately, at least at Athens, it was in significant part on the legal system that aged citizens depended to make what they could of the final chapters of their lives, because that legal system ensured their continuing care and civilized treatment by their grown children.

Suggested Readings

On the ancient Greek family, a readable account by a recognized authority is W. K. Lacey, *The Family in Classical Greece* (Ithaca, 1984; first published 1968). Among many writings on ancient Greek women, introductory or comprehensive studies include S. Pomeroy's pioneering *Goddesses, Whores, Wives, and Slaves: Women in Classical Antiquity* (New York, 1975); and, more recently, E. Cantarella, *Pandora's Daughters: The Role and Status of Women in Greek and Roman Antiquity*, trans. M. B. Fant with a foreword by M. R. Lefkowitz (Baltimore, 1987). D. M. Schaps, *Economic Rights of Women in Ancient Greece* (Edinburgh, 1979), and R. Just, *Women in Athenian Law and Life* (New York, 1989), deal incisively with specialized but transcendentally important aspects of the subject. Similarly focused are G. Sissa, *Greek Virginity* (Cambridge, Mass., 1990), and N. H. Demand, *Birth, Death, and Motherhood in Classical Greece* (Baltimore, 1994). Interpersonal dynamics within the household are speculatively treated by P. Slater, *The Glory of Hera: Greek Mythology and the Greek Family* (Princeton, 1992). An excellent collection of ancient sources in English is M. R. Lefkowitz and M. B. Fant, eds., *Women's Life in Greece and Rome* (Baltimore, 1982). Children in Greek antiquity have been well treated by M. Golden, *Children and Childhood in Ancient Athens* (Toronto, 1990), a work to which I am in several places indebted. On old age in Greece, the scholarly work referred to in the text is B. E. Richardson, *Old Age Among the Ancient Greeks* (Baltimore, 1933). A more recent and far more penetrating overview will be found in G. Minois, *History of Old Age: From Antiquity to the Renaissance* (Chicago, 1989), ch. 3, "The Greek World: Sad Old Age."

For a cross-cultural investigation by an authority on classical antiquity, see S. C. Humphreys, *The Family, Women, and Death: Comparative Studies* (London and Boston, 1983). For an accessible and well-documented overview of the entire life course, see the excellent work of R. Garland, *The Greek Way of Life* (Ithaca, 1990).

Chapter 8. Farmer, Crafter, and Soldier

With the general domestic context of the Athenian citizen in mind, it is now possible to turn to that same citizen's everyday life and, to a limited extent, to that of his dependents and of noncitizens as well. Not surprisingly, that life was centered on, if not entirely taken over by, work in one form or another. Naturally, the people of Attica found time for other activities—entertainments, athletics, socializing, high cultural pursuits, or travel—differing in degree and kind according to individual circumstances. But work was at the center. Unless we can first understand the Athenian in his (or her) capacity as a worker, activities on the periphery of that center will remain without reference point or meaning.

PHASES OF THE ATHENIAN CITIZEN'S LIFE COURSE

It would be helpful at the outset to isolate landmarks or turning points in the citizen's career to serve as a sort of skeleton on which to drape our discussion. As it happens, the life of the citizen male was periodically punctuated by various rituals, ceremonies, or thresholds of eligibility which served to mark an Athenian's entry into or exit from the successive phases of his public existence. Chapter 7 took the story of the young citizen up to his enrollment in his father's deme, whereby, following approval of the deme's decision by the courts and the Council, he acquired the status of citizen. From this point he was eligible to participate and vote in meetings of the Assembly. Here is our first landmark. However, although he had joined the sovereign Demos, the new citizen had yet to gain access to the full privileges of citizenship. That came later, at another turning point—the one that (if any) marked the beginning of full adulthood—a decade down the road, around age thirty. Both "state" and "society" are involved. Constitutionally, at thirty an Athenian first became eligible for membership in the Council of Five Hundred, for service in the court system as a juror, and for election to the generalship. At home, this was the age when an Athenian could expect his father (if his father was still alive) to turn over to him the family property—in most cases a farm. Although his parents would continue to reside with him, the son now assumed leadership of the household for the first time. Not surprisingly, the recommendations given by Greek writers from Hesiod on for the age of a male's first marriage converge, again, at age thirty. With the father's house in his ownership or control, the son was at last in a position to establish a family of his own.

The agreement between the timing of constitutional and domestic careers cannot be accidental; it reflects once again the symbiotic interdependency of state and society. Ownership of property and family leadership were evidently interpreted constitutionally as signifying eligibility to exercise the weightier responsibilities of government service.

The next major landmark occurred at age fifty-nine (the "sixtieth year"), when public and private schedules were again in synch. In that year, responsibility for military service ended and, for a single year, the aging citizen was subject to mandatory duty as an arbitrator. At home, if the typical career had proceeded on schedule, that same citizen entered his old age, as his first son (if born soon after his own marriage at age thirty) prepared to receive the family property and begin his new household.

Needless to say, except where minimum ages of eligibility were imposed by law, these demographic landmarks do not necessarily tell us anything about the life of any particular Athenian man. Many never saw thirty, much less sixty. Although marriage amounted to a culturally imposed universal, age at first marriage naturally varied, and the birth and gender of children were no more governable in antiquity than they are today. Some "handovers" took place before the father reached sixty—or never took place at all. And so on. These phases should be regarded as typical or modal only. At the same time, our skeletal career does have the useful effect of bringing into high relief an unsettling question about the lives of a great many Athenian men. What did they do between the acquisition of citizenship about age twenty and their full entry into Athenian state and society around age thirty? Although physically mature, men in this age bracket normally possessed no house or (if farms were in question) source of livelihood and, for that reason, could not marry and reproduce. Only the son of a very wealthy man would have had his own bachelor apartment in town. The typical son must have continued to live in his father's house, thereby undoubtedly giving rise to domestic conflict as the son grew impatient to assume leadership of the household. In addition, because all women of the citizen class, as we saw in Chapter 7, were off limits, one naturally wonders about possible sexual outlets during these years of youthful exuberance. Brothels, some maintained by the state, were within the reach of most, if not all, Athenian men. The rich also enjoyed the favors of the high-priced but cultivated noncitizen women euphemistically called *hetaerae*, or "escorts." Some scholars, too, have even suggested that it was during these years that ostensibly heterosexual men, either now married or later to marry, engaged in "bisexual" or "pseudohomosexual" pursuits (to borrow two terms used in the scholarly literature). Readers of some of the philosopher Plato's dialogues will recall such liaisons, characteristically involving an older "lover" pursuing a younger "beloved." (Arguing against such a suggestion is the fact that the "beloved" might be too young, the "lover" too old to fit into the span of ages under consideration here.)

But there is one activity that may with confidence be assigned to these years of frustration and conflict—active military service. Eligibility for call-up extended from about age twenty (after the completion of two years in the Ephebeia, or Youth Corps) to the sixtieth year, but it is self-evident that it was the younger, stronger, more compliant, and easily trained of these men who saw disproportionately more frequent service. (Since call-ups were by age groups—twenty-one-year-olds, twenty-two-year-olds, and so on—it was possible for the authorities to control the age composition of a mobilization.) Because men in their twenties had no wives or children, their deaths would not have had the same catastrophic consequences as in the case of older men. There would have been no property to be litigated among conflicting claimants; no orphaned (i.e. fatherless) children to be raised at state expense; no need for a widowed wife to return to her natal household with no guarantee that she could be betrothed again. Once past the high-risk years of military service, survivors to the fourth decade of life would then, on this model, be free to assume the responsibilities of family and property with relatively less danger of death.

FARMING AND THE CITIZEN FARMER

At Athens, the private ownership of land was, legally speaking, monopolized by members of the citizen class. When a foreigner received a grant of citizenship in Athens, the list of privileges accompanying the grant often included "possession of land and house," with the implication that such possession was the exclusive right of Athenians. What proportion of citizens, then, were actually able to make use of this right? Outside Athens, ownership of land was occasionally the basis of citizenship or at least of membership in a ruling elite. At Sparta, from the beginning of the Lycurgan regime that was in place in the archaic and classical periods, each citizen possessed a theoretically equal allotment of land. The produce it yielded permitted the Spartan to pay the dues on which the maintenance of his citizen status depended. At Syracuse and Samos, ruling classes were called Land Sharers, with the implication that it was precisely *landed* wealth that justified their social and political preeminence. No such rule or practice is known to have obtained at Athens (in fact, as we saw, the franchise had been extended to Solon's *thetes*, who in many instances must have been landless). Even so, it is clear that the great majority of Athenians possessed real property of significant value. In 403 B.C. it was proposed before the legislature that citizenship be restricted to landowners. The proposer noted that five thousand persons would be disfranchised under the terms of the restriction. Given a citizen body of thirty thousand, five-sixths will have been property owners; of twenty thousand, three-fourths. Classical Athens, for all its urban growth, its urban occupations, its industry, and its occasional rejection of rural ways and values, had remained a city of farmers.

The Athenian Farm

Smallholder or, to cite a synonymous archaic English term, *yeoman* best describes the condition of the typical Athenian farmer. To put it in economic language, it appears that most Athenian farms had stabilized at the *subsistence* level; that is, at the point at which production was just sufficient to sustain the owner and his family. No surplus, at least in typical years, would be produced. Such a farm, according to a recent study, would measure about 55 to 60 *plethra* (or roughly 5 hectares or 12½ acres). Significantly, this agrees with the minimum acreage that could profitably be worked by a yoke, or pair of oxen, the complement of draft animals ideally owned by Athenian farmers. Additional factors also tended to work against the preservation or creation of farms appreciably larger than a subsistence plot. Dowries in the form of farmland and the division of estates among two or more legitimate sons would have rapidly reduced larger holdings to smallholder dimensions. Another limiting factor was the supply of labor. If the owner, in the pursuit of the widely held ideal of self-sufficiency, hoped to work the land by himself (perhaps with the aid of family members), the acreage could not be large. Still other restrictions were imposed by, first, military service, which might require the owner's absence for months at a time; and, second and uniquely for Athens, the option of participation in the democratic institutions (Assembly, courts, magistracies, and especially the Council of Five Hundred), which would require one's physical presence in the urban center for periods ranging from a single day to a full year. To be sure, alternative sources of labor were available, but any recourse to them would tend to create an unwelcome loss of independence.

Of course, not every farm conformed to this model. Some, including any owned by the Solonian thetes, were appreciably smaller. These Athenians had no oxen but worked their tiny plots by hand and, by applying manure, kept the ground in continuous production rather than allowing portions to lie fallow. Nonetheless, these farms alone could not always have supported their owners, and the owners were probably often forced to supplement their incomes by other means, including selling their labor to more prosperous citizens at harvest or other peak-labor times. At the opposite extreme, some farms did exceed the scale of the subsistence operation, but by no great degree. A recent study has noted that the size of the largest known Athenian farms, about 300 plethra, agrees with the recommendations of the philosophers Plato and Aristotle that the largest estate not exceed the smallest by more than four or five times, respectively. These recommendations may reflect the actual conditions of the city of Athens, where the philosophers resided. The point is that, as ancient societies go, this is a modest degree of variation. One need only think of the enormous estates of late Republican Rome, worked by gangs of slaves captured in Rome's foreign wars. There were, of course, some very wealthy Athenians, but their wealth did not take the form of arable land holdings in Attica.

At no point, as in the case of Italy, had giant plantations been pieced together from the tiny plots of dispossessed smallholders. Athenian farmers had succeeded in holding their own against the forces of indebtedness, climatic change, or failure of nerve which constantly threatened to bring the subsistence farmer to ruin. This conclusion is ripe with ramifications. If the great majority of citizens were landowners, they could all participate, physically and emotionally, in a societal regime that attached great social and sentimental value to the ownership of land. Ideologically, these same facts made possible in the political sphere the upholding of the egalitarian ethos underlying many of the institutions and procedures of the democratic constitutional apparatus (see Chapter 6). The relative homogeneity and solidarity of the citizen body were ultimately grounded in the essentially uniform participation of those same citizens in a subsistence-scale agrarian economy. The ideals of Athenian democracy had had their beginnings in the fields of Attica.

Crops and Stock

In the early days of Athens, the principal crops had been cereals—wheat and especially barley. These had been, and probably remained, the plantings favored by the wealthy Eupatrid aristocrats who had laid claim to the rich farmlands of the plains of Attica. But the Mediterranean climate, in combination with the peculiar character of the topography and soils of Attica, permitted a far wider range of crops. By the time of Solon, parts of Attica were under cultivation with so-called cash crops, so called because, unlike the grain crops produced primarily for consumption by the owner-farmer himself, they were produced for sale on the market. The cash crops of ancient Athens are the trademark products of modern Greek agriculture, known to every alert visitor to the country (or to a Greek restaurant): the grapevine (for wine), the olive (for oil), and various fruits including the fig. Not only the weather of the region, but also the hilly, thin, and rocky earth of Attica, while useless for cereal crops, were particularly suitable to these new plantings. Once introduced, the vine, olive, and fruits enjoyed great success, rapidly raising the formerly disadvantaged owners of these farms to a level of considerable prosperity. These "new rich," as noted in Chapter 5, are believed by some historians to have been among the beneficiaries of Solon's new income-class system introduced early in the sixth century B.C.

Besides raising crops, Athenian farmers devoted much of their resources, effort, and time to stock raising. Again, the practice of modern Greeks accurately preserves the conditions prevailing in antiquity. Sheep, goats, pigs, and poultry were the primary forms of livestock. Milk and cheese from sheep and goats (visitors to modern Greece are sometimes surprised to observe the general absence of cow's milk and milk products) and probably eggs from poultry were staples of the subsistence diet. Sheep supplied wool. All livestock provided manure and, if and when slaughtered, hides. Meat was another matter. Animal flesh was not a regular component of the ancient Greek diet. Fish, at least in the urban (or coastal) settings, was far more frequently encountered. But the consumption of meat was mostly limited to the occasions of private or public sacrifices, particularly the latter, where numerous animals were slaughtered and their flesh divided among the attendees at public expense. The smallholder did not kill his sheep or goat—much less the oxen that pulled his plow—to put meat on the table. Pigs, it is true, were raised for consumption, but they are mentioned most often in the context of sacrifices or as being brought to market for sale. They were not normally raised for slaughter by individual farmer-breeders.

Farmers took care that their stock animals not make excessive demands on their arable land. If the animals were not penned and fed fodder, they could, as a recent work has emphasized, have been grazed in the woods, on otherwise useless wasteland, on the stubble of cereal crops, or on the weeds growing on fallow land before its next use. Larger animals, however, would have required a greater investment and, in the case of our smallholder, an excessive diversion of arable land to grazing. Most Athenians probably did not own more than the two oxen required for plowing, so the slaughter of either a bull or a cow was, again, entirely out of the question. It is for this same reason that horses, too, remained a highly prized luxury beyond the reach of all but the most prosperous Athenians. Besides, horses did not repay the investment as draft animals (the poor man's alternative to the ox was a mule or donkey), and of course horseflesh was not eaten.

Even given these limitations, a considerable range of options lay open for the Greek (and especially the Athenian) smallholder. This is one of the fundamental facts of ancient Athenian farming: the variety of options made possible for many farmers a *mixture* of crops and livestock. Two strategies now lay open. First, the farmer could, by careful selection of plant or animal, make adjustments according to peculiarities of soil, contour, or microclimate. Such considerations applied particularly in the case of more prosperous owners, whose holdings might be distributed over two or more distinct regions of Attica. Here the object was to maximize yield according to individual conditions. The second strategy might be characterized as "hedging your bets." The greater the variety of crop or stock, the less likelihood that an unforeseen change in conditions would wipe the owner out. The drought that kills one crop might spare another; the disease that strikes a hoofed animal might not affect poultry or honeybees. Nonetheless, some farmers did put all their eggs into one basket by specializing in a single crop. The advantages of doing so were volume and efficiency, but there was the risk of total disaster in a society that provided few safety nets. For the subsistence-level farmer, diversification, though resulting in lower yields, must have seemed a more attractive response to the dangers of living on the edge of ruin.

The Rural Village

It was stated above that the great majority (perhaps three-fourths or even five-sixths) of Athenians were landowners. Where did these landowners live? Note, first, that the word used here is not *farmer* but landowner. The two terms are not synonymous. Some Athenian farmers were tenants, working someone else's land in exchange for rent or a percentage of the produce. Conversely, a wealthy proprietor need have nothing to do with his land. He could live in the city, while directing through a bailiff the working of his land by hired labor or slaves. How many such absentee landlords there were we do not know, but some must have been among the many Athenians who, in the time since Clisthenes' reforms, had relocated to the urban center from their ancestral rural demes.

It was in the outlying villages, however, that the great majority of citizen smallholders surely continued to reside. There is more significance in this statement than might at first appear. Travelers in the rural United States, to illustrate the point, will encounter first one, then another isolated farmstead, with the farmer-owner's home and near it a barn, pens, silo, and sheds placed directly on the land itself. Such was *not* the pattern of settlement in ancient rural Attica. If isolated farmsteads ever existed in any significant numbers, they have left virtually no traces. Instead, citizen smallholders and their families lived in "nucleated" (or clustered) villages—the same villages that, with very few known exceptions, were institutionalized by Clisthenes as the demes of the new democracy. The majority of these (as shown, for example, by the quotas, based on citizen population, for the Council of Five Hundred) were very small, numbering a few hundred souls at most. Most demes probably resembled the town of Herakleion in the northeastern Peloponnese, where the author, as a field excavator for the University of California dig at the panhellenic sanctuary at Nemea, lived for a summer in the mid-1970s. At the heart of the village lay communal structures of various types and functions. Surviving inscriptions mention the agora (or meeting place), a courthouse, and (perhaps outside the actual village center) a theater or even a gymnasium, although in the smallest demes any such structures would have been on a modest scale, if they existed at all. Nearby were clustered the dwellings of the demesmen. Not much survives in the way of physical remains of these village infrastructures. Beginning in antiquity, buildings were frequently cannibalized for construction materials (such as stone blocks, wooden timbers, and roof tiles), and not many deme sites have been fully excavated, owing in part to the fact that they often lie beneath modern structures or developments. But the documented existence of either a meeting place (the agora) or a place of assembly (the theater) is adequate evidence of the communal solidarity of the local citizen farmer population. And again, as stated at the conclusion of Chapter 6, the demesman-farmer could find in that local community, by way of compensation for his continuing absence from the urban center, a rich offering of opportunities to engage in a common social, cultural, and political life not fundamentally dissimilar from its larger and more sophisticated version in Athens. The Athenian farmer's existence was characterized neither by isolation nor by a total absence of the amenities of urban life.

Agricultural Labor

The conclusion at which we have just arrived should not be allowed to obscure the fact that the primary occupation of the farmer and his family was agricultural or related labor. This labor had, first and importantly for our understanding of the human element of ancient Athenian farming, a temporal dimension. The archaic poet Hesiod's *Works and Days*, discussed in Chapter 2, is devoted in large part to instructing the reader on the proper timing of agricultural tasks; the poem is in effect a sort of calendar for agricultural activity. Furthermore, this calendar dictated, not only that certain types of labor fall at certain times of the year, but also that periods of intense labor alternate with other periods of relative idleness. At least that is what the poet seems to imply, for, after the harvest, which extended from midsummer to late fall, he instructs his reader "to let the slaves cool their heels and unyoke the pair of oxen." It was during winter, too, that the poet admonishes his farmer to avoid loafing at the blacksmith's—the ancient Greek equivalent of the general store with its wood stove and cracker barrel. But the point should not be overdrawn. There is after all, Hesiod concedes, work to be done, even in winter. For one thing, it was at this time that the vines had to be pruned. Probably there was always something to do, especially for the many smallholders who had gone the route of "mixed" farming, raising a variety of crops and livestock, each plant or animal on its own schedule. But this finding at once brings us back to the problem posed by the demands made on the citizen farmer's time and energy by nonagricultural pursuits. What about the activities of his deme community? What about military service? What about participation in the democratic government? How could the smallholder find the time and energy for either?

Alternative sources of labor were available to even the humblest of Athenian citizen farmers. Merely to identify them will shed light not only on agricultural practice, but also on the components and internal dynamics of the society as a whole.

Family members.   Intuitively, one would guess that all able-bodied members of the owner's household would be available to contribute their labor. With regard to children, it is important to remember that a daughter might marry and leave her father's house at an age as young as thirteen (see Chapter 7), whereas a son, as noted at the beginning of this chapter, did not typically marry until about age thirty and, even after marriage, continued to reside in his father's (now his own) house. Sons, in other words, were available, but daughters generally were not, at least not at an age at which they could be helpful.

The case of the farmer's wife, the other obvious candidate, is more problematic. At the close of Chapter 2, Hesiod, in the context of his normative blueprint for a farm not unlike that of the Athenian smallholder under consideration here, negatively characterized women as "no helpers in hateful poverty, but only in wealth," and then went on to compare human females to the drones of a beehive which (on his mistaken understanding of apiary society) stay at home, consuming the fruits of others' labors. (In still another picturesque passage he captures a young unmarried girl languishing at home before the fire while the storm rages outside.) Did not (as Hesiod suggests) free Athenian women engage in agricultural labor? Some isolated and parallel evidence suggests that they did. In the period after the Peloponnesian War, a court speaker relates that Athenian women went into the fields to tend the vines. True, these were hard times (especially as a result of the heavy loss of adult male lives in combat), but the fact that the incident could occur at all demonstrates that the "inside versus outside" division of space between females and males could be overridden, at least beyond the reach of the threatening environment of the city. Gardens (tilled to yield produce for home consumption and for sale in markets) were probably tended by women, if the evidence of parallel societies (with a comparable degree of female confinement) is applicable to the ancient Greek case. For what it is worth, the women of modern Greek villages (including the one in the Peloponnese where the author lived) regularly engage in outdoor agricultural labor. Hesiod's negative comments might therefore, as already suggested in Chapter 2, be put down to one man's animosity toward the world—toward his brother, the judges, and females in particular.

Paid free labor.   Demand for labor at peak periods probably usually exceeded by far the combined capacity of the owner's family members. Another option was to hire free workers, citizen or otherwise. Two status categories are in question. Metics—the resident aliens discussed in Chapter 5—could not own land, but nothing prevented them from working the lands of those who did. The second category comprises the poorer members of the citizen body more or less corresponding to Solon's bottommost class of thetes. Some owned no land at all; others, a small amount but not enough to sustain themselves. For both groups, opportunities for employment were probably seasonal and temporary, occurring especially at harvest time and in winter, when the vines had to be pruned. But there is little reason to suspect the existence of large groups of migrant workers such as those still found in the United States.

Slaves.   Slaves were available in Athens throughout the classical period for agricultural as well as other labor. Of course, since Solon's Shaking Off of Burdens, Athenian citizens were no longer enslaved for defaulting on debts secured by their persons—simply because loans of this kind were no longer legal. But non-Athenian slaves were, as we saw in Chapter 5, available in large numbers from foreign sources and at prices that put a slave or two within the reach of many Athenian smallholders. However, use of slaves brought with it disadvantages as well as advantages. On the plus side, slaves were not (like citizens) protected by civil rights, did not demand the respectful treatment usually accorded free Greeks (especially other Athenians), and, perhaps the critical point, were always at hand when the owner needed them. On the down side, slaves could fall sick or even die, escape, or be kidnapped, and they were certainly difficult to motivate. If, furthermore, slaves provided an adequate supply of labor in periods of peak demand, they must have been unprofitably idle much of the rest of the time. Use of slaves was not necessarily the attractive solution to the farmer's labor difficulties it might first appear to be.

The Mentality of Ancient Greek Farmers

Self-sufficiency. Given this range of options for procuring additional workers, it is obvious that no single simple profile could accurately portray the workforce on all the thousands of Athenian farms. If the truth be known, it would probably turn out to be a continuum of possibilities: from the relatively large estate of the absentee landlord worked by tenants, seasonal labor, and many slaves; to the smallholder assisted by family, a hired *thes*, and a slave or two; to the proud but impoverished poor citizen who did all the work himself. But despite this diversity, a general point, which applies to all Athenian farmers, deserves emphasis. It concerns the high value placed on "self-sufficiency" (Greek *autarkeia*), the notion that a man could, without reliance on others, obtain the necessities of life for himself and his family. This was, of course, an unattainable ideal for most. Surely nearly every farmer, as we have just seen, relied on the help of others, if only his wife and children. To sink into debt (as many did) rendered a farmer dependent on a creditor and brought him that much closer to ruin—and to total dependency on others. For the farmer who produced a surplus and took it to town for sale there arose a dependency not only on the availability of buyers for his goods but more generally on an alien urban culture. Nonetheless, farmers continued to pursue the ideal. Above all, as noted, the practice of "mixed" farming spread the risks imposed by the environment and so enhanced the chances that the smallholder would stay afloat. Probably most citizen farmers could hold their heads high, satisfied that their lands were free of debt and that they would be able (in accord with another cardinal moral principle) to pass the family property, undiminished in value, on to the next generation.

At the same time, it would not do to maintain self-sufficiency if that meant that the citizen owner's time, effort, and energy were monopolized by the requirements of his farm. If nothing else, the state looked primarily to citizens for fighting men; when called up, the farmer did not have the option of declining to serve. And the democratic government required, as we saw in Chapter 6, participation (voluntary participation, to be sure) by a high percentage of Athenians. In other words, self-sufficiency, which was an essentially private ideal, could not in this society be purchased at the cost of neglecting the demands or needs of the larger community of Athenians.

Conservatism.   Pursuit of the lofty ideal of *autarkeia* was perhaps the most conspicuous item in the attitudinal repertoire of Athenian farmers. But by no means does it tell the entire story. If, for one thing, self-sufficiency was to be achieved, the farmer's decisions—the decisions on which his success or failure in maintaining a subsistence level of productivity depended—had to reflect the realities of his physical and economic environment. Scholars are generally agreed that the net result of the workings of these environmental forces was a pronounced conservatism. By conservatism, in the present context, is meant a strong tendency to stick with the tried-and-true practices, routines, and methods that had proved satisfactorily effective in the past. With so little margin for error, an experiment of any kind carried with it an unacceptable element of risk. Failure, even on a small scale, could lead to indebtedness, and inability to repay the debt could initiate a slide down the slippery slope toward loss of some or all of the land. A new crop, a new implement or method, a variation in schedule—all must have been regarded with extreme suspicion. Reinforcing the reluctance to experiment was the ready availability of slave and other supplementary labor. If, that is, productivity could be enhanced by the purchase of a slave, what incentive would there be to innovate in the first place?

Nonetheless, the point should not be overstated. When we, from our vantage point of twenty-five hundred years of human progress, contemplate ancient Greek farming, all we see are opportunities for improvement. But virtually all of those improvements with which we are familiar are of comparatively recent origin, the products of the application of modern machinery, advanced animal husbandry, and sophisticated biological techniques. Obviously, the failure to make *those* improvements cannot be laid at the doorstep of the conservatism of ancient Athenian farmers. Furthermore, certain advances, however minor and incremental, were in fact made, particularly in the introduction of new crops. Mention has already been made, for example, of the innovating cash crops, the olive and grape vine. To this extent, it must therefore be granted, the Athenian farmer's resistance to change was not totally unbending. Generally, however, he emerges as a creature wedded to the ways that had always in the past served to avert the economic and personal disaster that lurked just around the corner. It was perhaps inevitable, too, that this habit of mind, springing from and maintained by the dominant concerns of his existence, should also have colored his and his family's attitudes in other areas of their lives as well. The phenomenon is clearly in evidence when, as in the comedian Aristophanes' so-called war plays, rural Athenians collide with their more sophisticated urban counterparts. A farmer's "conservatism" operated in the realms of his values, his religious beliefs, his political preferences, his view of history—in short, across the board of his life as an Athenian.

Attitude about work.   What was a farmer's (and his wife's and children's) attitude about work? Since their lives were centered on, in some cases indeed consumed by, agricultural labor, we will know little about the farming population unless we can answer this question. Our poet-farmer Hesiod, with characteristic (but not for that reason necessarily distorting) negativity, addresses the point. For him, work (by which he means, of course, farming work) is an unwelcome condition visited on people from heaven. "For the gods keep hidden from humans the means of livelihood. Otherwise you would easily do enough work in a day to live for an entire year without working at all." Thus the poet longingly looks back upon a lost utopian world order when the earth yielded a livelihood with virtually no effort on the farmer's part. He goes on to recount the sad tale of a fall from grace, of a downhill decline from a time "free from evils and hard work and miserable diseases," through ages of gold, silver, bronze, and heroes, finally ending in a fifth, and Hesiod's own, Age of Iron: "For now is a race of iron, and people never cease from toil and suffering by day nor from perishing by night." But, for all his negativity, Hesiod lives in the real world of the present. Rather than mope fruitlessly over an irrecoverable bygone paradise, he repeatedly asserts the value of doing the very thing he hates the most: working.

> Work! . . . in order that hunger may hate you, and chaste Demeter, the well-crowned, love you and fill your barn with livelihood; for hunger is appropriate to the shiftless man. Both gods and humans are angry with a man who lives in idleness.

> If the heart in your breast longs for wealth, do it my way and work with work piled upon work.

> Work the work which gods marked out for humans, lest you, in bitterness of heart, with your wife and children seek to obtain your livelihood from your neighbors and they neglect you.

> Do not put off work to tomorrow and the day after; for a lazy man does not fill his barn. Nor does the procrastinator. Industry helps work, but the dawdling man is always wrestling with ruin.

The point could not be clearer. But note what is absent from all these passages. There is no hint that work is of value *in itself.* Rather, the value of work resides exclusively in what work produces: the livelihood that, had it not been for the cruel intervention of the gods, would have come to the human race almost spontaneously. Work is a necessary evil. There is nothing uplifting or ennobling about it; that is an idea that belongs to another place and time. Hesiod's work ethic is entirely lacking in idealizing or romanticizing illusions.

Town Versus Country

The topographic and demographic diversity of classical Attica is a demonstrable fact. Of all the differences in question, the most obvious was that distinguishing "town" from "country"—the densely packed urban center focused on the Acropolis and Agora from the outlying plains, coastal strips, and hills of greater Attica. In the present case, however, the opposition between urban and rural should not be overdrawn. Ties of various kinds—social, constitutional, cultic, and economic—served to integrate the city and the countryside in a number of ways. Citizens who had migrated to the city retained links of kinship, marriage, friendship, and sentiment with their ancestral demes. The Clisthenic phyle, or "tribe," discussed in Chapter 6, combined into a single administrative unit citizens from the City, Coastal, and Inland regions. In the sphere of religion, major sanctuaries were in certain notable instances (especially the sanctuary of Demeter and Kore at Eleusis and that of Artemis at Brauron) situated in distant rural locations, to which city residents journeyed on sacred occasions. Absentee landlords living in town owned farms outside the city walls; and farmers from the rural demes came to town to sell their produce on a regular basis. And so on. It cannot be denied that to a meaningful degree Attica was a unified whole.

But this is not to say that there were no substantial differences between a citizen farmer and his urban counterpart. The agricultural lifestyle and routine imposed a distinctive outlook (as we have seen), as well as characteristic deportment, tastes, and manners. At the same time, the relative isolation of the village communities insulated the rural population from the newfangled innovations of the urban center. Aristophanes' comedies, which often involve interaction between rustic and city folk, repeatedly and consistently illustrate the point. A farmer in town could be identified by his dogskin cap; by his telltale aroma of grapes, figs, and wool; by his distinctive rugged speech; and in general by his behaving in a way that struck some townspeople as rude, ignorant, or even "barbarian." These country bumpkins (as an unkind urbanite might term them) knew nothing of the intricacies of forensic oratory, of atheistic scientific theories about the heavenly bodies or the causes of rain, or of the questions of epistemology and ethics being debated by Socrates and others in the Agora—the heady stuff that made the urban center the intellectual hotbed that it was. Differences as marked as these cannot be ignored or reduced, as some historians would suggest, to variations of social or economic status (as real as those variations sometimes were). The contrasting conditions of town and country had fostered two mutually antagonistic cultural styles.

How did the farmers themselves regard the town? It is perhaps not too great an exaggeration to say that it was a case of attraction and repulsion. Farmers needed a market where they could sell their surplus produce or obtain goods they could not produce themselves. To participate in government or in a legal action required a trip to the Pnyx or Agora. And these same democratic institutions offered an opportunity to supplement one's income by earning the small compensations offered by the treasury. In short, many a farmer probably could not live without the city. But that same city was viewed by that same farmer with profound distrust, if not outright hostility. The comedies of Aristophanes sympathetically portray the smallholder's point of view. When there is a military call-up, he suspects, farmers go to war while city types manage to finagle their way out of serving. When a farmer comes to town to sell his goods, he must always be on his guard against being cheated. One of his characters, Strepsiades, a farmer originally from a rural deme and incongruously married to a haughty and luxury-loving woman of the aristocratic Alcmeonidae, is driven deeply into debt by his reckless son who, under his mother's influence, has squandered his money on horses and dogs. When Strepsiades seeks instruction from Socrates in finding his way out of his predicament, he cannot understand the philosopher's teachings. This simple country boy is hopelessly out of his depth in this urban setting. Comedic portrayals apart, while, during the Peloponnesian War, farmers looked on helplessly as the Spartans pillaged their farms and, year after year, destroyed their crops, urbanites remained in relative security, their homes and possessions protected by the city fortifications.

Not surprisingly, if the city was a source of disgust, the farmer could find solace in his own rural existence. True, the work was hard, even debilitating. True, living on the brink of economic ruin was a constant source of anxiety. True, a hailstorm, an insect infestation, or an enemy army could suddenly wipe out a year's work—and income. But there were compensating pleasures. Listen, once again, to one of Aristophanes' characteristically sympathetic evocations of life in the country (the speaker is the farmer Trygaeus, the protagonist of the *Peace*):

> Remember, my good men, the ancient style of life,
> which she, Peace, once provided to us, and those
> long-gone cakes and figs and myrtle berries and
> sweet lees of wine and the bed of violets at the well
> and the olives for which we long. For the sake of all
> these, my good men, greet this goddess Peace!

A hard-nosed critic might try to undermine the credibility of such sentiments. Are they not the expected response to a protracted war (now entering its second decade), when farmers, forcibly confined within the walls of Athens, wistfully longed for the good old days? Are they not the product of an urban mentality (after all, the play, written by an urban poet, was produced in a theater on the slopes of the Acropolis before an urban audience), with its predictable idealization of a style of life outside its own experience yet admired from afar? Are they not the product of a nostalgic attachment to a rural economy which was increasingly being undermined by Athens' substantial dependency on imperial tribute and overseas trade? Perhaps, in varying degrees, these are all valid objections. But what continues to shine through is the strength and sincerity of the farmer's devotion to the land and to rural life—a devotion so genuine that neither Aristophanes nor his audience could possibly have denied its reality.

INDUSTRY

Not all Athenians—or other residents of Attica—earned their livelihood through farming and stock raising. Many citizens and noncitizens were engaged in various forms of nonagricultural employment that can conveniently be grouped under the general umbrella term *industry*. Numbers employed predictably elude us, but chances are that the total industrial workforce, if noncitizen as well as citizen, female as well as male, and child as well as adult are counted, was substantial. The reader should remember, too, that although such categories as agricultural or industrial serve a necessary analytic purpose, they do not necessarily correspond in a neat, one-to-one fashion to the realities of Athenian society. A farmer (or a dependent member of his family) might well have moonlighted in some industrial capacity, and (to look ahead to our final section) both farmers and industrial workers certainly served in the military organization.

Mining

As if to compensate for the relatively poor quality of much of its arable land, Attica was endowed with certain natural resources, without which—for all the talents, creative impulses, and efforts of the Athenian people—Athens could not have achieved preeminence among Greek city-states. To pick two obvious examples, stone quarries on Mount Hymettos and Mount Pentelikon provided the fine marble used in Athens' unparalleled monumental public architecture and its exquisite works of sculpture; and the clay beds north of the city supplied the potters whose decorated works set the standard for artistic excellence throughout the Mediterranean for generations. Even more essential for preeminence, since Athens' military might and balance of trade during the glory years of the classical period depended on them, were the rich deposits of silver in southeast Attica in and around the district of Laurium. A rich vein discovered during the decade between the two Persian invasions, early in the fifth century, bankrolled the construction of the fleet of triremes with which the Athenians almost single-handedly scored the decisive naval victory over Xerxes' fleet off the island of Salamis. In the absence of sufficient export commodities, Athens' silver was also exchanged for imported products, including the vital supply of grain upon which the population was absolutely dependent (see further, Chapter 9). The city's political freedom

and economic survival would have proved unobtainable but for this invaluable—and fortuitous—resource.

Who or what, then, actually owned the silver? The state owned it, in perpetuity. A farmer's ownership of the "land" did not extend beneath the surface, to mineral rights; hence no mine is ever found up for sale or included
in a dowry or inheritance. Who, then, worked the deposits? In keeping with
the government's general non-involvement in the economy (see Chapter 9),
the state made the mines available to private individuals on a leasing basis.
Several such leases, recorded on stone inscriptions from the fourth and third
centuries B.C., are preserved. According to their terms, the state leased a particular mine of a particular type ("new," "in operation," or "to be reopened")
to the lessor at the rate of $1/24$ or 4.16% of the silver recovered. Nonetheless,
even at this modest rate, mining, as a consequence of the risks involved, did
not always yield a satisfactory return. Other forms of investment, such as
moneylending and trade, continued to be more attractive to many rich capi-
talists.

Even so, a few Athenian lessors are known to have become rich from
the mining of the Laurium silver. Notable instances include the family of
Callias, reported to have been worth 200 talents and whose son Hipponicus
and grandson Callias were in succeeding generations regarded as the richest
men in all of Greece. Another is the general Nicias, said to have been worth
about 100 talents, with an annual income of about 10 talents produced by the
labor of 1,000 slave-miners. Noteworthy, too, is the fact that the family of
Callias (the case of Nicias is unclear on this point) had, prior to its involvement in mining, owned extensive agricultural land, held a prestigious hereditary priestly office, and indeed was identified as members of the pre-
Solonian Eupatrid ruling elite. These Athenians, in other words, were not
Johnny-come-lately entrepreneurs who on the strength of mining profits had
risen to prominence from outside the aristocracy. This fact cautions against
any excessively rigid assumptions about the elite's attachment to the land—
that is, to agriculture and stock raising—as the supposedly sole respectable
sources of income. To be sure, no Eupatrid largeholder would casually dispose of his land, nor was there reason to; a wealthy man with no inclination
toward farming could always put the farm under the supervision of a bailiff
and move to town. But the purchase of a mining lease to *supplement* a traditional landed income was another matter altogether. Besides, the hit-or-miss
nature of the mining business probably tended to favor the rich, because
they could minimize the risks by serially or simultaneously spreading their
efforts over several leases.

Who actually did the physical work of mining? Occasionally, a free citizen lessor is found working his lease. But the evidence overwhelmingly identifies the laborers as slaves. Numbers varied greatly. Nicias, again, owned 1,000
slaves for contract work in the mines; Callias' son Hipponicus, 600; and one
Philemonides, 300. At the other extreme, an enterprising but impecunious

entrepreneur might put a single slave to work on a tiny lease. And, to turn to another vital point, what about the conditions of these slaves' mining labor? Absent ancient testimony on the subject, one is thrown back on the findings of archaeologists and one's imagination. Excavations at Thorikos (a deme near the east coast, north of Cape Sounion) exposed, besides the mining facilities themselves (tunnels, ventilation shafts, cisterns, washing tables), housing accommodations probably intended for slaves, so these servile laborers, unlike some of their less fortunate Roman counterparts, were at least not kept permanently underground. But the narrow confinement of the low-ceilinged tunnels, the stuffy air filled with smoke from lamps, the threat of cave-ins, and the inevitable accumulation of ground water must have made the mine worker's existence difficult to endure. Nonetheless, at the conclusion of our discussion of industrial work, we will see that it was not these conditions alone, as horrible as they undoubtedly were, that accounts for the fact that the mines were worked by servile, rather than free, labor.

Industrial Workplaces

Besides the extraction of natural resources, many people were engaged in various types of manufacturing. Some of the products of this manufacturing activity will already be familiar to many readers: ceramic pottery, stone statuary, bronze armor and weapons, characteristic ancient Greek men's and women's garments, and so on. Again, our concern here is with the human element: the setting of industrial work, the social profile and status of the workers, and, last of all, the estimation in which this type of work (as opposed to agricultural labor) was held by the Athenian public.

To begin, let us identify the principal settings of industrial work and, in connection with each such setting, attempt to determine the character of its workforce. The available evidence may be conveniently grouped under three distinct headings: factories, shops, and household industry.

• *Factories.* Only a few sizable industrial establishments are known. Of these few, in only two or three instances is there any precise indication of the size of the workforce. The metic Cephalus (the father of the orator Lysias and his brother Polemarchus) owned a shield factory employing 120 slaves, with an inventory that at one time included 700 shields. Pasion, a freed slave (with metic status) who eventually received citizenship, also owned a shield factory; its income of one talent (6,000 drachmas) per year implies a large number of workers. The estate of the citizen father of Demosthenes (the famous orator) included at the time of his death a sword factory with 32 or 33 slaves and an income of 30 *minae* (one-half a talent); a couch factory staffed by twenty slaves with an annual income of 12 minae; and large stocks of factory materials. Additionally, new-rich "entrepreneurs" of the later fifth century, such as Cleon the tanner and Hyperbolus the lamp maker, owed their wealth to various industrial enterprises. This is as close as ancient Athens got to "heavy industry."

• *Shops.*   Shops, stalls, and tables, each typically producing or selling a single type of merchandise, proliferated in the general area of the Athenian Agora. Some dealt in produce or manufactured goods: foodstuffs of all kinds (in raw form to be transported home for preparation), wine, flowers and wreaths, garments, shoes and other leather goods, stone and metalwork, household furnishings, women's articles, figurines, books, and (for the well-heeled buyer) even horses. Services are not often mentioned, though we do hear of barbershops and, in the financial sphere, bankers and moneylenders (positioned at the "Tables" in the Agora). Human merchandise ran from cooks and other workers for hire, to prostitutes, to slaves for sale in the "Circles." There was a degree of organization, in that producers and sellers of a particular commodity tended to be clustered together; hence the frequent references to "The Fish," "The Birds," or "The Fresh Cheese" as locations or destinations. But the overall impression must have been one of a tightly packed jumble of commercial activity resembling an Eastern bazaar.

Not all activity in the Agora market area was strictly or even incidentally commercial. Contemporary sources reveal that citizens—that is, adult male Athenians—made a habit of congregating in or near the shops, sometimes a particular group in a particular shop or area. Thus the demesmen of Deceleia, when in town, used to hang out at the barbershop on the Street of the Herms. The same was probably true of noncitizens, metics, slaves, and perhaps visiting foreigners as well. Except for women and children of the citizen class (who, as we saw in Chapter 7, remained in the vicinity of their homes), a substantial portion of urban Athens was probably to be found in the streets of the market on any given day. No less than the institutions of the democratic government, the major state religious festivals, and athletic activity, the Athenian marketplace—superficially paralleling the modern suburban shopping mall—was a striking manifestation of Athenian life, public and (unlike the suburban shopping mall) out of doors.

To a gratifying extent, the lively scene just described, though based largely on written sources, has been partially confirmed and given specific illustration by the American excavations in the Agora. A particular concentration of commercial establishments was found to have lined the streets southwest of the Agora, at the base of the Areopagus Hill and between it and the Pnyx, the meeting place of the Assembly. The evidence consists primarily of traces of the production of pottery, metalwork, stone sculpture, terra-cotta figurines, and shoemaking, sometimes in association with the remains of structures probably to be identified as workshops. Interestingly, two of these establishments help bring to life the career of perhaps the best known of all Athenians: the philosopher Socrates. Socrates' father, and probably Socrates himself, were stone sculptors and probably worked in a shop like that on

"The Street of the Marble Workers" identified by the archaeologists. Socrates is also recorded to have visited a rein maker's shop and (to the point here) the shop of a cobbler named Simon. Excavators discovered in a structure of classical date a large number of hobnails and, in the street directly outside, a cup bearing the name of its owner—Simon! (Later sources reveal, incidentally, that Simon was himself a man of speculative bent and that he recorded in dialogue form some of his conversations with the philosopher.) No more striking illustration could be produced of the philosopher's—and probably of other Athenians'—practice of passing the time of day in commercial establishments.

• *Household industry.* Some or all of the workshops just described may also have doubled as the proprietor's residence. A similar arrangement may lie behind the occasional enigmatic mention in documents of a "house with workshop." Some scholars have, on this basis, imagined a widespread cottage-level industry, with hundreds, perhaps thousands, of Athenian households involved. No law, zoning ordinance, or societal ideal prohibited or even discouraged such a combination of domestic and commercial functions. The "workshop" need have been nothing more than a small shed adjacent to or built onto the dwelling. Nor is the labor force hard to imagine: the homeowner's wife, older children, elderly parents, and very likely a slave or two. To the extent that females were engaged as workers, this society's division of labor prompts the assumption that textiles and food items were among the goods produced. The combined production—as well as the numbers of hands involved—may have been immense.

The foregoing discussion deliberately blurs a fundamental distinction with regard to the workforce—that between the producer and the seller. This is appropriate inasmuch as Athenians themselves commonly made no differentiation between the two. The manufacturer and the retailer of a given item of merchandise were often identifiably the same person; the workshop (as in the case of the cobbler Simon) and the "store" were one and the same place. But the generalization needs qualification. For one thing, most ordinary domestic dwellings could not also have been retail outlets, to the extent that *free* women and children were involved. If producers, they would not have dealt as sellers on a face-to-face basis with buyers, certainly not with adult male buyers from outside the household; and, in any event, the use of domestic quarters for such a purpose is inconceivable (on the confinement of females, see Chapter 7). For another, where many of the known shops, stalls, or booths are in question, some were obviously outlets only, not sites of production. A farmer may have driven his pigs to market to sell, but the retailer who sold butchered pork from a stall was likely a different person altogether. In still other cases, there were probably middlemen who bought up the production of household shops to sell it "wholesale" to retailers. But, even so, many an

Athenian crafter, paralleling the practice of a modern American crafts fair, also played the complementary role of salesperson.

Order and Status

Additional dimensions of the workforce that need to be addressed are those of order and status. To begin with order, although the situation is complicated (since free and slave, male and female were sometimes found doing the same job), certain trends are nonetheless discernible. At all levels—factory, workshop, and home—citizens were engaged, but not in all capacities and not necessarily to the exclusion of noncitizens. Thus factory owners included not only Demosthenes' father and the politicians Cleon and Hyperbolus (all citizens), but metics (Lysias' family) and even ex-slaves (Pasion) as well. Obviously the monopoly citizens enjoyed in the ownership of "land and house" did not extend to the nontraditional industrial pursuits. Industry, unlike agriculture, was not a jealously guarded citizen monopoly. If anything, certain more traditionally minded aristocrats, permanently wedded to the land and its value system, probably made it a point of honor to avoid it.

And who worked in these factories? All the known employees were slaves. The same, again, applies to mine workers. The reason for this striking fact may not be immediately apparent. It is not necessarily a matter of the difficulty or desirability of the work, as one might suspect. True, the mines were as inhospitable a workplace as can be imagined, but there is no reason to think that employment in a potter's or a shield factory was any more disagreeable than subsistence-level farming. Nor is the explanation economic, because the cost of slave labor approximated the wages paid to free citizen workers. Rather, slaves tended to be employed in factories (and in mines and presumably all large operations) because the conditions of work were unacceptable to citizens (and to free Greeks generally). Why? All types of large-scale employment inevitably meant *dependency*—specifically in the form of dependency on (or subordination to) the owner of the workplace, a bailiff (the manager of a large farm), or a shop foreman. But Greeks, as we saw in our discussion of the farmer's mentality, valued the ideal of self-sufficiency, and self-sufficiency meant among other things that one was one's own boss. All smallholders, the self-employed farmers, already automatically fulfilled the ideal. While others (family members, hired workers, or slaves) worked under their direction, they themselves took orders from no one. No citizen or metic would voluntarily have endured so subservient a degree of dependency. It is no wonder there continued to be such a multitude of tiny workplaces and retail outlets (as well as farms).

It cannot be overemphasized that the negative view of certain types of employment grew out of the conditions of that employment (namely, dependency) and *not* out of the nature of the work itself. To be sure, a premium continued to be placed on working the land. Agriculture and stock raising were hallowed by their great antiquity. And because aristocrats who owned large estates continued out of choice, habit, or necessity to adhere to the traditional pursuits, lifestyle, and values, those citizens who aspired to aristocratic ways (and there were many, as suggested in Chapter 5) would naturally share that preference. No disgrace or even disapproval was attached to farming, however debilitating the labor or meager the income. Nonagricultural labor, however, was another matter. The Athenian philosophers, for example, evidence a demeaning attitude toward what they call "banausic" labor; that is, the crafts or trades. But this attitude may be in part a reflex of an extremely high valuation of the intellectual life, and is in any case not discernible in other departments of Athenian life. For example, artisans who signed their work obviously took pride in their achievements (and note that, in the case of decorated pottery, not only the painter, but the *potter* as well, sometimes signed the finished product). State religion embraced and ennobled the crafts. One need mention only the magnificent temple of Hephaestus, the smith god (in the close vicinity of which, incidentally, metalworkers established their foundries); and the cult of Athena, the patron divinity of crafts, in whose honor aristocratic girls wove a garment for the goddess each year to serve as the centerpiece in the procession of her great festival, the Panathenaia. No stigma, in short, adhered to employment in manufacturing *per se*, despite its relatively recent emergence and development.

But if productive labor—traditional or otherwise—was respectable as long as one was one's own boss, the same did not necessarily apply to the business of *selling* the products of that labor. Small-time retailers came in for particular criticism. As noted earlier in connection with farmers' attitudes toward the town, merchants were habitually suspected of cheating their customers, whether by overcharging, selling inferior products, or whatever. It is undeniable, for this reason alone, that retailers were held in low regard. When Aristophanes pokes fun at the dramatic poet Euripides by observing that his mother sold vegetables in the marketplace, he is alleging two different types of inferior status. First, although a free-born person of the citizen class, she had been driven outside the proper domain of respectable woman, her house, to seek employment. Second, that employment had taken the specific form of retail selling. But the same did not apply to business activity on a larger scale. Demosthenes' father is not known to have suffered loss of status because he owned factories designed to produce articles—couches and shields—for sale in the retail marketplace. The reason for the difference is obvious. The wealthy factory owner did not personally engage in the dirty business of haggling in the Agora, whereas the small-time retailer, who did, unavoidably confronted the wrath of a hostile public on a daily basis. (When, therefore, Aristophanes castigates Cleon, the owner of a tannery, he is unfairly tarring his victim with a brush actually meant for much humbler folk.) Citizens, as we saw, condemned metics and slaves, on purely statutory grounds and without regard for an individual's actual qualities, to a permanent condition of extreme social inferiority. But they could also harbor negative feelings about members of their own class whose activities habitually involved deceit or other dishonorable conduct.

THE MILITARY ORGANIZATION

Thus far, this chapter has considered two subjects, farming and industry, pursuits which correspond roughly to what we might call occupations. When due allowance is made for part-time employment and for the occasional piecing together of an income from various sources, it is fair to say that these occupations were pursued more or less on a full-time basis. But a major category of Greek public life remains, which must be treated in the context of this chapter—military service. To what extent military service counts as an "occupation" or full-time activity depends on the place and time one is considering. Beginning in the later classical period, Greek cities increasingly withdrew from using their own citizens in combat, preferring instead to rely on paid mercenaries. In time, noncitizen mercenaries emerged in many cases as bona fide professional soldiers and sailors. But the full-time *citizen* soldier or sailor was, in any period early or late, a rarity. Sparta comes the closest. There, the agricultural and industrial work of the society had been allocated to noncitizen subject allies (the perioikoi) and state-owned slaves (the helots) in order to allow the citizen elite (the Spartiatai) to pursue military activity on a twenty-four-hour-a-day basis. Sparta's case, however, was extreme and paralleled nowhere else in ancient Greece.

What about Athens? The question was addressed by the Athenian general Pericles in the *Funeral Oration* delivered early in the Peloponnesian War and recreated by the historian Thucydides. Pericles found Athens' approach to military policy to differ diametrically from that of its oligarchic rival, Sparta. Among other differences, the speaker makes the point that, whereas the Spartans (with their addiction to drilling) experience the hardships of war before war actually occurs, Athenians, despite their more relaxed attitude and with little preparation, face those same hardships "no less fearlessly than those who are always in laborious training." That is, as concerns our discussion, Athenians, otherwise engaged in civilian pursuits, only intermittently and temporarily turned to military activity and, having discharged their soldierly obligation, returned once again to those pursuits. Among other concerns, it will be worth our while to try to determine to what extent Pericles' estimation of Athenian practice was true to reality.

Military service was, first of all, an obligation incumbent upon, and a privilege normally accessible only to, Athenian citizens. Procedure left little opportunity for exceptions. All citizens were, from an early date, as we saw in Chapter 7, enrolled on the registers of their demes. It was with reference to these registers that the authorities assembled the names of those who had reached military age and, when a mobilization was ordered, determined the identity of those required to present themselves. No citizen could shirk his duty. Neither wealth nor its absence were factors. The rich served, mainly as horsemen and infantry; and even the poorest thetes, even though financially unable to arm themselves for service in the infantry, were eligible to serve in other capacities, especially as rowers in the fleet. Failure to serve, desertion, or cowardice in battle were all well-defined crimes and, upon their demonstration in a court of law, severely punished. True, as the comic poet Aristophanes testifies, some Athenians could and did object to a particular war on particular grounds, but no pacifist ideology is discernible at any time. There were no conscientious objectors in ancient Athens. All citizens served. But what about noncitizens? Note was just made of the future trend toward the employment of noncitizen foreign mercenaries. But already in the fifth century B.C., as we will see, metics and even slaves were engaged in military service under certain restricted conditions. Nonetheless, noncitizen roles often involved elements of either subordination (as in the case of slave rowers) or segregation (as probably in the case of metic infantry), thereby leaving largely intact the otherwise unchallenged citizen monopoly on military representation of the Athenian state.

Athenian fighting men were distributed over several branches of service: infantry (heavily armed hoplites and lightly armed slingers and skirmishers); naval officers, crews, and marines; and the cavalry. Each must be examined separately, for each possessed its own distinctive economic base, personnel, and ideological outlook. Whereas the various arms of some modern military organizations are roughly on a par in these (and other) respects, nothing could be further from the truth in the case of ancient Athens. Some of the most striking points of difference among the various segments of Athenian society were carried over into the requirements, personnel, status, and outlook of the land, naval, and mounted military forces.

Infantry

Armed foot soldiers fell into two broad classes. Of far lesser importance—military, political, social, and otherwise—were the light-armed troops, principally lightly armed soldiers, archers, and slingers. The more important group comprised the hoplites or heavy-armed infantry. The hoplites' military importance derived from their superior armament, advanced training, and greater numbers; their political and social importance, from the fact that, until later in the classical period, hoplites were obligated to purchase and maintain their own expensive bronze armor and weapons. Thus, as noted in Chapter 5, the hoplites come the closest to representing a sort of middle class of Athenian citizen society.

The hoplite panoply (helmet, breastplate, shield, greaves or shin guards, spear, and sword) and accompanying battle tactics were a product of the archaic age, when they replaced the more primitive mode of individual man-to-man combat illustrated, for example, by the Homeric poems. At the heart of hoplite warfare was the phalanx, the battle line of soldiers, one or more rows deep, each man standing shoulder to shoulder with his fellow citizens to right and left. Panoply and tactics were integrally related; neither made any sense without the other. An isolated hoplite, weighed down by heavy armor, unable to run any great distance, and defenseless from behind, was a military contradiction in terms. The hoplite's effectiveness depended entirely on his function within the phalanx, and the phalanx's effectiveness in turn on the hoplites' ability to perform precisely coordinated maneuvers. These facts imply the next point of significance about the hoplites: the necessity of lengthy training.

Late in the fourth century B.C., when Aristotle's *Constitution of the Athenians* was written, such training was provided by the so-called Ephebic College (*ephebos* being Greek for "young man"). Participation was compulsory for all Athenians who had reached the age of eighteen, and the curriculum ran for two years. During the first year, training in warfare was conducted by athletic trainers and specialized instructors in armed combat and in the use of the bow, javelin, and catapult. Upon completion of the training, the class of recruits gave a public military exercise before a meeting of the Assembly, after which they received a shield or spear from the state. The second year was spent on patrol and on duty at guardposts in and about Attica. Aristotle is emphatic on the point that the ephebes' service during these two years was continuous: they took their meals together and, to eliminate a handy excuse for absenting oneself, an ephebe could not (except in a few specified cases) be a litigant in a court proceeding. Two years of continuous military training and duty at this impressionable age would have had predictable effects. These Athenians, whether the sons of farmers or artisans, must have come out of the Ephebic College seeing themselves as in some sense full-fledged soldiers. That the Athenian state so regarded them as well is indicated by the ceremonial award of the spear and shield before the Assembly and by Aristotle's statement that only after graduation from the college did these young Athenians "join the other citizens," implying that military competence was a necessary precondition of citizenship.

Strictly speaking, eligibility for military service began with entry into the Ephebic College and ended at age fifty-nine—the landmark year mentioned at the beginning of this chapter. But, obviously, not all citizens falling within this four-decade span were on an equal footing, militarily speaking. To facilitate assignment of different age groups to appropriate tasks, the pool of citizens was divided into forty-two one-year cohorts, so that mobilizations and other assignments could be made according to age. It is believed, for example, that the relatively light and risk-free duty of manning the walls was assigned to ephebes (that is, eighteen- to twenty-year-olds) and to men in their fifties. Mobilizations for actual campaigns (and thus likely to involve combat) are known to have extended all the way to men in their forties, but our modal career identified men in their twenties as particularly likely candidates. Whatever the ages most susceptible to call-up for active duty, how much action a citizen actually saw depended on the circumstances. Was there a war going on? Wars could be lengthy; the Peloponnesian War lasted twenty-seven years, for example. Furthermore, expeditions were normally confined to the summer months, and even within these limits actual combat was far from continuous. When an army did set out, the length of its absence depended on multiple factors, the distance of the theater from home being an obvious one. (Thus one scholar's tabulation of the number of days for which soldiers about to depart on a campaign were requested to provide themselves with rations showed a variation between one and sixty.) It all depended. But in most years, on the average, the citizen soldier, whether farmer or artisan, was probably able, with the aid of substitute labor provided by family members, hired hands, or slaves, to incorporate military service into his civilian schedule.

The elements of hoplite warfare—the heavy armor and the phalanx battle line—imposed certain standards of conduct and attitude. Equality among members of the infantry was one. All soldiers wore the same armor; all performed much the same tasks; all (if not in a given battle, then over time) ran comparable risks. Another was cooperation. Equality need not imply cooperation, but the phalanx necessitated that each soldier subordinate any individualistic impulse to the collective tactical requirements of the group. For one thing, each man's unguarded right side (all hoplites carried the shield on the left arm) needed to be protected by the overlap of the shield of the man standing to his right. The soldier who turned in flight thus exposed his fellow soldier to danger and, by creating a gap in the line, gave the enemy an opportunity to break through—a potentially fatal development. Hence, as many historians agree, the showboating individualism of the Homeric chieftain confronting his adversary in a man-to-man duel was replaced by an egalitarian and cooperative code of conduct—and attitude. When one considers the large percentage of citizens engaged in hoplite service, it is obvious that the ideology implicit in Athens' democratic government was both partly rooted in and reinforced by the conditions imposed by many citizens' service in the infantry.

Hoplite warriors, even in a maritime state like Athens, enjoyed considerable prestige. After all, it was an Athenian hoplite phalanx that had repulsed the Persians at Marathon in 490 B.C., early in the history of the democracy. Not long thereafter, however, in the wake of the great sea victory a decade later at Salamis, Athens embarked on her transformation into a naval power. It was with a fleet that Athens would build and maintain its empire and, after the empire was built, would face its land-based adversary, Sparta. Nonetheless, traditionalists like Aristophanes, loyal to the agricultural regime of values, could—sixty or seventy years after the event—continue to hold up the "Marathon Fighters" as paragons of courage and moral rectitude. Their continuing high prestige was also evident in the use of metaphors drawn from hoplite warfare in works of literature and in the depiction of notable hoplite military victories in public monumental art and architecture. Yet not all citizens could become, or necessarily chose to become, hoplites. Mention has already been made of the light-armed troops; and, as we will see, many wealthy Athenians elected to join the cavalry. Nor, conversely, were all hoplites Athenian citizens. Although metics were not admitted to the Ephebic College, their service as hoplites during the fifth century is recorded. But there is no reason to think that the existence of either group—nonhoplite citizens or noncitizen hoplites—seriously compromised the high estimation enjoyed by the Athenian heavy infantry.

Naval Service

By the time of the outbreak of the Peloponnesian War, Athens, for all the glorification of the hoplite infantryman, had become a naval power—indeed, the greatest naval power in the Greek world. The great sea victory over the Persians off Salamis in 479 B.C. marked the beginning—and an enduring symbol—of the city's maritime regime. The Delian League, and the Athenian empire that emerged from that league, comprised a multitude of island and coastal cities and so presented the need for a substantial fleet for policing and tribute-collecting purposes. That same fleet provided the backbone for Athens' long struggle against Sparta in the Peloponnesian War. Traditionalists may have looked back nostalgically to the hoplite glory of Marathon, but the present and future of classical Athens depended on the navy.

Athens' naval establishment was not entirely independent of the organization of the land forces. The ten generals, elected one per phyle by the People each year, were generals of the navy as well as of the army. The Ephebic College (following its creation late in the fourth century B.C.) provided naval training in the form of ship races and naval war games. But by and large the distinctive demands imposed by the maintenance of a large navy led to the creation of separate organization and procedures.

Finances ranked high among these demands, because (leaving personnel aside for the moment) warships were very expensive to build and keep in a good state of repair. Early on, pure luck played a decisive part. A silver strike at Laurium led, in the period between the Persian Wars, to the financing of the construction of two hundred triremes—the ships that defeated the Persians at Salamis. Also, under the Empire, many of the allies at first contributed ships and crews to a navy commanded by Athenians, only later substituting cash payments in lieu of ships. Triremes built and maintained at Athens were financed by imperial tribute, by extraordinary war taxes imposed on the wealthy, and, most distinctively, by a form of the liturgy called the *trierarchy* (or "command of a trireme"). Each trierarch was presented with a hull and rigging and ordered to meet all additional expenses toward its maintenance for one year; as his title indicates, he also had to serve as its captain. In the fifth century, the trierarchs, normally assigned one per trireme, numbered about 400; later, when the expenses grew too great for one person, the burden was spread over the 1,200 richest citizens. So, a very substantial number of citizens served the navy in the capacity of involuntary sources of funding (as well as captains of their ships).

But it is with respect to personnel that the navy differed most markedly from the infantry. True, the role of citizens was conspicuous. Besides providing the great majority of trierarchs, citizens alone could be elected general, and the subordinate officers whose status is known were virtually all citizens as well. But it is with the tens of thousands of rowers that we are primarily concerned. Many rowers were drawn from the thetic citizen class (the bottommost tier in Solon's system), and particularly from the nonagricultural urban poor population. Serving on a volunteer (rather than a conscript) basis, these Athenians, probably in many cases not otherwise fully employed, exchanged their participation for pay. Citizens also figured as archers and marines, the latter being heavy-armed infantry soldiers of the hoplite class, but their small numbers, nominally ten per trireme versus a crew of two hundred rowers, rendered them a relatively insignificant segment of the total personnel on board.

Noncitizens were a significant presence. In contrast with the citizens' near monopoly on hoplite service, naval personnel were drawn in significant numbers from the metic and slave populations as well. Metics in a few cases are known to have held the trierarchic liturgy and occasionally crop up as naval contractors, helmsmen, shipwrights, ship's carpenters, and flute players (who marked the beat for rowers). Both metics and slaves joined the thetes as rowers. Both were paid, the latter under a lease arrangement between the state and the slaves' owners. Nor was pay the only available incentive for slave rowers. After the Athenian naval victory at Arginousae late in the Peloponnesian War, the government expressed its gratitude by not only freeing but also enfranchising those slaves who had rowed in the fleet. No less significant are the social aspects of the situation. The Athenian trireme shows us citizens, resident aliens, slaves (and, not mentioned so far, hired foreign mercenaries) cooperatively carrying out a shared task in a very confined space over what were often lengthy periods of time. It was a mixture of groups recalling the diverse labor forces at work on public building projects on the Acropolis and, at a humbler level, the side by side cooperation of free and slave in the domestic household. Plainly, the stratification of Athenian society, however tenaciously the boundaries were maintained in other areas, did not preclude the relaxation of differences of order or status when an individual's pursuit of gainful employment or the well-being of the commonwealth demanded it.

The Cavalry

Despite the long presence of the horse in Greece, the animal played only a minor role in the military organizations of the classical city states.

Regions with grassy plains suitable for horse raising, such as Thessaly, produced impressive corps of cavalry, but they were exceptional. In contrast, the land of Attica is hilly, rocky, and thin-soiled; and the needs of a growing human population dictated that what plainsland there was be given over to cereal production. Nor was the lack of suitable grazing the only factor militating against the development of an Athenian cavalry. Horse raising, then as today, entailed very considerable expense. Either private individuals or the state (or both) would be required to make a big investment. Combat, furthermore, obviously would also continually put that investment at risk. And cavalry warfare required highly skilled horsemen. Where were these horsemen, and these funds, to come from?

No cavalry corps is known to have existed at Athens before the middle of the fifth century B.C. Evidence for an earlier corps might be thought to be provided by Solon's income class system established in 594 B.C. The second of the four classes was called *hippeis*, or horsemen. But a *horse*man does not have to be a *cavalry*man, and Solon's title may reflect not a military role, but the prestige value, of the horse in Athenian society. When, 150 years later, an Athenian cavalry first leaves its mark on the historical record, it is 300 men strong. By the outbreak of the Peloponnesian War in 431 B.C., the number has grown to 1,200—1,000 cavalry plus 200 mounted archers. All of a sudden, one in about thirty Athenians is a mounted soldier. How had the factors working against the development of an equestrian force been overcome?

It was state subsidy that made such a development possible. That subsidy took two forms. Feed was provided for the animals—a not insignificant expense when the number of mounts had reached 1,200. As for the riders, the treasury gave the cavalryman a start by granting a loan (not a gift) toward the purchase of his horse. Because most (if not all) cavalrymen came from wealthy families, it may seem odd that such a loan was thought necessary. But the explanation is provided by the assumption underlying the modal career with which we began this chapter: that the twenties were the years of military service. If the recruit's father was still living, then he, the recruit, had typically not assumed ownership or control of his father's property. So the state put up the money for the purchase of the horse. When, after a dozen years or so, the horse had had its day, our rider, now in this thirties and having succeeded his father, probably retired from cavalry service. With the ancestral estate at his disposal, he was in a position to repay his cavalry loan to the treasury.

Cavalry service appealed only to aristocrats—the only Athenians with significant prior experience with horses. (Another attraction, unrelated to social class, was the relative safety of equestrian warfare when compared with the highly risky, but more prestigious, duties of the hoplite). Metics, furthermore, were excluded from the cavalry, and no slave, needless to say, ever mounted a horse in the service of Athens. The resulting heavy concentration of aristocrats accounts for the persistent oligarchic, antidemocratic tendency of the corps, in evidence throughout its existence. For example, late in the fifth century B.C., when twice, in 411 and 404/3, the democracy was temporarily interrupted by more restrictive oligarchic regimes, the cavalry on both occasions sided with the oligarchs. Finally, with the loss of the Peloponnesian War, many cavalrymen preferred to withdraw from public life rather than to continue to serve under the restored, but in their eyes discredited, democratic government.

The Athenian Military Organization: Ideology and Motivation

Infantry, navy, and cavalry, as we have seen, differed to an astonishing degree considering that they all represented the same state. Some of the economic and social factors accounting for these differences have been brought out in the foregoing discussion. But it is the pronounced ideological variations distinguishing hoplites, rowers, and horsemen that are most striking and justify a brief characterization.

• Hoplites.   Moderately prosperous, typically farmers, with a traditionally agricultural outlook. During the Peloponnesian War, they favored a return to peace and the resumption of cordial relations with their former ally, Sparta. They were opposed to any further extension of the Athenian empire.

• Rowers.   Poor, probably landless thetes residing either in the urban center or in the port town of Peiraeus. They supported "radical" democratic politicians like Pericles and (after Pericles' death) the "new" politicians, Cleon and others. During the Peloponnesian War, because naval activity meant continued employment, rowers favored persecution of effort against Sparta and, because increased tribute would be spent on the citizen body, expansion of the Empire.

• Horsemen.   Wealthy and often aristocratic landowners with a tradition of horsebreeding. They were ideologically committed to oligarchic constitutional arrangements.

Ideology, however firmly embraced, does not necessarily provide the full explanation for why a man fights, particularly if service (as for the thetes) is voluntary. Pay was undeniably a major contributing factor. Except for the cavalry (from which a recruit could be excused on grounds of insufficient wealth), all soldiers and sailors received some form of payment (even if only in the form of an allowance for provisions while on campaign). But the pay was viewed differently. For the hoplite, the small sum was probably regarded as compensation for lost income or inconvenience. His primary motivation was a combination of the personal (witness the appeals of battlefield speeches to protect family and property) and the patriotic (witness the lofty idealization of Athens in Pericles' *Funeral Oration*). Rowers, by contrast, propertyless and underemployed, saw naval service (like payments for Assembly attendance or court duty) as a source of otherwise unobtainable income. But wealthy horsemen, on whom a small payment (had it existed) would have had no effect, were probably motivated in part by the desire to maintain the aristocratic exclusivity that we saw in Chapter 5 underlay their lifestyle preferences.

Military service was plainly not, as at Sparta, the equivalent of a full-time job. The rise of the professional mercenary lay in the future. Still, besides its varying importance as a source of livelihood, military training and combat, even if only intermittent and short-lived, was part of a man's public identity in that it represented an opportunity to express a distinctive political or ideological outlook.

Suggested Readings

For a comprehensive and up-to-date overview of ancient Greek farming (the "recent study" to which reference is made several times above), see A. Burford, *Land and Labor in the Greek World* (Baltimore and London, 1993). Still valuable is the sketch of farming life in V. Ehrenberg, *The People of Aristophanes* (reprinted New York, 1962), ch. 3.

Industry is treated synoptically by R. J. Hopper, *Trade and Industry in Classical Greece* (London, 1979); and the crafts, by A. Burford, *Craftsmen in Greek and Roman Society* (London, 1972). For the excavation of the shops southwest of the Agora, see the report of R. S. Young, "An Industrial District of Ancient Athens," *Hesperia* 20(1951): 135–288; and, for less technical accounts, see the appropriate sections in the works on the Athenian Agora cited at the end of Chapter 3 of this textbook. For separate treatments by specialists on various crafts and industries, see C. Roebuck, ed., *The Muses at Work* (Cambridge, 1969). The industry about which we know the most, pottery, is addressed by T. B. L. Webster, *Potter and Patron in Classical Athens* (London, 1972), with Chapter 1 devoted to the potters and Chapter 20 to purchasers and patrons. Again, the treatment of traders and craftsmen in the comedies of Aristophanes in the work of Ehrenberg just cited, Chapter 5, is still valuable.

Study of the Athenian military has been conducted branch by branch. Virtually all aspects of land warfare are exhaustively treated by W. K. Pritchett in *The Greek State at War*, five volumes thus far published (Berkeley, 1971–present). For the administration (and other aspects) of the naval forces, see B. Jordan's able *The Athenian Navy in the Classical Period* (Berkeley and Los Angeles, 1975). The cavalry have been well handled by G. Bugh, *The Horsemen of Athens* (Princeton, 1988). Ehrenberg's Chapter 11, "War and Peace," adds valuable material and insight from Aristophanes.

Chapter 9. Athenian State and Society: The Economy

With the completion of our discussion of the principal occupations pursued both within and outside the home, it is now appropriate to turn to the larger economic setting of which such compensated labor was merely a part, however important a part. *Economy* here is understood in a broader sense. It includes not only the monetary economy, involving the exchange of money for goods or services, but also those sectors of ancient Athenian society that, even long after the introduction of coinage, persisted in more traditional modes of exchange and economic life generally. For the sake of clarity, however, we will begin with coinage, then proceed to income in the form of wages and compensation for services, and from income to the cost of living. With this more familiar material as a backdrop, we then return to our "average" Athenian, the subsistence farmer (and his household) and the economics of his precarious existence. With the subsistence household we will compare the contrasting economic situation of the wealthy liturgical class, then leave the domestic unit to consider briefly Athenian trade, the finances of the state government, and finally the impact of the Empire on Athenian public spending.

Chapter 3 opened our study of Athenian state and society by surveying their physical setting in terms of the "built environment." The present Chapter resumes (and completes) that introduction by examining the economic base that alternately limited and enabled the Athenians in the pursuit of their domestic and public lives.

THE COINAGE OF CLASSICAL ATHENS

Ancient Greek opinion ascribed the invention of coinage to the Lydians in southwestern Asia Minor. The surviving numismatic record shows that, as least as far as Greece is concerned, that opinion was correct. The earliest known Greek coins, struck by cities neighboring the Lydians, date to the later seventh century B.C. As for Athens, Aristotle attributed to Solon (his archonship traditionally dated to 594 B.C.) a reform of Athenian coinage, implying that coins had existed even earlier. But numismatists have generally rejected Aristotle's claim, preferring to place the earliest Athenian coins at least a generation or more later than the lawgiver. A historiographical observation is in order. Ahistorical retrojections are not uncommon in Athenian affairs, particularly where Solon is concerned. Greeks generally loved to ascribe cultural innovations of unknown origin to some "first founder"; and, in Athens' case, Solon was particularly favored as the originator of classical Athenian institutions. But more pressing here is the question of why coinage was introduced into the Athenian economy *at all,* whatever the particular circumstances of its introduction.

The Uses of Coinage

It was once thought that, because coins in later antiquity served as a medium of exchange and did so at all levels of economic transactions, they must have been created in order to serve just this purpose—to make possible a monetary economy. This assumption is now widely questioned. True, minted coinage did serve the very useful function of guaranteeing uniformity and genuineness of value in terms of weight and fineness (that is, purity) of precious metal content. A lump of silver might weigh anything. And who knew whether the silver was pure or debased? But all else is open to question. Numismatists note, for example, that small denominations—the small change that one would expect to circulate in abundance if transactions were being made with the aid of coinage—are missing in the numismatic records of some cities. Besides, different kinds of reasons are at hand to explain the introduction and early use of coins, particularly coins of large denomination. They could be used to facilitate large payments by a state to a foreign party. (The hiring of a mercenary army would become a familiar example in later times). Or they would be convenient for merchants or traders buying or selling in large quantities. Put to such uses, large denominations were less what we call "coins" than ingots stamped by the issuing authority to guarantee their weight and purity. Furthermore, because all denominations bore an advertisement of the issuing state (in Athens' case, for example, an owl or a head of Athena), coinage was also an expression of civic consciousness, or even patriotic pride. A coin proclaimed the identity and authority of the issuing entity and therefore possessed a certain propaganda value. But as a purely practical device for enabling economic transactions at the level of the ordinary citizen, its effect was long delayed. Only in the later half of the fifth century B.C., as evidenced graphically by the comedies of the Athenian poet Aristophanes, did the smaller denominations begin to play a noticeable role in everyday economic life. And even when they did, the original purposes of coinage, just mentioned, lost none of their importance.

The Value of Athenian Coinage

At various times and places ancient Greek coins were minted from electrum (a natural alloy of gold and silver used in certain early emissions), gold, silver, and bronze (a synthetic alloy of copper and tin). In classical Athens, only two of these metals were in regular use: bronze for small denominations and silver generally (but not exclusively) for the larger. Gold, not commonly found in the Greek homeland region, was confined to a few extraordinary mintings and never in ordinary circulation. As a basis for further discussion, the denominations of classical Athenian coins may be briefly described:

• The *obol* was the unit of small-change currency. Greek *obolos* means "spit" (a long metal instrument), reflecting the fact that such objects had served as a medium of exchange before the origins of coinage. Fractional coins were worth ⅛, ¼, ⅜, ½, and ¾ an obol.

• The *drachma,* or "handful" (of "spits"), was equivalent to six obols. Higher denominations were the didrachm (two drachmas), tetradrachm (four drachmas), and decadrachm (ten drachmas), although of these only the tetradrachm was ever in general use.

• Two additional terms, *mina* and *talent,* denoted large units of value which did not correspond to any actual piece of currency. A mina was equivalent to one hundred drachmas, a talent to sixty minas or six thousand drachmas.

Our next task is to get some idea of what these denominations were worth. Two different approaches have been tried. One, quite unsatisfactory in its results, is to measure the precious metal content of an obol or drachma and then calculate the current value of that much bronze or silver. An example will illustrate the fallacy of this method. Take the tetradrachm, weighing in at about sixteen grams of pure silver. The current value of silver is about $5.65 per troy ounce. At thirty grams per ounce, an average tetradrachm would weigh just over one-half ounce and be worth $3.01 (more precisely, 53 percent of $5.65). Now, as we shall shortly see, a typical wage in the classical period was one drachm, or one-quarter of a tetradrachm, per day of work. Was a free Athenian citizen's full day of labor worth only 75¢?

WAGES, COMPENSATION, AND THE COST OF LIVING

A better way to measure the value of Athenian money is to calculate the nature and amount of work it took to earn a given sum. Fortunately, some headway can be made here, as contemporary sources preserve specific figures of three distinct kinds: (1) wages paid by the Athenian treasury for skilled and unskilled labor on public building projects; (2) compensation, again paid by the treasury, for service in the organs of the democratic government; and (3) compensation (including a ration allowance) for active service on military campaigns. A small selection of this evidence, shown in Table 9–1, will be sufficient for our purposes.

Table 9–1.   Wages and Compensation in Classical Athens

TYPE OF PAYMENT	DATE	PROJECT OR SERVICE	PAY OR COMPENSATION (PER DAY)
Wages for labor on building projects	409–407 B.C. 329/8–327/6 B.C.	Erechtheum Eleusis	1 drachma (skilled labor) 1¹/₂ drachmas (unskilled) 2 drachmas (semiskilled) 2¹/₂ drachmas (skilled)
Compensation for government service	Before 420s B.C. 420s and later Introduced 390 B.C. By 393 B.C. By 320s	Jury duty Jury duty Assembly Assembly Assembly	2 obols per day 3 obols per day 1 obol per meeting 3 obols per meeting 1 drachma for ordinary meeting; 1¹/₂ drachmas for "principal" meeting
Compensation for military service	450 to 400 B.C.	Active duty	No more than 3 obols (including ration allowance)

If one compares the earlier (fifth-century) and later (fourth century) figures, it is obvious that considerable inflation of wages and compensation had occurred. For the sake of simplicity, let us take 1 drachma per day as a working number: that was the wage for one day's skilled work, paid for both free and slave labor at the end of the fifth century. Note, too, that the disbursements for government or military service were not, strictly speaking, wages, but *compensation.* Thus there was no reason why these payments (around 3 obols or ¹/₂ drachma at the end of the fifth century) should have equaled contemporary *wages* for skilled manual labor. So, we now have an idea of what it took to earn 1 drachma. We will not, however, push the inquiry further by taking the step of equating that one day's labor with the value of one day's labor in today's United States. Who, after all, is to say what a day's work in present-day America is worth? Is it the wages of the minimum-wage worker, of the trade unionist, or of a highly skilled professional? But even if the value of one drachma is left at one day's gainful employment, we are still able to determine just what could be bought with the proceeds of that employment.

Here, again, we are fortunate, for sufficient evidence (both documentary and literary) is at hand concerning the prices of familiar commodities at or near the end of the fifth century to allow us to form a general impression of the cost of living in Athens. Table 9–2 sets out a selection of this evidence.

To form an idea of the cost of living, certain assumptions and calculations are necessary. It is assumed, first, that a house and land were owned outright, whether through inheritance or dowry or both. For the calculation of the cost of food, let us assume, in line with our discussion in Chapter 7, a fam-

Table 9–2.   The Cost of Living in Classical Athens

	ITEM	*PRICE*	*DAYS OF LABOR*
Food	15 lbs. wheat	1 drachma	1 day
	24 lbs. barley	1 drachma	1 day
	3 qts. olive oil	1 drachma	1 day
	4 qts. olives	1 obol	¹⁄₆ day
	4 qts. figs	1 obol	¹⁄₆ day
	1 gal. wine (domestic, unwatered)	1 drachma	1 day
Fuel: firewood	70 lbs. cut wood	¹⁄₂ drachma	¹⁄₂ day
Clothing	Tunic	7–10 drachmas	7–10 days
	Cloak	About 10 drachmas	About 10 days
	Pair of shoes or sandals	6–8 drachmas	6–8 days
Furniture	Bed	6–8 drachmas	6–8 days
	Bench	5 drachmas	5 days
	Table	4–6 drachmas	4–6 days
	Painting	5–10 drachmas	5–10 days
	Curtain or hanging	10 drachmas, 1 obol	10 ¹⁄₆ days
Stock animals	Ox or cow	About 50 drachmas	About 50 days
	Sheep	10–19 drachmas	10–19 days
	Goat	10–12 drachmas	10–12 days
Slaves	Adult (male or female)	About 174 drachmas	About 174 days
	Young child	72 drachmas	72 days
Building materials	1,000 bricks	36–40 drachmas	36–40 days
	Beam or rafter	1 drachma, 4 obols– 2 drachmas, 3 obols	1–3 days
	Load-bearing beam	17 drachmas	17 days
	Roof tile	1 drachma	1 day
Weapons	Bow	7 drachmas	7 days
	Bow and quiver	15 drachmas	15 days
	Shield	20 drachmas	20 days

ily of four: the parents and two children. A recent estimate based on fourth-century prices puts the average daily cost of barley (more commonly encountered than the more expensive wheat) for such a family at 1.65 obols. With olives or figs, honey, olive oil, and wine added, the total comes to about 2.5 obols per day. But, to the nuclear parent-child component must be added elderly paternal grandparents and very likely a small number of slaves. Firewood (or charcoal), too, was an expensive necessity in deforested Attica. Not included in our estimate, however, are vegetable produce, which was probably usually provided from a household garden or (as is still the case in modern Greece) by picking greens in the wild; milk and cheese supplied by the household's sheep or goat; and meat. With regard to the last item, it was noted in Chapter 8 that privately owned livestock was not normally slaughtered for home consumption. Public religious festivals with their animal sacrifices were, again, an alternative source of meat, although animal flesh, especially fish, were available for sale in the market to those who could afford it. The upshot is that even an extended family with slaves could be fed for not much more than, say, 1 drachma per day.

Additional significant expenses were undoubtedly subject to great variation. From the examples given in the tables it is clear that clothing was expensive, but garments and shoes were well made, mended when necessary, and expected to last. Besides, carding, spinning, and weaving were standard female domestic tasks, so presumably the simple everyday garments worn by most Greek men and women were often made at home. Furniture, like the house itself, was passed from generation to generation by inheritance or dowry and probably therefore not a frequent expense. Animals and slaves were another matter. Not every farmer could afford, at 50 drachmas each, the two oxen prescribed by Hesiod for plowing, but a sheep or goat was within the reach of any household with a worker earning as much as 1 drachma per working day. An adult slave, if purchased at the price given in Table 9–2 (the average sale price of a number of slaves auctioned in 415 B.C.), cost more than three times the price of an ox. (The recorded sale price of a slave child, at 72 drachmas, reflects the contemplated cost of raising the child to a productive age.) Now, historians disagree regarding the number of slaves owned by an average household. But 174 drachmas, if measured against an income of 1 drachma per day, could easily represent the total annual wages of the family's principal wage earner. Accordingly, it is difficult to imagine how many less prosperous households, if entirely dependent on such income, could manage to accumulate a surplus large enough to purchase even a single slave. Cost must have severely limited the availability of servile labor to the lower economic echelons of Athenian society.

Once-in-a-lifetime expenses, of course, inevitably occurred. To mention one affecting a substantial portion of the citizen population, those Athenians aspiring to service as hoplite soldiers were obligated, before the assumption of this expense by the state treasury, to outfit themselves with armor. As the price of a shield, 20 drachmas, suggests, the outlay involved was hardly insignificant. To consider a still greater, perhaps the ultimate, expenditure, what about the Athenian who, leaving his father's house, hoped to establish his own farm or urban residence? Land, despite the general social prohibition on its sale, was nonetheless available. So were houses. But even the lowest attested prices for both put them beyond the reach of all but the most well-to-do segment of upper-class society. A man might decide to build his own house on his father's property, but if he did, a single load-bearing beam, reflecting the scarcity of timber, would set him back 17 drachmas. The remaining lumber, bricks, roof tiles, and furnishings would accumulate to a staggering total. (One estimate, for example, put the cost of merely *furnishing* a two-story townhouse at 650 drachmas!) These economic realities underscore one of the assumptions underlying the citizen life course set out at the beginning of Chapter 8. Grown sons did not normally set out on their own but awaited the retirement or death of their fathers; only at that time did they assume control or ownership of a house or land.

The assumption built into the figures in Table 9–2 is that a citizen (or metic or slave) could earn 1 drachma per day for skilled labor at the end of the fifth century B.C. But care must be taken not to read more into that assumption than is warranted by the facts. All such wage-earning employment (as well as compensation for government service) was available only to those with ready access to the workplaces or seat of government in the urban center. In addition, the laborers did not work every day of the year nor, if they did work daily for a long stretch on a funded public project, could they expect such opportunities always to be available. Besides, the frequent official religious festival days must have exerted a powerful temptation to take a day off now and then. As for government service, the assembly met only forty times a year and, while the courts were in session perhaps as many as two hundred days of the year, no citizen member of the pool of jurors could count on being selected to sit on a panel and, unless he was so selected, he of course would not receive his 2 or 3 obols. Military pay was disbursed only for active duty on campaigns, so it, too, was a chancy on-again, off-again proposition. On the positive side, many a family had reserves in the form of an inheritance or dowry, although these were safeguarded by a strong societal ideal that each generation pass on the household's property undiminished to the next. Additional income might be earned by family members other than the male head of the household; and, as noted in the preceding Chapter, domestic cottage industry was probably a frequent source of significant income.

In conclusion, the variables are so numerous that no simple profile of "household economy" is possible and, if the full truth were known, we would probably be confronted with a multitude of varying financial arrangements. But we have perhaps succeeded in identifying the principal parameters conditioning the fortunes of the great bulk of Athenian citizen households.

THE ECONOMY OF SUBSISTENCE FARMING

Thus far we have considered the cost (and the resulting standard) of living in terms of typical earnings from skilled wage labor. Not all Athenians, however, supported themselves by such fixed daily wages. The incomes of the crafts workforce were certainly less regular and subject to all sorts of fluctuations. And of course, as noted in Chapter 5, the great majority, perhaps as much as three-fourths, were landowners, and of these a high percentage were certainly subsistence-level farmers. By and large, these farmers had little involvement in the cash economy. Strictly speaking, the term *subsistence*, taken at face value, implies that the farmer (and his supplementary household labor force) themselves produce all the daily necessities of life and thereby become independent of all potential sources of supply, including the cash market. Nothing needs to be purchased, and because the subsistence farmer by definition produces no surplus, he has nothing to sell. Naturally, in this case as in others, such a formalistic model, though indispensable as an analytic tool, bears little relation to reality (nor was it ever intended to). Farmers often *were* engaged in the business of the marketplace: to purchase tools or other commodities they could not manufacture themselves; to sell off the surplus of the occasional bumper crop; or, even on a regular schedule, to dispose of produce specifically grown on a cash-crop basis for sale. But our present concern is with subsistence farming considered in isolation from any contacts with the urban cash economy, however common or substantial the latter may have been. With assistance from an excellent recent study, it will be possible to reconstruct this economic environment in its main lines.

"Subsistence Crisis Insurance"

The basic problem with which the subsistence farmer had to deal was *change*, usually *unpredictable* change. The obvious changes in question were environmental, especially those involving the climate, insect infestations, soil exhaustion, erosion, and so on. But changes in the human social and political environment also had to be reckoned with, such as when kin or neighbors, one's village, the state, or even a foreign power made demands on the farmer's resources. If, then, you, the farmer, are already operating at the subsistence level of production, how do you deal with the certainty that, sooner or later, some damaging alteration of the natural or human environment is bound to occur? Unless precautions are taken, a serious loss of production might result, perhaps necessitating the incurring of debt. Any property used to secure such debt would thereafter be at risk until the debt was repaid. If land had been put up as security, then, in the event of default, the loss of the land would be a fatal blow to the household's economic and social future. Risks as great as these dictated a cautious, bet-hedging approach which, though perhaps ruling out the possibility of windfall surpluses, did minimize the risk and offer a reasonable guarantee of survival.

Various risk-reducing strategies—"subsistence crisis insurance," to use a phrase now well established in the field—were adopted. One, already men-

tioned in Chapter 8, was to spread one's crops over a number of widely separated holdings of farmland. Such fragmented holdings could, and did, easily grow up as a consequence of the accumulation of land through inheritance and dowry—especially dowry, because the woman might bring into
marriage a plot from a geographically remote area. Differences in location,
topography, contour, soil, or local microclimate would on the average tend
to even out the deleterious effects of a sudden environmental change.
Another strategy was to diversify crops on the same piece of ground. Vines,
figs, and olives could be grown in close proximity; and specific mention is
made in contemporary sources of growing cereal crops between rows of
trees or grapevines. The change that destroyed one crop might spare another. Stock raising, too, could be viewed as a sort of insurance policy in that,
in the event of a crop failure, animals could be selectively sold off or slaughtered for consumption. To do so of course meant the loss of a productive
sheep, goat, ox, or cow from which it would take some time to recover. But
with any luck the short-term sacrifice could be compensated for by better
yields in future years. These examples are sufficient to illustrate the point,
made earlier in Chapter 8 in our discussion of conservatism, that the economics of subsistence farming involved constant careful observation of
one's environment, shrewd calculations, and above all a cautious, risk-mini-
mizing attitude.

But there was also a purely human dimension to the farmer's calculations. Risk could be reduced by forming interlocking ties of mutual dependency with other persons, groups, or institutions. Given such ties, one could
appeal to them for assistance in times of crisis. The phenomenon operated
throughout the various sectors of Greek society.

Beyond the walls of one's own abode, a farmer looked first, of course, to
his own kinspeople. Greek literary sources consistently acknowledge the
mutual obligations of kin. These obligations extended not only to consanguineal (blood) kin but also to affinal (marriage) relations as well. In fact, affinal relations might well prove more useful to a farmer than his blood kin,
since, whereas parents, siblings, and children probably lived close by, his wife's
kin might dwell in a more distant region—a region not subject to the same
pattern of risk factors as his own.

Should one's kin fail to provide the necessary relief, appeal could be
made to more remote groups, one being the immediate neighbors. The tit-
for-tat basis of good relations with the neighbors and the value of such relationships are succinctly expressed by Hesiod in the *Works and Days*.

> Invite your friend to a feast, but leave your enemy out. And especially invite him
> who lives near you, for if anything goes wrong at your place, neighbors come
> right away, but kinsmen are slow to arrive. A bad neighbor is as great a pain as a
> good one is a great blessing. The man who enjoys a good neighbor has a valu-
> able possession. Not even an ox would die were it not for a bad neighbor. Take
> a fair measure from your neighbor and pay him back four square with the same

measure, or add a little, if you can. That way, if you are in need afterwards, you may count on him for help.

Neighbors by definition are a matter of proximity of residences. Friendships, however, are another phenomenon altogether. The sort of friendship with which we are concerned here is not that based *solely* on mutual affection but rather, among other factors, on the likelihood that one's friend might, in a subsistence crisis, be able and willing to provide assistance. A Greek, as numerous texts show, sought out and nurtured friendships in the expectation of reciprocation if and when assistance should be necessary. Again, Hesiod lays bare the underlying dynamic.

> Do not profit from dishonesty. Ill-gotten gain is as bad as bankruptcy itself. Be friends with the friendly, and visit the man who visits you. Give to one who gives, but do not give to the one who does not give. A man gives to the generous, but no one gives to the stingy. Giving is a good thing, but mere taking is a bad thing and a bringer of death.

Gift giving was not the only means of creating a bond of friendship. Ancient Greeks, like modern Greeks, fostered amity through social means, especially shared meals at the host's home (as Hesiod acknowledges in the first line of the penultimate passage). Friendship could even be cemented by a bond of fictive or pseudokinship, a tendency illustrated and paralleled by the modern practice of inviting persons outside the family to be the godparents of one's children. In any event, friendships, however created and maintained, could, like affinal relations, be particularly valuable sources of "subsistence crisis insurance" in that, unlike blood kin or neighbors, you could *select* them with a view to their possible future usefulness—for example, with reference to their location, their resources, the particular crops or stock they raised, and so on. We are a long way from the affective bonds familiar in modern Western societies.

"Patrons" and "Clients"

The three categories thus far considered—kin, neighbors, and friends—exhibit a common feature. Generally speaking, they all share the social and economic status of our subsistence farmer and, for that very reason, might prove of only limited value to him in time of need. Should there be a crisis, they are all in the same boat. Hence the importance to our farmer of "vertical" as well as "horizontal" links of mutual dependency or obligation; that is, of individuals placed much higher up the socioeconomic ladder of Athenian society.

As before, we are dealing with a number of different kinds of societal phenomena. The simplest of these, and the one we should expect to encounter in Greece on the basis of practice in comparable societies, ancient Rome in particular, is the patron-client relationship. Typically, the relationship is an asymmetrical one based on mutual obligation and reciprocity between a superior and an inferior party. In the ancient Greek case, our "patron" could of course be a wealthy member of the elite, especially a largeholder whose abundant resources of land, stored grain, or livestock could help his subsistence-level "client" through a crisis. By way of reciprocation, the "client" could repay the favor by various means: labor or other assistance when needed; support in the political arena (including canvassing and voting); and social deference, the latter extending particularly to public acknowledgment of his patron's superior (and of his own correspondingly inferior) status. But, oddly enough, though the basic preconditions of clientism are present in ancient Greece, such vertical relationships are hardly ever explicitly acknowledged, at least not in the quasi-institutionalized form the example of ancient Rome would lead one to expect. Indeed, the Latin terms *patron* and *client* have no known Athenian analogues. Explanations for the absence of the expected terminology are, however, at hand. Perhaps clientism existed, but it was considered a social blunder (at least on the part of the patron) to call attention to the fact—hence the silence of the sources on the topic. Alternatively, to mention an even more attractive approach, perhaps clientism, going by some other name, was submerged in a foreign institutional context that has hidden its existence from us.

Such an "institutional context" was in fact at hand in the form of the various associations of Athenian citizens. Some of these, such as the *genos* or clan, were private and voluntary groups open only to upper-class males. But the memberships of others, like the phratry, or "brotherhood," to one of which every Athenian citizen belonged from an early age (see Chapter 7), cut across all social and economic barriers. The same was true of the demes, or constitutionalized villages, which, because every citizen was enrolled in one deme or another, embraced all members of the local citizen community, from the poorest beggar to the wealthiest aristocrat. The upshot is that the phratry or deme provided a setting for the interaction of potential "patrons" and "clients," of rich and poor, of the elite and outsiders, who would not otherwise have naturally come into contact with one another, at least not on the basis of a shared membership in a single organization. That shared membership, it has been suspected, made possible, perhaps even encouraged, the formation of links of mutual obligation and reciprocity which in other, comparable societies went by the name of "clientism."

A still more elevated source of "subsistence crisis insurance" existed; namely, the state itself. The Athenian state played the role of patron to a dependent "client" citizen body, especially to its more vulnerable members, including subsistence farmers. The most straightforward example is the liturgy, the compulsory public service performed at the holder's personal expense, imposed by the state on all of Athens' wealthier citizens. Besides training dramatic lyric choruses and outfitting warships, the holders of the liturgy benefited the lower classes more directly and viscerally by providing entertainments (the so-called agonistic liturgies) and, most to the point here, an occasional good meal in the form of the liturgy called *hestiasis,* or "dining."

The wealthy benefactor, forced into the role of patron, wined and dined at his own expense *all* the members of his phyle or tribe—a full one-tenth of the citizen population! By accepting the meal, furthermore, the tribesmen assumed the burden of reciprocal obligation to him—and, indirectly, to the state—of clients. More often, the state dispensed with the intermediary and in its own name staged for public benefit sometimes magnificent religious festivals which invariably featured the sacrifice of animal victims and the consumption of their flesh by the participants.

THE RICH

To pass from the subsistence farmer to the rich is to enter an entirely different world. It is the difference between dependency and relative independence, between a narrowly circumscribed range of choices and considerable freedom of opportunity, between debilitating manual labor and the option of cultivated leisure, and, to put the matter in societal terms, between the social inferiority of the "client" and the social superiority of the "patron." Nonetheless, the findings of earlier chapters caution against any exaggeration of these differences. The houses of the rich and of the poor did not differ greatly in scale or appointment (see Chapter 3). Farms varied in size by no more than four or five times (see Chapter 7). And, perhaps most importantly, it seems that even low-ranking citizens aspired to much the same cultural ideals and held the same values as their more prosperous fellow Athenians (see Chapter 5). This was not ancient Rome.

In Chapter 5 we considered alternative ways of defining the rich, settling on the class of holders of the liturgy. It has been estimated that late in the fifth century B.C., the liturgical class at Athens comprised about six hundred citizens, or roughly 2 to 3 percent of the citizen population at that time. Put in terms of the units of currency mentioned at the beginning of this chapter, these six hundred citizens possessed personal fortunes—total net worth—of about 3 or 4 talents or more. It will be recalled that 1 talent was equivalent to six thousand drachmas, and 1 drachma was the pay for one day's skilled labor on a public works project late in the fifth century B.C. Thus, in terms of their wages or other comparable income, the subsistence farmer or laborer must have regarded the fortunes of the rich as almost unimaginably great. No smallholder could rationally expect that, simply by working hard or efficiently, he could ascend to the lofty heights of the liturgical class.

Sources and Uses of Wealth

Accordingly, the reader might naturally wonder what were the sources or forms of the wealth of the rich. Much of the answer to this question has already been provided in previous chapters.

• *Land.* The rich often owned land. But what was it good for? Since there was no legal prohibition on the selling or purchase of real estate (except that neither land nor houses could be owned by noncitizens), farmland could theoretically be converted to cash or another form. Yet this was unlikely to happen, as aristocrats depended on estates as a source of their traditional agrarian identity and in many cases certainly retained strong sentimental attachments to them. But unless the estate could be put to profitable, cash-generating use, a "land-poor" owner was the likely result. Normal sources of income from land included rent-paying tenants, the efficient use of slave labor, and the sale of cash crops.

• *Mining leases.* Some citizens amassed personal fortunes through leasing silver mines from the state and exploiting them profitably with slave labor. See Chapter 8.

• *Rents.* Both buildings and land were commonly rented out for profit. "Tenements" (multiple family dwellings) were mentioned in our discussion of the archaeological record of ancient Athens in Chapter 3. Renters of land included the so-called tenant farmers just mentioned, who worked another citizen's property, sometimes (as before Solon) in exchange for a percentage of the produce, but more usually for payment in cash.

• *Importing and exporting.* Trade will be discussed shortly. Specific figures on profits and the numbers of individuals involved are totally lacking, but some of the more successful were not citizens but metics.

• *Money-lending.* Both citizens and noncitizens are recorded to have loaned out money at interest, the best-known instance being the so-called *bottomry loan* (to be discussed shortly in connection with the importation of grain). Banking activity of other forms is attested, but the participants were almost always non-Athenians, even freedmen and slaves.

• *Industry.* What little evidence there is for large-scale factories in Athens was set out in Chapter 8. These establishments were devoted to the manufacture of such goods as tanned leather, lamps, furniture, metal items, armor, and so on. Despite this diversity of products, however, Athenian industrial establishments—and with them mining operations—shared a common feature: the use of slaves, often in large numbers. Large-scale slave labor could be highly profitable. Estimates of the ratio of profit to the expense of maintaining slaves range as high as nearly 100 percent in a single year. Those owners who profited from such investments were often *parvenu* outsiders who employed their newly acquired leisure and freedom by turning to democratic politics and thereby becoming the "new politicians" of late fifth-century Athens. Cleon, the tanner, who emerged as a leading demagogue in the wake of the death of the aristocrat Pericles, is merely the most famous of this class of successful entrepreneurs.

What did the rich, whether inheritors of "old" money or "nouveaux riches," do with their wealth? To begin, two negatives, both prompted by the parallel experience of the ancient Romans, should be mentioned. Rich Athenians did not buy up the small plots of indebted or impoverished fellow citizens and consolidate them into giant, unified plantations. Nor did they, in the pursuit of domestic comfort, routinely construct palatial mansions or baronial rural villas. But a short yet representative list of things they did do with their money would include horse breeding (and the entry of chariot teams in such "international" events as the games at Olympia and Delphi); for rural residents, the purchase and maintenance of townhouses in Athens for themselves or family members; expensive forms of entertainment (including the cost of imported wines, decorated pottery, and servants); the retention of expensive itinerant teachers in rhetoric and philosophy, called "sophists"; the dowering of daughters; and the accumulation of property to be bequeathed to sons. To these must be added, of course, the civic outlays involved in purchasing one's armor (or cavalry horse), liturgies, and other forms of taxation.

What is missing from this list? Capital investment. The closest Athenians came to such investment was the purchase of slaves, yet here they had little choice. Generally speaking, free labor for use in industrial settings certainly was not, as a consequence of the high valuation of independence by the citizen and metic classes, available. The idea of spending money in order to make more money had not yet seen its day. Rather the trend was to *consume* one's surplus wealth, especially in conspicuous advertisement of one's station in the societal order. Hence the popularity of luxurious dinner parties or symposia, the display of horses, and the private financing of public monuments (when, for example, a holder of a liturgy wished to commemorate the victory of his chorus in a tragic or dithyrambic competition).

Sometimes, however, such expenditures did approximate an investment, but an investment of a political or social rather than an economic nature. A large dowry might bring in its train all the advantages of a link with another family of standing or reputation equal to (or higher than) one's own. Instruction in rhetoric or philosophy, over and above its educational or moral value, could prepare one's able and enterprising son for success in democratic politics. A victory at Olympia with a four horse chariot could, as the ambitious politician Alcibiades was not the only one to realize, be converted into support at the polls or in plebiscites. But the public liturgy, although imposed by governmental authority and thus hardly a voluntary expenditure, provides the clearest example. We saw above how the subsistence farmer, by "investing" in kin, neighbors, friends, or patrons, could, in return for the payment of his "premium," purchase a form of insurance against the unhappy possibility of a crop failure or other calamity. The principle underlying such arrangements was, again, reciprocity. For the rich, the liturgy could be made to serve essentially similar purposes.

"Investment" in a tragic chorus, in the equipping of a trireme, or in a public feast could be repaid at some future date by the grateful recipients. And when would that be? When the rich donor needed the support and good will of the wider citizen public—above all, if he was a politician, in an election or, as forensic texts explicitly inform us, should the former holder of the liturgy ever be a litigant before a popular jury.

The Precarious Condition of the Wealthy

Even though the payment of a liturgy can be crudely conceptualized as a premium paid on an insurance policy, the fact remained that it could represent a serious drain on the donor's resources, especially for those who, in their enthusiasm to increase their popularity, exceeded the legal minimums as to frequency or amount expended. But this was but one of a number of factors that rendered the financial stability of the rich as precarious as that of the subsistence farmer. Very few of the family fortunes of the liturgical class are known to have survived beyond the second generation—by one scholar's count, only about 5 percent. Even allowing for the certainty that, because of our fragmentary or incomplete record, not all such families were adequately documented over time, this is a very low number.

Some of the causes of personal financial collapse are easy to guess. Besides the liturgies, there were other (true) taxes to be paid (see "The Athenian State Treasury," below). As we saw in Chapter 7, estates upon inheritance were divided equally among legitimate sons, so obviously the survival to adulthood of more than one heir could have a catastrophic effect. Measures were sometimes taken to prevent such division of the family property. For example, two sons could decide to share the estate, jointly residing in their father's house with their families and working the land (or running a business) in partnership. Or, again as we saw in Chapter 7, first cousins could marry in order to reunite an already-divided farm and work it more efficiently. At best, however, these temporizing measures merely served to delay the inevitable. Additionally, there were the hazards that beset any money-making enterprise. The loss of a vine orchard to disease or to an enemy invasion, the desertion of a slave workforce, or a financial loss (say, the failure of a creditor to repay a substantial loan) could, among a multitude of other possibilities, bring a family's prosperity to an abrupt end. By no means could it be said that the rich had necessarily realized the much sought-after ideal of self-sufficiency, which so successfully eluded the subsistence farmer.

IMPORTS AND EXPORTS

The land of Attica, as previously emphasized, was ill suited for the production of cereal crops. As the population—citizen, metic, and slave—grew and became progressively more urbanized, the capacity of the land to provide adequate grain (wheat and especially barley) was far outstripped by the number of mouths to feed. The solution to the problem was to increase grain imports. This turned out to mean the seeking of distant suppliers. Athens' Aegean neighbors were not producing large surpluses; even if they had been, if the potential supplier did not enjoy easy access to the sea, the prohibitive expense of land transportation would have driven prices up to unacceptable levels. As it worked out, the bulk of the grain needed was imported by ship from remote locations in the Black Sea region, the Levant, Egypt and Libya, and Sicily.

Other major import items were in different ways critical to the city's economy and security. Slaves, of necessity, were virtually all imported. Since Solon's legislation, the enslavement of Athenians had been illegal; and, for economic reasons, the house-breeding of existing slaves to produce the next generation of servile labor is believed to have been impracticable. Some slaves (as their recorded given names suggest) were Greek, but the great majority were brought in from peripheral civilizations, especially from Thrace, Scythia, and various kingdoms and regions of Asia Minor. The remaining major category of import might be styled "strategic materials." By the fifth century B.C., Attica had lost much of its forests, but large quantities of timber were needed for the construction of the ships on which Athens' military supremacy was utterly dependent (sizable lumber was also needed for use in buildings, especially large public structures, but also for framing private houses). Ships also required certain metals, pitch (for caulking hulls), and vermilion (for painting them)—all not generally available locally. For timber and metals, the two big items, the principal suppliers were Thrace and Macedon to the north of the Greek orbit. From these examples alone it is clear to what a great extent Athens' domestic well being, not to mention its continuing military superiority, rested on the maintenance of a constant, large stream of imports from mostly distant, overseas suppliers.

Not surprisingly, the Athenian government did not leave the administration of import traffic to the chances of the marketplace. The grain trade in particular was closely regulated, first through a number of very specific laws. It was an offense punishable by death for an Athenian resident to ship grain to any harbor other than Peiraeus. Any ship that entered Peiraeus carrying grain was required to unload there at least two-thirds of its cargo (that is, only one third could proceed to any other destination). Once the grain was in Peiraeus, furthermore, the amount that any one individual was allowed to purchase was limited in order to prevent unscrupulous individuals from controlling or manipulating the market. To ensure the observance of these (and similar) laws, and perhaps to monitor prices and profits, a special board of "grain police" was created (whereas most other market activity came under the jurisdiction of the all-purpose board called the "market regulators"). Ten times a year the so-called principal meeting of the Assembly was *required* to consider any questions relating to the food supply. Nor was the state's intervention confined to the boundaries of Attica. Through diplomatic or political means, friendly relations were cultivated with foreign suppliers, notably, Thrace, Macedon, the Crimean Bosporus, and Egypt. An Athenian colony named Amphipolis was eventually, after repeated attempts, established near the mouth of the Strymon, providing access at once to the hinterland of Thrace and Macedonia and control over the land route along the northern shore of the Aegean. Scyros, Lemnos, and Imbros, islands lying along the sea lanes between Athens and the Black Sea, were seized or settled by cleruchies of Athenian citizen colonists. It is abundantly evident that, where Athens' vital imports were concerned, the private and public sectors were inextricably intertwined.

On the other hand, the *financing* of the import trade, in particular the grain trade, was subject to market forces, however serendipitous. The crucial element was the distinctive Athenian maritime loan (or, to cite a more specific but arcane technical term, *bottomry loan*). Reduced to its essentials, the complex financial arrangements falling under this heading amounted to the provision of capital at interest for the purchase of a cargo of grain. The loan could be made either to the ship owner or the trader. If to the ship owner, the security for the loan was his ship and, if they were slaves, its crew; if to the trader, the security was the cargo of grain itself. The fact that the security took such forms—the ship or the cargo—put the lender in a (to our minds) peculiar position. If the ship or cargo was lost at sea, the lender had no legal claim against the borrower; he had to write the loan off as a total loss. To compensate for such risks, accordingly, very high interest rates—up to 30 percent for an out-and-back voyage of only two or three months' duration—were charged. To recoup the costs of the loan, the borrower was compelled to sell the grain in Peiraeus at a very hefty markup. At the same time, too, climatic or political disturbances could seriously and without warning affect the supply of grain available. As far as is known, the resulting rise and fall of prices were not subject to governmental intervention. Athens did not normally regulate the price of grain or, what amounted to the same thing, as in imperial Rome, distribute it at subsidized prices or at no cost. Rather, the role played by the state was confined to efforts to maintain satisfactory relations with the suppliers. In succeeding centuries, the People would make a regular practice of conferring honors upon foreign states or individuals supplying Athens with grain at favorable prices, especially in times of famine or other crises.

Given these very substantial imports, how did Athens achieve a satisfactory balance of trade? It is appropriate to note, first, that it may well never have occurred to the Greeks themselves to wonder about such a balance, for as far as we know no records were kept that might reveal either balance or imbalance. Nonetheless, this is no reason why we should not inquire about the nature and extent of the Athenian export market.

Solon, back in the early sixth century B.C., had sponsored a law prohibiting the export of any crop other than olive oil. Presumably his principal purpose was to prevent the exportation of vital foodstuffs, obviously including grain. But olive oil was (or eventually would be) produced in abundance and was much in demand elsewhere. Except for this one product, however, it is difficult to identify major Athenian export commodities. Wine (a natural possibility in view of Attica's suitability to viniculture) had been excluded by Solon, and although Athenian *amphorae* (a common type of large vessel used for transport of various products) are found all over the Mediterranean, there is no good reason to believe that they had been used to hold wine (or, for that matter, any other particular product). In Chapter 8, we reviewed some of the evidence for factories and the so-called cottage industry, but there is no trace or written record of the exportation of the Athenian leather goods, furniture, lamps, lyres, armor, or textiles that those workplaces are known to have produced.

Pottery is the major exception. From the sixth century and throughout the classical period, Athens virtually monopolized the Mediterranean fine ceramic market. Remains of Attic pottery are found far and wide, accompanied by very little evidence of possible competitors. At the same time, one must be careful not to overemphasize the importance of ceramic goods for the Athenian economy. For one thing, because fired pottery is virtually indestructible (while nearly everything else decomposes over time), it is overrepresented in the archaeological record. The total value of the exported product may therefore not in fact have been great (when measured against the sum of all imports), despite the conspicuous presence of Athenian wares at so many sites all over the Mediterranean. (Significantly, too, the workforce needed to manufacture the estimated sum productivity of Athenian potteries may not have been large; informed estimates range in the low hundreds, only a very small percentage of the total free and servile workforce.)

By the standards of the ancient Aegean, Athens was a very wealthy city. Yes, it may be true after all that, by accident of preservation or discovery, a substantial export commodity has escaped our attention. But this is not the only possible explanation for the apparent absence of a balancing export business. Athens was rich enough to run a substantial trade deficit, and, in the absence of record keeping, such a deficit could easily have gone undetected. Such ignorance (and lack of interest) would fit in comfortably with the *general* ignorance of (and lack of interest in) large-scale economic conditions by all ancient Greek governments. Only the need to feed the home population and to maintain the military armament (in Athens' case, the navy) seems to have stirred these governments to take notice and then, having taken notice, to intervene by legal, political, or military means.

THE ATHENIAN STATE TREASURY: INCOME AND EXPENDITURE

If the Athenians lacked a comprehensive grasp of their overall finances, they did realize, on a day-to-day basis, the necessity of a regular flow of revenue into the treasury. The major sources of revenue are easily enumerated. The silver mines, owned by the state and leased to citizens in exchange for a payment calibrated to the type of mine, remained active throughout the classical period. Taxes, low by modern Western standards, included a 2 percent duty on all goods, both imports and exports, passing through the port of Peiraeus; a sales tax on goods sold in the Agora; and a tax on goods sold by the city itself (as, for instance, in auctions of confiscated properties). Fines were imposed by the law courts. Foreigners engaged in commercial transactions in the Agora were assessed a fee; and all metics, male and female, paid an annual poll (or "head") tax. Funds for emergency military use were raised by an extraordinary tax on property called the *eisphora,* a rare exception to the tendency not to tax the persons or property of citizens. These were the main sources of revenue, but our data are not adequate to allow us to estimate its absolute dimensions.

Against income was set a staggering array of expenditures. From our discussions in Chapter 6, it is already evident that Athens' democratic government was itself maintained only at great cost. Besides the expected overhead outlays necessary to sustain an organization of any kind, there was the compensation, mentioned more than once previously, of up to a full drachma (or, later, even more) a head per day, distributed on a regular basis to thousands of participants in the legislative, magisterial, and judicial systems. Such pay was both compensation for lost income and, in most cases, an indirect form of public welfare. The same may be said of the so-called *theoric* payments enabling citizens to participate in civic religious festivals and, indeed, of the festivals themselves which, as noted earlier, furnished participants with periodic portions of sacrificial meats (as well as entertainments). On occasion, in contrast with the general noninterventionist policy noted earlier, cash or grain was distributed to the citizen body in times of crisis. Throughout antiquity, but particularly under the Periclean regime of the mid- and later fifth-century B.C., public building projects involving enormous expenditures on materials and labor were undertaken. Maintenance of a military apparatus and the actual conduct of warfare, too, made exorbitant demands on the financial resources of Athens. Mention has just been made of the importation of strategic materials, notably timber and metals required for the construction of naval warships. Fighting forces had to be paid while on duty, and at great total cost. A single trireme typically employed about 170 rowers earning up to 1 drachma per day each. A fleet of 100 triremes would cost 17,000 drachmas, or nearly 3 talents per day for the rowers alone, to keep in operation; even at the prevailing lower scales of pay, a single trireme would drain the treasury at the rate of about 1 talent per month of operation.

THE ATHENIAN EMPIRE

No mention has been made of the Athenian Empire, the alliance of tribute-paying allied Aegean maritime states over which Athens exercised leadership from the foundation of the so-called Delian League (out of which the Empire developed) in 478 B.C. immediately following the end of the Persian Wars. The Empire remained intact until the end of the Peloponnesian War and the capitulation to Sparta in 404 B.C. The tribute, paid in cash by all allies except for a few who continued to provide ships for the allied fleet, was, from the year 454 B.C. when the Delian League treasury was transferred from the island of Delos to Athens, subject to administration by the Athenian legislature—that is, by the People of Athens. It was a very substantial sum. For the year 431 B.C., on the eve of the outbreak of the Peloponnesian War, Thucydides states that the combined annual tribute was 600 talents. Another classical writer, Xenophon, gives 1,000 talents as the total of imperial and domestic revenues. For the 400 talents raised from nonimperial sources we have already identified the principal taxes, rents, fees, and so forth. The question that has always been asked is whether, and in what ways and to what extent, the imperial tribute, *too,* was employed to support the domestic economy of the city of Athens?

First let it be acknowledged that very substantial expenses were incurred in the operations of the Delian League, even if those operations sometimes worked to the detriment of the allies themselves. The cost to the imperial treasury of two allied military operations is recorded. When Poteidaea, a member of the Empire, revolted in 432 B.C. following a dramatic increase in its tribute, it was reduced by Athens at the cost of 2,000 talents. Earlier, Samos, another member, had revolted in 441 B.C., and its suppression under Pericles' leadership set the treasury back 1,200 talents. When such figures as these are measured against a nominal annual combined tribute of 600 talents, it is obvious that the Empire itself (at least as defined by Athenian interests) was the principal beneficiary. Personnel expenses incurred in the administration of the Empire were also large. Aristotle, again, states that 700 Athenians were at a single time engaged "overseas"—presumably as nonmilitary imperial officials. At the time of the outbreak of the Peloponnesian War, this would have been about 1 of every 40 Athenians!

These officials may have been necessary for the operation of the Empire, but they were also Athenian citizens profiting from otherwise unobtainable gainful employment. Additional direct benefits to Athenians from imperial operations and administration are easy to identify. The imperial fleet kept open the trade lanes that brought the vital grain supply to the imperial capital. Land in the form of cleruchy allotments was distributed to landless Athenian thetes (and perhaps also to zeugitai), providing them with a self-sufficient income and relieving Athens of some of its dependent poor. When in 427 B.C. the island of Lesbos revolted and was reduced by an imperial military force, farms were confiscated and given to Athenian citizens (to whom the former Lesbian owners, while still working the land, paid a rent). At home, the dockyards employed Athenian citizens (and other residents of Attica) building, maintaining, and outfitting the imperial squadrons. Because delegations from all allied states were compelled to journey each year to deliver their tribute, and because allied states were required to use the Athenian court system, the local economy benefited indirectly from the regular presence of so many visitors spending money brought from outside Attica.

It is more difficult to estimate to what extent imperial tribute went toward subsidizing expenditures at Athens *unrelated* to Delian League activities or objectives. During Pericles' time, political debate focused on the expenditure of tribute moneys on the monumental buildings, including the Parthenon, under construction at that time on the Acropolis. Although we lack direct contemporary testimony, our suspicions are legitimately aroused by the exceedingly lavish and unparalleled extravagance of all-marble construction and by the costly elaborate sculptural programs, in combination with the fact that it was it at just this time—that is, when the accumulated surplus was large and funds were not yet needed to wage the ruinous war against Sparta—that the projects were undertaken. It is immaterial, of course, whether the Parthenon, for example, was paid for directly out of the Delian League treasury or out of domestic revenues while other routine expenses, such as defense, were met by tribute. Either way, the allies were compelled to pay against their wills for Athena's temple and other embellishments of the imperial capital. Another extravagance was pay for government service. Direct democracy was expensive, for if a high level of participation of a mostly poor citizen body was to be achieved, the participants would have to be compensated. If, alternatively, these payments are viewed as primarily a form of social welfare, and the democracy merely the excuse, the conclusion is the same. The money had to come from somewhere, and the typical ancient Greek city-state was simply not capable of meeting demands on its treasury of such dimensions over so long a period. Was it the Empire, then, that made possible the only direct democracy in a major polity in Western history?

Suggested Readings

For a general account of ancient Greek coinage, see C. M. Kraay, *Archaic and Classical Greek Coins* (Berkeley, 1976). Use has been made here of the study by M. M. Markle, "Jury Pay and Assembly Pay at Athens," *History of Political Thought* 6 (1985): 265–297. The prices cited in the table are taken mostly from the inscriptional evidence for the sale of the property of the Hermokopidai in 415 B.C.; see W. K. Pritchett, "The Attic Stelae," pt. II, *Hesperia* 25 (1956): 178–317. The complex mechanics of subsistence farming, sketched only briefly above, are splendidly set out by T. W. Gallant, *Risk and Survival in Ancient Greece: Reconstructing the Rural Domestic Economy* (Palo Alto, 1991). Mention was made at the end of Chapter 5 of J. K. Davies, *Wealth and the Power of Wealth in Classical Athens* (New York, 1981); the work is relevant here to the sources, uses, and instability of Athenian fortunes. For an overview of the ancient Greek economy, perhaps the best treatment is M. M. Austin and P. Vidal Naquet, *Economic and Social History of Ancient Greece* (London, 1977). The finances of the Empire are well treated by R. Meiggs, *The Athenian Empire* (Oxford, 1972), ch. 14.

Epilogue: State and Society
in the Hellenistic Era

The preceding, greater part of this textbook has been concerned with Greece's first city, Athens, during the classical period (ca. 525–322 B.C.). Thereafter, Greek antiquity extends through two lengthy eras, the Hellenistic (322–27 B.C.) and, with Greece's absorption into the *imperium Romanum*, the Roman (27 B.C.–A.D. 476). It is with the Hellenistic that we will briefly occupy ourselves here, as we note some of the major trends that serve to justify the traditional periodization of ancient Greek history, especially where significant departures from the state and society of Classical Athens are in question. But the reader should realize that the term Hellenistic, a modern coinage with no exact ancient equivalent, is customarily used in connection with the dissemination of Greek culture across the territories of the East conquered by the Macedonian king Alexander the Great (died 323 B.C.). The thorny question of the nature and extent of this process of dissemination continues to be investigated by historians, archaeologists, and other specialists—and will be for some time to come. However, the focus of the following brief account will continue to be the state and society of old Greece, especially Athens.

THE ATHENIAN STATE: THE DEMOCRACY

It will be obvious from the discussion ending in Chapter 9 that Athens' loss in 404 B.C. of the war against Sparta and its allies, and, with the loss of that war, the surrender of the Empire, was a fiscal event of catastrophic proportions. Suddenly the regular flow of tribute into Athens was terminated. Surprisingly, it is not as easy as one might think to gauge the impact of the loss of tribute on the Athenian economy—or, more remotely, on the functioning of Athenian state and society. Still, there are signs that that impact may not have been so catastrophic after all. For one thing, very expensive naval operations no longer had to be financed, and the seven hundred imperial posts staffed by Athenians that were reported by Aristotle no longer existed. The expenditure of funds (whether imperial or domestic) on the Periclean building program on the Acropolis had already ceased, eliminating a major drain on the treasury. Besides, there is one impressive positive indication that Athens, despite the absence of the tribute-paying allies, remained financially solvent. Pay for service in the democratic organs of the central government was not interrupted. Indeed, it was increased, for it was only after the loss of the war, sometime between 403 and the late 390s B.C., that pay for attendance in the

Assembly was inaugurated, first at the low level of one obol, later rising incrementally to one drachma (six obols), or even one and a half drachmas (nine obols) for the principal meetings by the time of the composition of Aristotle's *Constitution of the Athenians* in the 330s B.C. By no means had the shutoff of imperial tribute bankrupted the Athenian democracy.

Furthermore, the introduction of pay for attendance in the Assembly reveals the continuing maintenance of one of the ideals of the democracy noted in Chapter 6: the high level of citizen participation. In fact, it is highly likely that the purpose of the payment was precisely to counter sagging attendance. After all, the quorum of six thousand represented a sizable percentage of the Athenian citizen body, and because, with the end of the Peloponnesian War, fewer matters of pressing urgency needed to be debated and voted on, the quorum must have become increasingly difficult to obtain. Further, the preservation of another of those classical ideals—the democracy's pervasive egalitarianism—is reflected in the institution of new procedures to increase the randomness of the allocation of jurors and of presiding magistrates to the courts (although, admittedly, the immediate object was less ideological than designed to lessen the possibility of tampering).

But other changes challenged in different ways some of the democracy's underlying principles. Certain of the boards, most significantly the board of generals, were gradually taken over by "experts"—in the case of the generals, professional career soldiers in contrast to the politicians who had filled the *strategia* during the fifth century. Popular democracy had been founded on amateurism, but no longer. Concurrently, the tie between the boards and the public organization, whereby one member of each board of ten was chosen from each of the ten phylai, was loosened and in some cases eventually abandoned altogether. Such developments compromised the principle, which went all the way back to Clisthenes, that the personnel of government represent more or less evenly the various constitutional segments of the polity. Equally seriously, the cardinal democratic principle of collegiality was forsaken in at least one vital area—fiscal administration—with the emergence of single officers placed in virtually unchallenged control of the city's finances (first the administrator of the theoric fund, later the political leader Lycurgus). Most of these innovations were in place by the time of the composition of Aristotle's *Constitution of the Athenians* in the 330s B.C. The author of this work believed that he was describing essentially the same government that Clisthenes had created at the end of the sixth century, but the fact remains that considerable erosion of certain of its guiding principles had already occurred.

What drove the process of decline evidenced in these procedural variations? *Demokratia*, taken literally, meant fundamentally an equitable distribution of power (*kratos*) over an entire citizen body (the *demos*). Such a distribution implied nothing necessarily about soundness of judgment in making decisions, about expertise appropriate to the task at hand, or about efficiency. Since the symptoms of change occurred in the most sensitive areas of military organization and financial administration, it is evident that it was precisely these concerns that were prompting the surrender of some of the government's more radically egalitarian features.

In this somewhat altered condition the democracy carried on until 322 B.C. when, following the Macedonian takeover, the government was suppressed. Nonetheless, surprisingly, the organs of Clisthenes' constitution survived more or less intact. There was still a legislature of Council and Assembly, and at least some of the boards continued to be constituted and to operate. But this was at best a hollow shell of a government, a mere form without content, an apparatus without a function to perform. The fact that Athens' policies and undertakings were now, and would continue to be under Roman rule, subject to approval by a higher power had impaired the democratic impulse. If *demokratia* was the distribution of power among the people, unless there was effective power to wield, the reason for participation by the people no longer existed, certainly not to the same degree.

The decline of the democratic spirit in postclassical times can be illustrated, even measured, in various ways. One such way involves the segments of the citizen body, especially the phylai and the demes—the tribes and constitutionalized villages that we first met in Chapter 4. It will be recalled that these segments served not only as units of statewide administration but were also *internally* organized as more or less self-sufficient associations. During the heyday of the democracy in the fifth and fourth centuries, the phyle associations and deme associations met regularly to conduct their associational business. These meetings resulted, particularly later in this period, in the promulgation of the acts of the assembled in the form of decrees inscribed on stone. Such decrees are relatively frequent before and after the year 322 B.C. For the phylai, about forty decrees survive prior to this date, but only about a dozen follow it (through the end of antiquity). For the demes, over a hundred predate the end of the fourth century, but only a third of that number are dated later than that time. At the associational level, democracy was slowly dying on the vine. Doubtless this was merely a reflex of the larger phenomenon of the city of Athens' losing political independence and autonomous control over both internal and external policies. The citizen members of the phylai and demes met less often and passed fewer decrees simply because of the apathy that sets in when a people comes to realize that it is powerless to alter the basic conditions of its existence.

THE HELLENISTIC GREEK WORLD: SOCIETY

Citizenship and the Citizen Body

Society of the classical period, at Athens and elsewhere, had been centered on the city-state, certainly as far as the citizen class was concerned.

Athenians, as we have seen, maintained an exclusive relation with their polis, while the very definition of citizenship in terms of descent from citizen parents prevented penetration of the elite inner circle by outsiders. Citizens enjoyed a generally uncontested monopoly over the functions of the city, notably (with significant relevance to the future) including military service. Nor did the impact of the city-state end with a citizen's exercise of a few core public duties. It was observed in the Introduction that many activities that modern Westerners have come to categorize as "private" and properly lying outside the reach of government were in ancient Greece actually organized and sustained by the central government. Large-scale entertainments, religious celebrations, and much associational activity are three vitally important examples. The daily lives of Athenian citizens and their family members revolved around, and were deeply embedded in, the structure and ethos of a small and isolated, but autonomous, city-state.

Much of this changed with the rise of the monarchies. Citizenship, for one thing, lost much of its former exclusivity. The privilege of official membership in the citizen body was no longer so jealously guarded, at least outside Athens. It will be recalled, for example, how rare were the grants of *politeia* conferred upon foreigners by the Athenian legislature. In the Hellenistic era, such grants increased in frequency, both to individuals and to the citizen bodies of entire cities (the latter type being called an isopolity or "equal citizenship"). Although both types of enfranchisement were potential only, requiring that the honoree physically relocate to the granting city and simultaneously surrender his existing citizenship before assuming active exercise of the new one, the frequency of the grants must have resulted in a Greek's thinking in less rigid and exclusive terms about his public identity.

Demographic trends worked in the same direction. A well-known statement of the Hellenistic historian Polybius declares that "in our times the whole of Greece has suffered a shortage of children and hence a decrease of population, in consequence of which some cities were deserted and agricultural produce was in short supply." The historian ascribes the trend to failure to marry or, when marriage did occur, to the parents' failure to raise more than one or two of any children that were born. Such failure he ascribes in turn to ambition, greed, and laziness. It is obvious from the specific content of this final moralizing remark on the driving forces of depopulation that the trend related only or primarily to people of means; that is, to the citizen elites of the Greek cities. But their failure to reproduce themselves in sufficient numbers was probably at least in part compensated for by two countervailing trends: the increasing manumission of slaves and the immigration of foreigners. Eventually, at least some of these two latter groups (or their descendants) would be enfranchised as full citizens. Such internal change of the civic or even the ethnic composition of a citizen body is a far cry from the strict application of the rule of descent in classical Athens, which had ordained that each new generation of citizens be the lineal blood descendants of the immediately preceding generation.

The Individual

The changing composition of the citizen class was over time attended by dramatic changes in the duties of the individual citizen. Perhaps the most dramatic such development occurred in the area of military service. Increasingly, Greek cities elected not to field forces of citizen soldiers (as dictated by the classical ideal of the conscript militia) but instead to hire mercenaries—paid professional fighting men. This development was another blow to the definition of what it meant to be a citizen. It contributed to the erosion of the importance of membership in a particular polis; and, most relevantly to the present point, it precipitated the dislocation of large numbers of citizens in many communities. The poor, the unemployed, the son who had not inherited property sufficient to sustain life could sever ties with their ancestral cities and seek their fortunes abroad in the service of a foreign power. Owing to this (and other) trends, the deracinated Greek was to become an all-too-familiar figure on the Hellenistic social landscape.

The severing of the tie between state and individual ramified across the spectrum of Hellenistic Greek society. Two examples derive particular significance from the foregoing account of classical Athens. During the sixth and fifth centuries, an athlete, if victorious in a panhellenic competition (such as the Olympic games), received a hero's welcome back in Athens; he had enhanced the city's reputation in the eyes of his fellow Greeks. But by Hellenistic times, quasiprofessional athletes, not closely associated with any particular city, were pursuing "international" careers as they hopped from meet to meet, amassing victories and prizes. Similarly, actors on the stage of classical Athens performed before their fellow citizens and, if the play won a prize, brought glory to an Athenian playwright and Athenian chorus master. But the Hellenistic period witnessed the rise of professional companies of actors touring from theater to theater about the Aegean region. No longer was the polis the sole reference point for distinction or achievement.

Another major discernible trend concerns free women, although its extent is open to doubt. It is a remarkable fact, particularly when one has in mind the restrictive conditions obtaining in classical Athens, that by the late Hellenistic period women are recorded as receiving grants of citizenship and even holding magistracies. Some historians have traced this remarkable development to the high visibility and decisive influence of the Hellenistic queens, especially those of Macedonia (Olympias, the mother of Alexander the Great, for example). By a sort of "trickle-down" process, nonroyal women would have been inspired by these high-profile exemplars to assert themselves within their own communities. Thus the queen who engineered the accession of her son to the throne and now ruled from behind that throne would have paved the way for the enfranchisement or appointment of other, less highly placed women throughout the Greek world. But there are difficulties with this at first attractive scenario. The Hellenistic queens do not make convincing role models, because they were not themselves power holders but exerted whatever influence they possessed *through men*, their husbands and sons. Often, too, these queens, as in the Macedonian court, resorted to deceit, even to murder and other unsavory means, in order to gratify their lust for power. Were such figures really the role models emulated by Greek women aspiring to positions of legitimate authority in other cities? In any event, these newly enfranchised or appointed women were very few in number, and in some of these few cases sufficient evidence is available to prompt a wholly different explanation for their rise in this Greek "man's world." They were wealthy, and their cities enfranchised or bestowed magisterial titles upon them in order to gain access to that wealth. By the later Hellenistic period, some magistracies had become virtual liturgies, with the occupant expected to meet all expenses of the office out of personal funds. What more natural way was available to tap these hitherto inaccessible potential sources of public revenue?

Chances are, then, that the condition of all women was unchanged—except for a very few women resident in cities where, unlike Athens, the law permitted their ownership of appreciable property. Nor was the condition of men significantly altered beyond the effects of the escape-valve mechanism for the release of excess population provided by mercenary service and other opportunities abroad. After all, no technological innovation, sudden and dramatic acquisition of wealth, or abrupt ideological shift had occurred which might radically transform the nature of work; the allocation of that work by age, gender, or rank; or the cultural standards that we have seen in operation in classical Athens. At the level of the individual and the domestic unit, the lives of free Greeks probably remained much as they had been before.

Hellenistic Associations

The same does not apply, however, to higher tiers of the Greek social organization. Note was made in the preceding section of the decline of the phylai and demes—segments of the Athenian citizen body—as internally organized tribal or village communities. It was suggested that such decline was due to a more general decline in the meaning and value of democratic institutions. But by no means did organized associational activity come to an end, either at Athens or elsewhere in Greece. Associations of several types were now flourishing, but all, unlike the phylai or demes, were more or less independent of the central governmental apparatus. While nominally religious, the guiding purposes of the new groups were quite varied. Some were social; some were artistic or cultural; some were commercial in their orientation. In a few cases commemorated by inscriptions on stone, a wealthy benefactor established a foundation to be maintained in perpetuity by his or her descendants and to be concerned primarily with fostering a cult of the heroized founder. Still another type was the philosophical school in Athens established by the last will and testament of the philosopher-founder.

Underlying this diversity were two pervasive and strikingly innovative trends. Most obviously to the student of the ancient sources, the memberships of some of these associations, in contrast with the all-adult male citizen composition of the demes (for example), were opened up to women and resident foreigners. Thereby the voluntary associations acknowledged the social reality of a more diverse community and institutionalized that diversity in the shape of a formally structured organization. The second, closely related trend has to do with the varying degrees of separation between these new inclusive groupings and the governments of the city-states in which those groupings were found. In contrast with the general integration of state and society emphasized throughout this book, the Hellenistic associations operated more or less independently of the public authority. These associations were serving a function—the provision of a communal structure for a heterogeneous population—that the city-states themselves, as long as citizenship was confined to an adult male hereditary elite, could not or would not serve. Though regrettably not well documented or understood in detail, these organizations may represent the most innovative and distinctive development of Hellenistic society.

THE HELLENISTIC GREEK POLIS: EDUCATION, ECONOMY, AND CULTURE

At the topmost tier, the culture of the city-state closely resembled in its main lines that of its classical predecessor. At Athens, the physical infrastructure and its attendant functions sketched in Chapter 3 remained mostly intact. But in two specific institutions, a shift in function (in the one case) and emphasis (in the other) occurred. The result was a change in the character of the social and especially the intellectual experience of younger men, and even women, of the citizen class.

The Ephebic College, once (as we saw in Chapter 8) the mandatory two-year regimen of military training for young Athenians about to enter the citizen body, was over time drastically transformed. By the end of the fourth century B.C., training had ceased to be compulsory; soon thereafter, the curriculum was reduced to a single year. With the suspension of the daily allowance of four obols paid to ephebes by the state, membership predictably shrank to a wealthy minority. Since by now, furthermore, Athens had long ceased to be a military power, instruction shifted from its previous military focus to education, including literature and philosophy. Eventually, as if to mark the final surrender of its original purpose, even foreigners were admitted to the college. But the more important point is the positive one—that an attempt had been made to provide formal education in a public setting, even though, characteristically, access was available only to a wealthy male minority.

Not unlike the reorientation of the Ephebic College was the transformation of a second civic institution: the gymnasium. As we saw, it had started out as a venue for physical exercise (its chief component, the *palaestra*, for example, was specifically dedicated to wrestling), but probably as a development of its natural use as a place for social exchanges, the classical gymnasium became the favored haunt of intellectuals, especially including some of the philosophers, at least in Athens. During the Hellenistic period, the latter, nonathletic function was expanded into a general educational role, eventually resulting in the emergence of the gymnasium as a bona fide public school. In a few documented cases outside Athens, the gymnasium is known to have accepted students, sometimes girls as well as boys, from childhood through early adulthood.

But how, especially if one bears in mind the nearly total absence of educational institutions throughout the classical period, did such schools now become possible? Expensive, large gymnasium buildings with elaborate interior fixtures had to be constructed and maintained. Teachers had to be paid their salaries. For athletic training, the onerous duty of providing olive oil and powder (to apply to the skin before exercising, particularly wrestling) had to be borne. Where did the funds come from?

In classical Athens, such public expenses had typically been met by wealthy citizens who had been tapped to perform a liturgy, the mandatory public service performed at the personal expense of the holder that we met in Chapter 9. This same system continued in operation in the Hellenistic period, but with even greater intensity. The Hellenistic age was an era witnessing a dramatic widening of the economic gap between the rich and the poor, resulting in increasing dependency of the lower classes on the city and of the city, in turn, on the resources of its wealthier citizens. Governments looked to men (and, as we have just seen, even a few women) of substance to underwrite the expense of those activities, such as education, on which the well-being of the community depended. Thus, for example, the gymnasium was often kept in operation by the personal contributions of its gymnasiarch, the holder of the liturgy of the gymnasium; he supplied the olive oil, paid the teachers, and so on. True, the funding had originated in the private sector, but even so the gymnasium, like other institutions supported by the liturgical system, remained public in orientation through its participation in communitywide contests and festivals. At first, as in the classical period, individual benefactors were animated by a personal interest in the activity in question, or by civic-mindedness, or at least by a desire to reap the rewards of recognition and enhanced prestige. But over time, predictably, as the liturgies became excessively burdensome, they lost their glamorous aura and came to be regarded as a mere tax to be avoided if at all possible.

As the Hellenistic city-state sought to address its internal financial demands in part through the exploitation of the resources of its wealthier citizens, it simultaneously engaged in economic relations with the outside world, both within and beyond the Greek orbit. As a result of these external contacts, the period witnessed a general breaking down of the earlier insularities and a movement toward greater interconnectedness of the local economy with both the immediate and the larger eastern Mediterranean region. Additional factors, including large-scale demographic trends and the movements of various types of "culture carriers" (emissaries, tourists, athletes, pilgrims, and so on), worked to the same end—a decline of the old particularism and the rise of a *koine,* or "common," Hellenistic civilization. But the detailed account of the "one world" of Hellenism which was now emerging and would soon begin its lengthy journey beyond the limits of old Greece is another story, to be told in another book.

Suggested Readings

The classic treatment in English of the Hellenistic period is W. W. Tarn, *Hellenistic Civilisation,* 3rd ed., revised by G. T. Griffith (London, 1952). A more recent treatment, by a leading authority, is F. W. Walbank, *The Hellenistic World,* rev. ed. (Cambridge, Mass., 1993). For the Cambridge Ancient History account, see, in the second edition, vol. 7, pt. 1, *The Hellenistic World* (Cambridge, 1984), with Chapter 8, by J. K. Davies, devoted to "Cultural, Social and Economic Features of the Hellenistic World."